LADIES'
HomeJournal®

all-time
favorites

Meredith Consumer Marketing
Des Moines, Iowa

Ladies' Home Journal® All-Time Favorites

Meredith® Corporation Consumer Marketing
Vice President, Consumer Marketing: David Ball
Consumer Product Marketing Director: Kathi Prien
Business Director: Ron Clingman
Associate Director, Production: Al Rodruck

Waterbury Publications, Inc.
Editorial Director: Lisa Kingsley
Creative Director: Ken Carlson
Contributing Project Editors and Writers: Mary Williams, Lois White
Associate Editor: Tricia Laning
Associate Design Director: Doug Samuelson, Bruce Yang
Production Assistant: Mindy Samuelson
Contributing Copy Editors: Terri Fredrickson, Gretchen Kauffman, Peg Smith
Contributing Indexer: Elizabeth T. Parson

Ladies' Home Journal® **Magazine**
Editor-in-Chief: Sally Lee
Creative Director: Jeffrey Saks
Food and Entertaining Editor: Tara Bench
Assistant Food Editor: Khalil A. Hymore

Meredith Publishing Group
President: Tom Harty
Executive Vice President: Andy Sareyan
Vice President, Manufacturing: Bruce Heston

Meredith Corporation
President and Chief Executive Officer: Stephen M. Lacy

In Memoriam: E.T. Meredith III (1933–2003)

Pictured on the front cover:
Almond Flower Cake (recipe on page 257)
Photography by Jay Wilde

Contents

19

88

138

269

From the Editor

Every woman has a personal collection of classic, go-to recipes she relies on for a variety of occasions, whether it's bringing appetizers to a friend's party, baking a cake for a holiday celebration, or whipping up a fast and simple dinner for her family on time-crunched weeknights. And that's what we hope *Ladies' Home Journal All-Time Favorites* will be to you: a timeless source of inspiring, delicious dishes that appeal to everyone. We carefully selected recipes to fit every need or occasion in your life, from fast breakfasts and Sunday brunches to tempting holiday treats and easy 30-minute meals.

Naturally, nutrition played a role in our picks as well. You've told us that living a healthy lifestyle is one of your greatest priorities, which is why you'll find many light, balanced meal ideas in this cookbook and in the pages of *Ladies' Home Journal* every month. When you see this heart symbol ♡, you'll know that recipe is low in fat and sodium and high in fiber.

Of course, you'll find plenty of splurge-worthy dishes and desserts in here too; after all, treats can be part of a healthy diet. We believe in moderation, not deprivation! We all want to make something special and indulgent for ourselves and for the people we care about from time to time, such as the gorgeous Almond Flower Cake on our cover (recipe, page 257).

We're thrilled about this collection and we know you will be too. Happy cooking—and eating!

Sally Lee, Editor-in-Chief
Ladies' Home Journal® Magazine

Breakfast & Brunch

APPLE AND CREAM CHEESE-STUFFED FRENCH TOAST

until golden brown, turning once. Repeat with the remaining 1 tablespoon oil, 1 tablespoon butter, and 2 sandwiches.

6. Stir maple syrup into the remaining apple mixture. Serve French toast with apple mixture. **MAKES 8 SERVINGS**

Per serving: 690 cal., 38 g total fat (16 g sat. fat), 216 mg chol., 345 mg sodium, 78 g carbo., 4 g fiber, 13 g pro.

Oat Pancakes ♡

Prep: 25 minutes **Cook:** 4 minutes per batch

1¼ cups regular rolled oats
¾ cup all-purpose flour
½ cup whole wheat flour
1 tablespoon baking powder
¼ teaspoon salt
3 egg whites
2¼ cups buttermilk
2 tablespoons canola oil
2 tablespoons honey (optional)
1 teaspoon vanilla
   Nonstick cooking spray
   Light pancake syrup (optional)

1. In a large bowl combine oats, all-purpose flour, whole wheat flour, baking powder, and salt. Make a well in the center of flour mixture; set aside.

2. In a medium bowl beat the egg whites with a fork; stir in buttermilk, oil, honey (if desired), and vanilla. Add egg white mixture all at once to flour mixture. Stir just until moistened (batter should be lumpy). If you prefer softened oats, cover batter and allow to stand at room temperature for 15 to 30 minutes.

3. Coat an unheated griddle or heavy skillet with nonstick cooking spray. Preheat on medium-high heat. For each pancake, pour about ¼ cup of the batter onto the hot griddle or skillet. Spread batter into a circle about 4 inches in diameter. Cook on medium heat for 4 to 6 minutes or until the pancakes are golden, turning to cook second sides when pancakes have bubbly surfaces and edges are slightly dry. If desired, serve with syrup.

MAKES 8 (2-PANCAKE) SERVINGS

Per 2 pancakes: 229 cal., 6 g total fat (1 g sat. fat), 3 mg chol., 257 mg sodium, 34 g carbo., 4 g fiber, 10 g pro.

Apple and Cream Cheese-Stuffed French Toast

Start to Finish: 1 hour

1 8-ounce package cream cheese, softened
4 tablespoons powdered sugar
2 teaspoons ground cinnamon
½ teaspoon ground ginger
5 baking apples (about 2¼ pounds), peeled, cored, and cut into ⅛- to ¼-inch slices
¾ cup granulated sugar
6 tablespoons butter
4 eggs, lightly beaten
1 cup whole milk
1 1-pound loaf brioche or soft French bread, cut into eight ¾-inch slices
½ cup chopped pecans, toasted
2 tablespoons vegetable oil
½ cup maple syrup

1. In a medium bowl stir together cream cheese, powdered sugar, ½ teaspoon of the cinnamon, and the ginger. Set aside.

2. In a large bowl toss together apples, granulated sugar, and 1 teaspoon of the cinnamon. In a large skillet melt 4 tablespoons of the butter on medium heat. Add apple mixture; cook about 8 minutes or just until apples are tender, stirring occasionally. Remove skillet from heat.

3. Spread a heaping ¼ cup of the cream cheese mixture on each of 4 bread slices. Top each with 2 tablespoons nuts and 6 to 8 of the cooked apple slices. Cover with the remaining 4 bread slices.

4. In a 3-quart rectangular baking dish mix eggs, milk, and the remaining ½ teaspoon cinnamon. Soak sandwiches, 2 at a time, in the egg mixture for 10 minutes, turning once.

5. Heat a griddle or large skillet on medium-high heat. Add 1 tablespoon oil and 1 tablespoon butter to the skillet. Add 2 sandwiches and cook for 6 to 8 minutes or

DANISH PUFFCAKE

BRUNCH BLINTZES

Brunch Blintzes

Prep: 30 minutes **Bake:** 15 minutes
Oven: 350°F

1½ cups fat-free milk
1 cup all-purpose flour
1 egg
  Nonstick cooking spray
1 15-ounce carton light ricotta cheese
2 tablespoons low-sugar orange marmalade
⅛ teaspoon ground cinnamon
1 8-ounce carton light sour cream
  Shredded orange peel (optional)
1½ cups fresh raspberries and/or blueberries

1. For crepes, in a medium bowl combine milk, flour, and egg; beat with a rotary beater or wire whisk until smooth. Lightly coat an unheated 6-inch skillet or crepe pan with nonstick cooking spray. Preheat on medium heat. Remove skillet from heat and pour in about 2 tablespoons of the batter. Lift and tilt skillet to spread batter evenly. Return skillet to heat; cook for 30 to 60 seconds or until crepe is browned on bottom. Turn out onto paper towels. Repeat with remaining batter to make 15 crepes total. When necessary, coat skillet with additional nonstick cooking spray, removing the skillet from heat before coating.
2. Preheat oven to 350°F. Lightly coat a 15×10×1-inch baking pan with nonstick cooking spray; set aside.
3. For filling, in a medium bowl combine ricotta cheese, orange marmalade, and cinnamon. Spread about 2 tablespoons of the filling on the unbrowned side of a crepe. Fold in half. Fold in half again, forming a wedge. Place in prepared pan. Repeat with remaining filling and crepes, overlapping as necessary to fit in pan.
4. Bake for 15 to 20 minutes or until heated through. To serve, spoon sour cream onto blintzes. If desired, sprinkle with orange peel. Top with berries. **MAKES 15 BLINTZES**

Per blintz: 101 cal., 3 g total fat (2 g sat. fat), 27 mg chol., 51 mg sodium, 12 g carbo., 1 g fiber, 5 g pro.

Danish Puffcake

Prep: 10 minutes **Bake:** 18 minutes
Oven: 425°F

4 tablespoons butter, melted
4 eggs
½ cup all-purpose flour
½ cup whole milk
  Dash salt
3 tablespoons fresh lemon juice
  Melted butter (optional)
¼ cup powdered sugar
1 cup fresh blackberries (6 ounces)

1. Preheat oven to 425°F. Place the 4 tablespoons melted butter in a very large ovenproof skillet. Place skillet in the oven while it preheats.

2. In a blender combine eggs, flour, milk, and salt. Cover and blend about 30 seconds or until a thin batter forms.
3. Remove skillet with butter from oven. Add batter to skillet, tilting skillet to spread batter evenly. Return skillet to oven. Bake for 18 to 20 minutes or until pancake is puffy, golden, and set.
4. Serve from skillet or transfer pancake to a plate. Drizzle with lemon juice and, if desired, additional melted butter. Sprinkle with powdered sugar. Serve immediately with berries. **MAKES 4 SERVINGS**

Tip You can also use a large skillet, but bake pancake for 20 to 22 minutes.

Per serving: 300 cal., 18 g total fat (10 g sat. fat), 245 mg chol., 121 mg sodium, 26 g carbo., 3 g fiber, 10 g pro.

CHOCOLATE WAFFLES

Waffles

Prep: 15 minutes
Bake: Per waffle baker directions

1¾ cups all-purpose flour
  2 tablespoons sugar
  1 tablespoon baking powder
  ¼ teaspoon salt
  2 eggs, lightly beaten
1¾ cups milk
  ½ cup vegetable oil or butter, melted
  1 teaspoon vanilla
    Maple syrup or fresh fruit

1. In a medium bowl stir together flour, sugar, baking powder, and salt. Make a well in the center of the flour mixture; set aside.
2. In another medium bowl combine eggs, milk, oil, and vanilla. Add egg mixture all at once to the flour mixture. Stir just until moistened (batter should be slightly lumpy).
3. Add batter to a preheated, lightly greased waffle baker according to manufacturer's directions. Close lid quickly; do not open until done. Bake according to manufacturer's directions. When done, use a fork to lift waffle from baker. Repeat with remaining batter. Serve warm with syrup or fresh fruit. **MAKES TWELVE TO SIXTEEN 4-INCH WAFFLES OR SIX 7-INCH WAFFLES**

Per waffle: 191 cal., 11 g total fat (2 g sat. fat), 38 mg chol., 137 mg sodium, 19 g carbo., 1 g fiber, 4 g pro.

Chocolate Waffles Prepare as above, except decrease flour to 1½ cups, increase sugar to ¼ cup, and add ⅓ cup unsweetened cocoa powder with the flour mixture. Fold ¼ cup miniature semisweet chocolate pieces into the batter. (You may need to lightly coat the waffle baker with nonstick cooking spray between each waffle to prevent sticking.) If desired, serve with plain yogurt and fresh raspberries and/or blueberries.

Breakfast Bread Pudding

Prep: 30 minutes **Bake:** 40 minutes
Stand: 15 minutes **Oven:** 325°F

  5 to 6 slices whole wheat cinnamon-swirl
    bread or cinnamon-raisin bread
    Nonstick cooking spray
1½ cups fat-free milk
  3 eggs
  2 tablespoons sugar
  1 teaspoon vanilla
  ¼ teaspoon ground nutmeg
  1 5.5-ounce can apricot nectar or peach
    nectar (⅔ cup)
  2 teaspoons cornstarch

1. Preheat oven to 325°F. Cut enough of the bread into cubes to make 4 cups. Place bread cubes in a shallow baking pan. Bake about 10 minutes or until bread is dry, stirring once. Cool on a wire rack.
2. Lightly coat six 6-ounce soufflé dishes or custard cups with nonstick cooking spray. Divide bread cubes among the prepared dishes. In a medium bowl combine milk, eggs, sugar, vanilla, and nutmeg; beat with a rotary beater or wire whisk. Pour milk mixture evenly over bread cubes. Press lightly with the back of a spoon to thoroughly moisten bread.
3. Place soufflé dishes in a 13×9×2-inch baking pan. Place baking pan on oven rack. Carefully pour hot tap water into the baking pan around dishes to a depth of 1 inch.
4. Bake for 30 to 35 minutes or until a knife inserted near centers comes out clean. Transfer dishes to a wire rack. Let stand for 15 minutes.
5. Meanwhile, for sauce, in a small saucepan gradually stir apricot nectar into cornstarch until combined. Cook and stir over medium heat until thickened and bubbly. Reduce heat. Cook and stir for 2 minutes more.
6. If desired, remove puddings from soufflé dishes. Spoon sauce over warm puddings.
MAKES 6 SERVINGS

Per serving: 178 cal., 4 g total fat (1 g sat. fat), 107 mg chol., 179 mg sodium, 27 g carbo., 3 g fiber, 9 g pro.

Farmer's Casserole ♡

Prep: 25 minutes **Bake:** 40 minutes
Stand: 5 minutes **Oven:** 350°F

> Nonstick cooking spray
> 3 cups frozen shredded hash brown potatoes
> ¾ cup shredded Monterey Jack cheese with jalapeño peppers or shredded cheddar cheese (3 ounces)
> 1 cup diced cooked ham or Canadian bacon
> ¼ cup sliced green onions (2)
> 1 cup refrigerated or frozen egg product, thawed, or 4 eggs, lightly beaten
> 1½ cups fat-free milk or one 12-ounce can evaporated fat-free milk
> ⅛ teaspoon black pepper

1. Preheat oven to 350°F. Coat a 2-quart square baking dish with nonstick cooking spray. Arrange potatoes evenly in the bottom of the dish. Sprinkle with cheese, ham, and green onions.
2. In a medium bowl combine egg product, milk, and pepper. Pour egg mixture over potato mixture in dish.
3. Bake, uncovered, for 40 to 45 minutes or until a knife inserted near the center comes out clean. Let stand for 5 minutes before serving. **MAKES 6 SERVINGS**

Farmer's Casserole for 12 Prepare as above, except double all ingredients and use a 3-quart rectangular baking dish. Bake, uncovered, for 45 to 55 minutes or until a knife inserted near the center comes out clean. Let stand for 5 minutes before serving.

Make-ahead directions Prepare as above through Step 2. Cover and chill for up to 24 hours. Bake, uncovered, in a preheated 350°F oven for 50 to 55 minutes or until a knife inserted near the center comes out clean. Let stand for 5 minutes before serving.

Per serving: 208 cal., 6 g total fat (3 g sat. fat), 27 mg chol., 610 mg sodium, 23 g carbo., 2 g fiber, 17 g pro.

Scrambled Eggs

Start to Finish: 15 minutes

> 4 eggs
> ¼ cup milk, half-and-half, or light cream
> ⅛ teaspoon salt
> Dash black pepper
> 1 tablespoon butter

1. In a medium bowl whisk together eggs, milk, salt, and pepper. In a large skillet melt butter on medium heat; pour in egg mixture. Cook, without stirring, until mixture begins to set on the bottom and around edge.
2. With a spatula or a large spoon, lift and fold the partially cooked egg mixture so that the uncooked portion flows underneath. Continue cooking on medium heat for 2 to 3 minutes or until egg mixture is cooked through but is still glossy and moist. Remove from heat immediately. **MAKES 2 SERVINGS**

Per serving: 213 cal., 16 g total fat (7 g sat. fat), 441 mg chol., 339 mg sodium, 2 g carbo., 0 g fiber, 14 g pro.

Greek-Style Scrambled Eggs Prepare as directed, except cook and stir 2 cups fresh baby spinach in the butter until limp. Add egg mixture and continue as directed. Sprinkle with ½ cup crumbled feta cheese with garlic and herbs and red onion slivers after the eggs begin to set.

Cheese and Onion Scrambled Eggs Prepare as directed, except cook 2 tablespoons sliced green onion in the butter for 30 seconds; add egg mixture. Fold in ⅓ cup shredded cheddar or Swiss cheese after eggs begin to set.

SCRAMBLED EGGS WITH
TOMATOES AND PEPPERS

Scrambled Eggs with Tomatoes and Peppers ♡

Start to Finish: 20 minutes

     1 tablespoon olive oil
 ½ cup chopped onion (1 medium)
 ½ cup chopped red or green sweet pepper
 ½ cup chopped, seeded tomato
     2 cups refrigerated or frozen egg product,
        thawed, or 8 eggs
 ⅓ cup fat-free milk
 ¼ teaspoon salt
 ⅛ teaspoon black pepper

1. In a large skillet heat olive oil on medium heat. Add onion and sweet pepper; cook for 4 to 6 minutes or until tender, stirring occasionally. Stir in tomato.

2. Meanwhile, in a medium bowl beat together egg product, milk, salt, and black pepper with a wire whisk or fork. Add egg mixture to onion mixture in skillet. Cook on medium heat, without stirring, until mixture begins to set on bottom and around edge.

3. With a spatula or a large spoon, lift and fold partially cooked egg mixture so that the uncooked portion flows underneath. Continue cooking on medium heat for 2 to 3 minutes or until egg mixture is cooked through but is still glossy and moist. Remove from heat. Serve immediately. **MAKES 4 SERVINGS**

Per serving: 114 cal., 4 g total fat (1 g sat. fat), 0 mg chol., 386 mg sodium, 7 g carbo., 1 g fiber, 13 g pro.

Ham and Cheese Skillet

Start to Finish: 25 minutes

        Nonstick cooking spray
     1 cup chopped cooked ham (5 ounces)
 ½ cup sliced green onions or chopped onion
 ½ cup chopped green or red sweet pepper
     6 eggs
 ¾ cup low-fat cottage cheese
 ⅛ teaspoon black pepper
     2 plum tomatoes, thinly sliced
 ¼ cup shredded reduced-fat cheddar
        cheese (1 ounce)
        Sliced green onions (optional)

1. Preheat broiler. Lightly coat an unheated 10-inch ovenproof skillet with nonstick cooking spray. Preheat skillet on medium heat. Add ham, the ½ cup green onions, and the sweet pepper. Cook and stir about 4 minutes or until vegetables are tender and ham is lightly browned.

2. Meanwhile, in a medium bowl beat eggs with a rotary beater or wire whisk. Beat in cottage cheese and black pepper. Pour over ham mixture in skillet. Cook on medium-low heat. As egg mixture sets, run a spatula around the edge of the skillet, lifting egg mixture so the uncooked portion flows underneath. Continue cooking and lifting edge until egg mixture is almost set but still glossy and moist.

3. Broil 5 inches from heat for 1 to 2 minutes or until eggs are set. Arrange tomato slices on eggs. Sprinkle cheese over tomato. Broil for 1 minute more. If desired, garnish with additional green onions. **MAKES 6 SERVINGS**

Per serving: 148 cal., 7 g total fat (3 g sat. fat), 228 mg chol., 581 mg sodium, 5 g carbo., 1 g fiber, 16 g pro.

Southwest Skillet

Start to Finish: 20 minutes

- 2 tablespoons sliced almonds
- 1 tablespoon olive oil or vegetable oil
- 1 yellow sweet pepper, seeded and cut into thin bite-size strips
- 1 fresh jalapeño, seeded and chopped*
- 4 medium tomatoes (about 1¼ pounds), seeded and chopped (about 3 cups)
- 1 teaspoon chili powder
- ½ teaspoon ground cumin
- ¼ teaspoon salt
- 4 eggs
- 1 medium ripe avocado, halved, seeded, peeled, and sliced (optional)

1. In a large skillet toast almonds on medium heat for 4 to 5 minutes or until lightly browned, stirring occasionally. Remove almonds from skillet; set aside. In the same skillet heat oil on medium heat. Add sweet pepper and jalapeño; cook and stir about 2 minutes or until tender. Stir in tomatoes, chili powder, cumin, and salt. Cook, uncovered, for 5 minutes, stirring occasionally.

2. Break 1 of the eggs into a measuring cup. Carefully slide egg onto tomato mixture. Repeat with remaining eggs, spacing eggs as evenly as possible.

3. Simmer, covered, on medium-low heat for 3 to 5 minutes or until the egg whites are completely set and yolks begin to thicken but are not hard. If desired, top with avocado. Sprinkle with the almonds. **MAKES 4 SERVINGS**

*Tip Because chile peppers, such as jalapeños, contain oils that can burn your skin and eyes, wear plastic or rubber gloves when working with them. If your bare hands do touch the chile peppers, wash your hands well with soap and water.

Per serving: 157 cal., 10 g total fat (2 g sat. fat), 212 mg chol., 230 mg sodium, 9 g carbo., 3 g fiber, 9 g pro.

SPINACH AND CHEESE OMELET

Spinach and Cheese Omelet ♡

Prep: 10 minutes **Cook:** 8 minutes

- Nonstick cooking spray
- 2 cups refrigerated or frozen egg product, thawed, or 8 eggs
- 2 tablespoons snipped fresh chives, Italian (flat-leaf) parsley, or chervil
- ⅛ teaspoon salt
- ⅛ teaspoon cayenne pepper
- ½ cup shredded reduced-fat sharp cheddar cheese (2 ounces)
- 2 cups fresh baby spinach leaves or torn fresh spinach
- 1 recipe Red Pepper Relish

1. Coat a 10-inch nonstick skillet with flared sides with nonstick cooking spray. Heat skillet on medium heat.

2. In a large bowl beat together egg product, chives, salt, and cayenne pepper. Pour into prepared skillet. Immediately begin stirring the eggs gently and continuously with a wooden spoon or plastic spatula until mixture resembles small pieces of cooked egg surrounded by liquid egg. Stop stirring. Cook for 30 to 60 seconds more or until egg is set but shiny.

3. Immediately sprinkle with cheese. Top with 1 cup of the spinach and ¼ cup of the Red Pepper Relish. With a spatula, lift and fold one side of omelet partially over filling. Arrange remaining spinach on warm platter. Transfer omelet to platter. Top with remaining Red Pepper Relish. **MAKES 4 SERVINGS**

Red Pepper Relish In a small bowl combine ⅔ cup chopped red sweet pepper, 2 tablespoons finely chopped green onion or onion, 1 tablespoon cider vinegar, and ¼ teaspoon black pepper.

Per serving: 122 cal., 3 g total fat (2 g sat. fat), 10 mg chol., 404 mg sodium, 7 g carbo., 3 g fiber, 16 g pro.

FRESH TOMATO OMELETS
WITH MOZZARELLA CHEESE

Fresh Tomato Omelets with Mozzarella Cheese

Start to Finish: 20 minutes

    4 eggs
    ⅛ teaspoon salt
    ⅛ teaspoon black pepper
       Nonstick cooking spray
    4 tomato slices
    ¼ cup shredded reduced-fat mozzarella
       cheese (1 ounce)
    1 teaspoon snipped fresh oregano or
       ¼ teaspoon dried oregano, crushed

1. In a small bowl combine eggs, salt, and pepper; beat with a rotary beater or wire whisk. Coat an unheated 8-inch nonstick skillet with nonstick cooking spray. Preheat on medium heat. Pour half of the egg mixture into the hot skillet.

2. Using a wooden spoon or plastic spatula, immediately begin stirring egg mixture gently but continuously until mixture resembles small pieces of cooked egg surrounded by liquid egg. Stop stirring. Cook 30 to 60 seconds more or until egg mixture is set but shiny.

3. Place 2 tomato slices on half of the egg mixture in skillet. Top with half of the cheese. Using a spatula, lift and fold opposite edge of the omelet over tomato slices. Sprinkle with half of the oregano. Transfer to a warm plate.

4. Repeat with the remaining egg mixture, tomato slices, cheese, and oregano to make second omelet. **MAKES 2 SERVINGS**

Per serving: 228 cal., 13 g total fat (4 g sat. fat), 432 mg chol., 398 mg sodium, 11 g carbo., 3 g fiber, 18 g pro.

Tex-Mex Spinach Omelet

Start to Finish: 25 minutes

    4 eggs
    1 tablespoon snipped fresh cilantro
       Dash salt
       Dash ground cumin
       Nonstick cooking spray
    ¼ cup shredded Monterey Jack cheese with
       jalapeño peppers, reduced-fat cheddar
       cheese, or reduced-fat Swiss cheese
       (1 ounce)
    ¾ cup fresh baby spinach leaves
    1 recipe Corn-Pepper Relish

1. In a medium bowl combine eggs, cilantro, salt, and cumin; beat with a rotary beater or wire whisk until frothy.

2. Coat an unheated 10-inch nonstick skillet with flared sides with nonstick cooking spray. Preheat skillet on medium-high heat.

3. Pour egg mixture into hot skillet; reduce heat to medium. Using a wooden spoon or plastic spatula, immediately begin stirring the eggs gently but continuously until mixture resembles small pieces of cooked egg surrounded by liquid egg. Stop stirring. Cook for 30 to 60 seconds more or until egg mixture is set and shiny.

4. Sprinkle with cheese. Top with three-fourths of the spinach and half of the Corn-Pepper Relish. Using a spatula, lift and fold an edge of the omelet partially over filling. Top with the remaining spinach and the remaining Corn-Pepper Relish. Cut omelet in half; transfer to plates. **MAKES 2 SERVINGS**

Corn-Pepper Relish In a small bowl combine ¼ cup chopped red sweet pepper; ¼ cup frozen whole kernel corn, thawed; 2 tablespoons chopped red onion; and 1 tablespoon snipped fresh cilantro.

Per serving: 232 cal., 15 g total fat (6 g sat. fat), 438 mg chol., 322 mg sodium, 8 g carbo., 1 g fiber, 17 g pro.

TEX-MEX SPINACH OMELET

ASPARAGUS-ZUCCHINI FRITTATA

Omelet de Provence

Start to Finish: 30 minutes

Nonstick cooking spray
2 cups sliced fresh mushrooms
3 tablespoons sliced green onions
1 clove garlic, minced
4 eggs
¼ teaspoon herbes de Provence or dried thyme or basil, crushed
⅛ teaspoon salt
Dash black pepper
1 teaspoon olive oil
¼ cup shredded part-skim mozzarella cheese (1 ounce)
1 medium plum tomato, chopped
1 tablespoon finely shredded Asiago cheese
Fresh parsley (optional)

1. Lightly coat an unheated 6- to 7-inch nonstick skillet with flared sides with nonstick cooking spray. Preheat skillet on medium heat. Add mushrooms, onions, and garlic; cook and stir until mushrooms are tender. Using a slotted spoon, remove mushroom mixture from skillet; set aside. If necessary, drain skillet; carefully wipe out skillet.
2. In a medium bowl whisk together eggs, herbes de Provence, salt, and pepper.
3. Add half of the oil to the skillet; heat skillet on medium heat. Pour half of the egg mixture into skillet. Using a wooden spoon or plastic spatula, immediately begin stirring eggs gently and continuously until mixture resembles small pieces of cooked egg surrounded by liquid egg. Stop stirring. Cook for 30 to 60 seconds more or until egg mixture is set and shiny.
4. Sprinkle with half of the mozzarella. Top with half of the mushroom mixture. Continue cooking until cheese begins to melt. Using spatula, lift and fold edge of omelet partially over filling. Remove from skillet; keep warm.
5. Repeat with the remaining oil, egg mixture, mozzarella, and mushroom mixture. Top omelets with tomato, Asiago cheese, and, if desired, parsley. **MAKES 2 SERVINGS**

Per serving: 255 cal., 16 g total fat (6 g sat. fat), 436 mg chol., 422 mg sodium, 8 g carbo., 2 g fiber, 21 g pro.

Asparagus-Zucchini Frittata ♡

Prep: 30 minutes **Bake:** 40 minutes
Stand: 10 minutes **Oven:** 350°F

Nonstick cooking spray
1½ pounds fresh asparagus, trimmed and cut into 1-inch-long pieces
1 medium yellow sweet pepper, cut into strips
⅓ cup chopped onion
¼ cup bottled roasted red sweet peppers, drained and chopped
1 small zucchini, halved lengthwise and sliced ¼ inch thick (about 1 cup)
10 eggs
1 cup fat-free milk
2 tablespoons snipped fresh dill or ½ teaspoon dried dill
1 teaspoon salt
½ teaspoon black pepper

1. Preheat oven to 350°F. Coat a 3-quart oval or rectangular baking dish with nonstick cooking spray; set aside.

2. In a large saucepan bring about 1 inch water to boiling. Add asparagus, sweet pepper strips, and onion. Return to boiling; reduce heat. Simmer, covered, about 1 minute or until crisp-tender. Drain well. Stir in roasted red peppers. Evenly spread asparagus mixture in prepared baking dish. Layer zucchini slices on top.
3. In a large bowl beat eggs with a rotary beater or wire whisk until combined. Beat in milk, dill, salt, and black pepper. Pour over vegetables in baking dish.
4. Bake, uncovered, for 40 to 45 minutes or until a knife inserted near center comes out clean. Let stand for 10 minutes before serving. If desired, garnish with fresh dill sprigs. **MAKES 6 SERVINGS**

Per serving: 176 cal., 9 g total fat (3 g sat. fat), 353 mg chol., 527 mg sodium, 11 g carbo., 3 g fiber, 15 g pro.

BACON 'N' EGG POCKETS

Breakfast Taco Roll-Ups ♡

Start to Finish: 20 minutes

   Nonstick cooking spray
⅓ cup chopped celery
⅓ cup chopped green sweet pepper
1 cup chopped cooked ham (5 ounces)
1 8-ounce can crushed pineapple (juice pack), well drained, or ¾ cup finely chopped apple
1 cup reduced-fat shredded cheddar cheese (4 ounces)
8 6-inch whole wheat or plain flour tortillas, warmed*

1. Lightly coat an unheated small nonstick skillet with nonstick cooking spray. Preheat skillet on medium heat. Add celery and sweet pepper; cook and stir until tender. Stir in ham and pineapple. Cook and stir until heated through. Remove from heat. Stir in cheese.
2. Spoon about ¼ cup of the ham-cheese mixture in the center of each warmed tortilla. Roll up tortillas. **MAKES 8 SERVINGS**

*Tip To warm tortillas, preheat oven to 350°F. Wrap tortillas tightly in foil; bake about 10 minutes or until warm. Or wrap tortillas in white microwave-safe paper towels; microwave on high about 30 seconds or until tortillas are softened.

Per serving: 136 cal., 6 g total fat (2 g sat. fat), 18 mg chol., 507 mg sodium, 17 g carbo., 9 g fiber, 12 g pro.

Bacon 'n' Egg Pockets ♡

Start to Finish: 15 minutes

2 eggs
4 egg whites
3 ounces Canadian bacon, chopped
3 tablespoons water
2 tablespoons sliced green onion
⅛ teaspoon salt
   Nonstick cooking spray
2 large whole wheat pita bread rounds, halved crosswise
½ cup shredded reduced-fat cheddar cheese (2 ounces) (optional)

1. In a medium bowl combine eggs, egg whites, bacon, the water, green onion, and salt. Beat with a wire whisk until well mixed.

2. Lightly coat an unheated large nonstick skillet with nonstick cooking spray. Preheat on medium heat. Add egg mixture to skillet. Cook, without stirring, until mixture begins to set on the bottom and around edge. Using a spatula or a large spoon, lift and fold the partially cooked eggs so the uncooked portion flows underneath. Continue cooking about 2 minutes or until egg mixture is cooked through but is still glossy and moist. Remove from heat immediately.
3. Fill pita halves with egg mixture. If desired, sprinkle with cheese. **MAKES 4 SERVINGS**

Per serving: 162 cal., 4 g total fat (1 g sat. fat), 118 mg chol., 616 mg sodium, 18 g carbo., 2 g fiber, 13 g pro.

BREAKFAST PIZZA

Salami and Provolone Burrito Wraps

Start to Finish: 25 minutes

- 4 eggs
- ¼ cup milk
- 1 tablespoon snipped fresh basil
- ¼ teaspoon salt
  Dash black pepper
- 1 tablespoon butter
- 2 ounces salami, chopped
- ½ cup bottled chopped roasted red sweet peppers, drained
- 4 8-inch flour tortillas, warmed (see tip, page 24)
- ½ cup shredded provolone cheese (2 ounces)

1. In a medium bowl whisk together eggs, milk, basil, salt, and black pepper. In a large skillet melt butter on medium heat; pour in egg mixture. Cook, without stirring, until mixture begins to set on the bottom and around edge. With a spatula or large spoon, lift and fold the partially cooked egg mixture so that the uncooked portion flows underneath. Stir in salami and roasted peppers. Continue cooking for 2 to 3 minutes or until egg mixture is cooked through but is still glossy and moist. Remove from heat.
2. Divide egg mixture among warm tortillas, spooning it down the center of the tortillas. Sprinkle with cheese. Roll up tortillas.

MAKES 4 WRAPS

Per wrap: 354 cal., 19 g total fat (8 g sat. fat), 243 mg chol., 821 mg sodium, 28 g carbo., 0 g fiber, 18 g pro.

Bacon Burrito Wrap Prepare as above, except add 1 tablespoon snipped fresh cilantro in place of the basil. Add 4 strips bacon, crisp-cooked, drained, and crumbled, in place of the salami; ¼ cup sliced green onions in place of the roasted red peppers; and ½ cup shredded Monterey Jack cheese with jalapeño peppers in place of the provolone cheese. If desired, top eggs with salsa; roll up tortillas.

Breakfast Pizza

Prep: 25 minutes **Bake:** 15 minutes
Oven: 400°F

- 4 ounces plain or peppered bacon, diced
- ½ cup chopped green sweet pepper
- ¼ cup sliced green onions (2)
- 1 12-inch prebaked pizza crust
- 1 8-ounce tub cream cheese
- 2 eggs
- 1 cup cubed cooked ham
- 1 cup shredded cheddar cheese (4 ounces)

1. Preheat oven to 400°F. In a large skillet cook bacon until crisp. Remove bacon from skillet; drain on paper towels. Drain skillet, reserving 1 tablespoon drippings. Cook sweet pepper and onions in reserved drippings until tender. Drain; set aside.
2. Place pizza crust on a large baking sheet; set aside. In a small bowl beat cream cheese with an electric mixer on medium just until smooth. Add eggs, 1 at a time, beating until combined. Spread cream cheese mixture over pizza shell. Sprinkle with bacon, green pepper, and green onions. Top with ham.
3. Bake for 15 to 20 minutes or until cream cheese layer is set. Sprinkle with cheddar cheese. Bake for 3 to 4 minutes more or until cheese is melted. Cut into wedges to serve.

MAKES 6 TO 8 SERVINGS

Per serving: 410 cal., 27 g total fat (13 g sat. fat), 126 mg chol., 635 mg sodium, 29 g carbo., 1 g fiber, 16 g pro.

Mushroom-Artichoke Pizza Prepare as above, except omit bacon, sweet pepper, and green onions. In a large skillet cook and stir 2 cups fresh mushrooms, sliced, in 1 tablespoon olive oil on medium-high heat until golden. Substitute cooked mushrooms for ham and add ½ cup marinated artichoke hearts, drained and coarsely chopped, and ½ cup slivered roasted red sweet peppers. Substitute shredded Italian-blend cheese for the cheddar cheese.

BANANA CRUNCH MUFFINS

Banana Crunch Muffins

Prep: 25 minutes **Bake:** 16 minutes
Cool: 5 minutes **Oven:** 375°F

- 2¼ cups all-purpose flour
- ¾ cup granulated sugar
- 2 tablespoons butter
- ¼ cup chopped pecans
- ⅓ cup packed brown sugar
- 1½ teaspoons baking soda
- ¼ teaspoon salt
- ¼ teaspoon ground cinnamon
- ¼ teaspoon ground nutmeg
- ½ cup butter
- 1 egg, lightly beaten
- 1 cup mashed bananas (2 medium)
- ⅓ cup milk

1. Preheat oven to 375°F. Grease twelve 2½-inch muffin cups; set aside. For topping, in a bowl stir together ¼ cup of the flour and ¼ cup of the granulated sugar. Cut in the 2 tablespoons butter until mixture resembles coarse crumbs. Stir in pecans; set aside.

2. In a medium bowl stir together the remaining 2 cups flour, the remaining ½ cup granulated sugar, the brown sugar, baking soda, salt, cinnamon, and nutmeg. Using a pastry blender, cut in the ½ cup butter until mixture resembles coarse crumbs. Make a well in center of the flour mixture; set aside.

3. In a small bowl combine egg, bananas, and milk. Add egg mixture to flour mixture all at once; stir just until moistened (batter should be lumpy). Spoon batter into prepared muffin cups, filling each three-fourths full. Sprinkle topping evenly over batter.

4. Bake for 16 to 18 minutes or until golden and a wooden toothpick inserted in the centers comes out clean. Cool in muffin cups on a wire rack for 5 minutes. Remove muffins from cups. Serve warm. **MAKES 12 MUFFINS**

Per muffin: 285 cal., 12 g total fat (7 g sat. fat), 44 mg chol., 285 mg sodium, 42 g carbo., 1 g fiber, 2 g pro.

Blueberry Streusel Coffee Cake

Prep: 30 minutes **Bake:** 35 minutes
Oven: 350°F

- 1½ cups packed brown sugar
- 1 cup coarsely chopped nuts
- 4 teaspoons ground cinnamon
- 1 8-ounce carton sour cream
- 1 teaspoon baking soda
- ¾ cup granulated sugar
- ½ cup butter, softened
- 3 eggs
- 1 teaspoon vanilla
- 2 cups all-purpose flour
- 1½ teaspoons baking powder
- 2 cups fresh or frozen blueberries, thawed
- 1 recipe Powdered Sugar Icing

1. Preheat oven to 350°F. In a bowl stir together brown sugar, nuts, and cinnamon; set aside. In another bowl stir together sour cream and baking soda; set aside. Grease a 13×9×2-inch baking pan; set aside.

2. In a large mixing bowl beat granulated sugar and butter with an electric mixer on medium until well mixed. Beat in eggs and vanilla. Beat in flour and baking powder until well mixed. Add the sour cream mixture; beat until combined.

3. Spread half of the batter evenly in the prepared pan. Sprinkle blueberries over batter. Sprinkle half of the nut mixture over the blueberries. Drop remaining batter into large mounds on top of filling. Carefully spread batter over the nut mixture and blueberries. Sprinkle the remaining nut mixture over batter.

4. Bake for 35 to 40 minutes or until a wooden toothpick inserted near the center comes out clean. Drizzle with Powdered Sugar Icing. Serve warm or let cool on a wire rack. **MAKES 16 SERVINGS**

Powdered Sugar Icing In a small bowl stir together ½ cup powdered sugar, 2 teaspoons milk, and ¼ teaspoon vanilla. Stir in enough additional milk, 1 teaspoon at a time, to make icing drizzling consistency.

Per serving: 345 cal., 14 g total fat (6 g sat. fat), 61 mg chol., 184 mg sodium, 51 g carbo., 2 g fiber, 4 g pro.

SPICED MAPLE PULL-APARTS

MONKEY BREAD ROLLS

Spiced Maple Pull-Aparts

Prep: 20 minutes **Bake:** 40 minutes
Cool: 10 minutes **Oven:** 350°F

- 1 cup packed brown sugar
- 2 teaspoons pumpkin pie spice
- 1 teaspoon instant espresso powder (optional)
- ½ cup butter, melted
- 1 teaspoon vanilla
- 3 11-ounce packages (12 each) refrigerated breadsticks
- 2 tablespoons maple syrup

1. Preheat oven to 350°F. Meanwhile, generously grease two 9×5×3-inch loaf pans or dishes; set aside.

2. In a medium bowl stir together brown sugar, pumpkin pie spice, and, if desired, espresso powder. Sprinkle 1 tablespoon of the brown sugar mixture into each prepared loaf pan; tilt pans to distribute sugar across the bottoms and along sides. Shake any excess brown sugar mixture back into the remaining brown sugar mixture. Set loaf pans and remaining brown sugar mixture aside. In a small bowl stir together butter and vanilla.

3. Unroll breadstick dough and separate into 36 strips. Roll each strip into a spiral, starting from a short side.

4. Dip each spiral into the butter mixture; roll in the brown sugar mixture to coat. Place 18 of the dough spirals in each loaf pan, arranging spirals in 2 layers in each pan. Sprinkle any remaining brown sugar mixture over the tops. Stir maple syrup into the remaining butter mixture; drizzle over spirals.

5. Bake about 40 minutes or until puffed and brown. To prevent overbrowning, cover loosely with foil during the last 10 minutes of baking. Cool in pans for 10 minutes; remove from pans. Cool slightly on wire racks; serve warm. **MAKES 18 PULL-APARTS**

Per pull-apart: 239 cal., 8 g total fat (5 g sat. fat), 14 mg chol., 410 mg sodium, 39 g carbo., 1 g fiber, 4 g pro.

Monkey Bread Rolls

Prep: 30 minutes **Bake:** 20 minutes
Oven: 350°F

- ½ of a 34.5-ounce package frozen cinnamon sweet-roll dough or frozen orange sweet-roll dough (6 rolls)
- ⅓ cup chopped pecans
- ¼ cup butter, melted
- ½ cup sugar
- ¼ cup caramel-flavor ice cream topping
- 1 tablespoon maple-flavor syrup

1. Grease a large baking sheet. Place frozen rolls about 2 inches apart on prepared baking sheet. (Discard frosting packets or reserve for another use.) Cover rolls with plastic wrap. Refrigerate overnight to let dough thaw and begin to rise.

2. Preheat oven to 350°F. Generously grease twelve 2½-inch muffin cups. Divide pecans evenly among the muffin cups; set aside.

3. Using kitchen scissors, cut each roll into 4 pieces. Dip each piece in melted butter, then roll in sugar. Place 2 dough pieces into each prepared muffin cup. Drizzle rolls with any remaining melted butter; sprinkle with any remaining sugar. In a small bowl stir together ice cream topping and maple syrup; drizzle over rolls.

4. Bake about 20 minutes or until rolls are golden brown. Cool in muffin cups on a wire rack for 1 minute. Invert onto a large platter. Cool slightly; serve warm. **MAKES 12 ROLLS**

Per roll: 252 cal., 12 g total fat (4 g sat. fat), 11 mg chol., 373 mg sodium, 36 g carbo., 0 g fiber, 2 g pro.

FRUIT AND YOGURT PARFAITS

Berry-Banana Smoothie

Start to Finish: 10 minutes

  1 cup orange juice
  1 cup frozen unsweetened strawberries, raspberries, and/or blackberries
  1 medium banana, peeled and cut up
  ¼ cup plain low-fat yogurt
      Fresh strawberries, sliced (optional)
      Fresh mint (optional)

1. In a blender combine orange juice, frozen berries, banana, and yogurt. Cover and blend until smooth.
2. To serve, pour into 2 glasses. If desired, garnish with fresh strawberries and fresh mint. **MAKES 2 (ABOUT 9-OUNCE) SERVINGS**

Per serving: 151 cal., 1 g total fat (0 g sat. fat), 2 mg chol., 24 mg sodium, 34 g carbo., 3 g fiber, 4 g pro.

Fruity Oatmeal

Start to Finish: 15 minutes

  2 cups water
  ¼ teaspoon salt
  1 cup rolled oats
  1 cup chopped apple or chopped, peeled peach
  ¼ cup raisins or snipped whole pitted dates
  1 teaspoon vanilla
  ¼ teaspoon ground cinnamon
      Fat-free milk (optional)

1. In a medium saucepan bring the water and salt to boiling. Stir in oats, apple, raisins, vanilla, and cinnamon. Reduce heat. Simmer, uncovered, for 3 minutes (for quick oats) or 5 minutes (for regular oats), stirring occasionally. Remove from heat. Cover and let stand for 2 minutes before serving. If desired, serve with fat-free milk. **MAKES 4 SERVINGS**

Per serving: 140 cal., 2 g total fat (0 g sat. fat), 0 mg chol., 151 mg sodium, 28 g carbo., 4 g fiber, 4 g pro.

Fruit and Yogurt Parfaits

Start to Finish: 20 minutes

  ½ cup chopped nectarine or peeled peach
  1 6-ounce carton plain fat-free yogurt
  ½ teaspoon vanilla
  ½ cup bite-size shredded wheat biscuits, coarsely crushed
  ⅛ teaspoon ground cinnamon
  2 teaspoons sugar-free maple-flavor syrup or light maple-flavor syrup
  1 tablespoon sliced almonds, toasted
      Fresh nectarine or peach slices (optional)

1. Place chopped nectarine in a small bowl. Stir in yogurt and vanilla.
2. Spoon half of the yogurt mixture into two 8- to 10-ounce parfait glasses. Top with crushed shredded wheat biscuits; sprinkle with some of the cinnamon. Drizzle with maple syrup. Spoon remaining yogurt mixture over all. Top yogurt with almonds and remaining cinnamon. If desired, garnish with nectarine slices. **MAKES 2 SERVINGS**

Per serving: 118 cal., 2 g total fat (0 g sat. fat), 2 mg chol., 75 mg sodium, 19 g carbo., 2 g fiber, 7 g pro.

Appetizers & Snacks

POLENTA WITH PEPPERS AND OLIVES

Polenta with Peppers and Olives

Prep: 25 minutes **Bake:** 10 minutes
Oven: 350°F

- 1 16-ounce tube refrigerated cooked polenta
- 2 tablespoons olive oil
- 1 cup red, green, and/or yellow sweet peppers cut into thin strips
- ⅛ teaspoon salt
- ⅛ teaspoon crushed red pepper
- ¼ cup pitted kalamata olives, coarsely chopped
- 2 tablespoons finely shredded Parmesan cheese
- 1½ teaspoons snipped fresh rosemary

1. Preheat oven to 350°F. Trim ends of polenta; discard trimmings. Cut polenta into 12 slices (each about ½ inch thick). Brush both sides of polenta slices with 1 tablespoon of the oil. Place polenta slices on a baking sheet. Bake for 10 to 15 minutes or until heated through.
2. Meanwhile, in a medium skillet heat the remaining 1 tablespoon oil on medium heat. Add sweet pepper strips, salt, and crushed red pepper. Cook and stir until pepper strips are tender, stirring occasionally. Stir in olives.
3. To serve, spoon pepper mixture over warm polenta. Sprinkle with shredded Parmesan cheese and rosemary. **MAKES 12 SERVINGS**

Per serving: 52 cal., 4 g total fat (1 g sat. fat), 3 mg chol., 124 mg sodium, 4 g carbo., 1 g fiber, 1 g pro.

Hummus and Cucumber Bruschetta

Prep: 25 minutes **Bake:** 10 minutes
Oven: 400°F

- 12 ¼-inch slices baguette-style French bread
  Olive oil nonstick cooking spray
- 1½ teaspoons Italian seasoning, crushed
- ¼ teaspoon garlic powder
- ⅓ cup finely chopped English cucumber
- 2 tablespoons plain low-fat yogurt
- 1½ teaspoons lemon juice
- 1½ teaspoons snipped fresh oregano or ½ teaspoon dried oregano, crushed
- ⅓ cup hummus
- ¼ cup chopped bottled roasted red sweet pepper, drained
  Snipped fresh oregano (optional)

1. Preheat oven to 400°F. Arrange baguette slices in a single layer on a large baking sheet. Lightly coat baguette slices with nonstick cooking spray. Combine Italian seasoning and garlic powder; sprinkle over bread slices. Bake about 10 minutes or until slices are crisp and lightly brown. Let cool.
2. Meanwhile, in a small bowl combine cucumber, yogurt, lemon juice, and 1½ teaspoons fresh or ½ teaspoon dried oregano. Spread some of the hummus on each toasted baguette slice; top with cucumber mixture and roasted red pepper. If desired, sprinkle with additional fresh oregano.

MAKES 4 SERVINGS (3 BRUSCHETTA EACH)

Per bruschetta: 126 cal., 3 g total fat (0 g sat. fat), 0 mg chol., 296 mg sodium, 21 g carbo., 1 g fiber, 5 g pro.

Pepper Cheese with Apricots ♡

Prep: 15 minutes **Chill:** 4 to 24 hours

- 1 16-ounce carton plain low-fat yogurt (see tip, bottom right)
- ¼ cup finely snipped dried apricots
- 1 tablespoon honey
- ¼ to ½ teaspoon coarsely ground black pepper
- ½ of an 8-ounce package reduced-fat cream cheese (Neufchâtel), softened
- 1 tablespoon finely chopped pistachio nuts
- 48 low-fat whole grain crackers

1. Line a large strainer sieve with a double thickness of 100%-cotton cheesecloth. Place strainer over a medium bowl. Stir together yogurt, apricots, honey, and pepper. Spoon mixture into strainer. Cover and chill for 4 to 24 hours or until mixture is firm.

2. Discard any liquid in bowl; wash and dry bowl. Transfer yogurt mixture to the clean bowl; stir in cream cheese. Sprinkle with nuts. Serve with crackers. **MAKES 12 SERVINGS (2 TABLESPOONS DIP WITH 4 CRACKERS PER SERVING)**

Per serving: 123 cal., 5 g total fat (2 g sat. fat), 9 mg chol., 138 mg sodium, 17 g carbo., 2 g fiber, 5 g pro.

Mediterranean Veggie Dip

Prep: 15 minutes + making yogurt cheese
Chill: 24 hours

- 1 recipe Yogurt Cheese
- ¼ cup chopped bottled roasted red sweet pepper
- ¼ cup crumbled reduced-fat feta cheese
- 2 tablespoons thinly sliced green onion
- 2 tablespoons chopped pitted kalamata or black olives
- 2 tablespoons snipped fresh Italian (flat-leaf) parsley
- 2 teaspoons snipped fresh oregano or ½ teaspoon dried oregano, crushed
- 6 cups carrot sticks, broccoli florets, cucumber spears, and/or sweet pepper strips

1. In a small bowl combine Yogurt Cheese, roasted sweet pepper, feta cheese, green onion, olives, parsley, and oregano. Cover and chill for up to 24 hours. Stir before serving. Serve with vegetables. **MAKES 12 SERVINGS (2 TABLESPOONS DIP WITH ½ CUP VEGETABLES PER SERVING)**

Yogurt Cheese Line a yogurt strainer, sieve, or a small colander with three layers of 100%-cotton cheesecloth or a clean paper coffee filter. Suspend lined strainer, sieve, or colander over a bowl. Spoon in one 16-ounce carton plain yogurt.* Cover with plastic wrap. Chill for at least 24 hours. Remove from refrigerator. Drain and discard liquid. Store, covered, in refrigerator for up to 1 week. Makes about 1 cup.

*Tip Use a brand of yogurt that contains no gums, gelatin, or fillers. These ingredients may prevent the whey from separating from the curd to make cheese.

Per serving: 50 cal., 1 g total fat (1 g sat. fat), 3 mg chol., 103 mg sodium, 7 g carbo., 1 g fiber, 3 g pro.

SUGAR 'N' SPICE FRUIT DIP

Citrus Salsa with Baked Chips ♡

Prep: 20 minutes **Bake:** 8 minutes
Oven: 400°F

  4 corn tortillas
     Nonstick cooking spray
  ½ cup chopped grapefruit segments
  ½ cup chopped orange segments
  ½ cup chopped tomato
  ½ cup chopped cucumber
  2 tablespoons chopped green onion (1)
  2 tablespoons snipped fresh cilantro
  ¼ teaspoon crushed red pepper
  ¼ teaspoon salt

1. Preheat oven to 400°F. For chips, lightly coat one side of each tortilla with nonstick cooking spray. Cut each tortilla into 8 wedges. Arrange on an ungreased baking sheet. Bake for 8 to 10 minutes or until lightly browned and crisp. Let cool.
2. For salsa, in a small bowl gently stir together grapefruit, orange, tomato, cucumber, green onion, cilantro, crushed red pepper, and salt. **MAKES 8 SERVINGS (¼ CUP SALSA AND 4 CHIPS EACH)**

Make-ahead directions Prepare chips as directed in Step 1. Place chips in an airtight container; cover and store at room temperature for up to 3 days. Prepare salsa as directed in Step 2. Spoon salsa into an airtight container; cover and store in the refrigerator for up to 4 hours.

Per serving: 44 cal., 0 g total fat, 0 mg chol., 80 mg sodium, 10 g carbo., 2 g fiber, 1 g pro.

Sugar 'n' Spice Fruit Dip ♡

Start to Finish: 15 minutes

  ½ cup tub-style light cream cheese, softened*
  ½ cup light sour cream*
  ¼ cup low-sugar raspberry preserves or orange marmalade
  1 teaspoon finely shredded lemon peel or orange peel (optional)
  ¼ teaspoon ground cinnamon, nutmeg, or allspice
  5 cups desired fruit dippers, such as clementine orange segments; strawberries; cut-up, peeled kiwifruit; raspberries; apple slices; pear slices; and/or banana slices

1. In a medium bowl beat cream cheese and sour cream with an electric mixer on medium speed until smooth. Stir in preserves, lemon peel (if desired), and ¼ teaspoon cinnamon until well combined. If desired, sprinkle with additional cinnamon. Serve with fruit dippers.
MAKES 10 SERVINGS (2 TABLESPOONS DIP WITH ½ CUP DIPPERS PER SERVING)

***Tip** If desired, substitute 1 recipe Yogurt Cheese (page 39) for the sour cream and cream cheese.

Per serving: 89 cal., 3 g total fat (2 g sat. fat), 9 mg chol., 68 mg sodium, 14 g carbo., 2 g fiber, 2 g pro.

Hot Artichoke Spread

Prep: 30 minutes **Bake:** 30 minutes
Oven: 350°F

- ¾ cup finely chopped onion
- 2 cloves garlic, minced
- 1 tablespoon butter
- 2 8-ounce packages reduced-fat cream cheese (Neufchâtel), softened
- 1½ cups grated Parmesan cheese
- ¼ cup milk
- ¼ cup light mayonnaise
- ¼ cup light sour cream
- ¼ teaspoon freshly ground black pepper
- 3 cups chopped fresh spinach leaves
- 1 14-ounce can artichoke hearts, drained and chopped
  Toasted sliced French bread or bagel chips

1. Preheat oven to 350°F. In a medium skillet cook onion and garlic in hot butter for 3 to 4 minutes or until tender. Set aside to cool.
2. In a large bowl stir together cream cheese, Parmesan cheese, milk, mayonnaise, sour cream, and pepper. Stir in spinach, artichokes, and onion mixture. Spread mixture in a 10-inch quiche dish or deep-dish pie plate or use 2 smaller au gratin dishes.
3. Bake for 30 to 35 minutes (20 to 25 minutes if using au gratin dishes) or until heated through and beginning to brown. Serve with French bread. **MAKES ABOUT 5 CUPS**

Per 2 tablespoons spread: 58 cal., 4 g total fat (2 g sat. fat), 14 mg chol., 138 mg sodium, 2 g carbo., 0 g fiber, 2 g pro.

Hot Sausage and Mushroom Spread

Prepare as directed in Step 1, except omit the butter and cook 8 ounces bulk hot Italian sausage, 2 cups sliced fresh mushrooms, and ½ cup chopped green or red sweet pepper with the onion and garlic; drain off fat. Set sausage mixture aside to cool. For Step 2, substitute 1 cup shredded mozzarella cheese (4 ounces) for 1 cup of the Parmesan cheese and omit the artichokes.

BAKED SANTA FE DIP

Baked Santa Fe Dip

Prep: 20 minutes **Bake:** 25 minutes
Oven: 350°F

- 2 cups shredded cheddar cheese (8 ounces)
- 1 cup shredded Monterey Jack or mozzarella cheese (4 ounces)
- 1 8.75-ounce can whole kernel corn, drained
- ½ cup light mayonnaise dressing or salad dressing
- 1 4-ounce can diced green chile peppers, drained
- 2 teaspoons finely chopped canned chipotle chile peppers in adobo sauce
- ¼ teaspoon garlic powder
- 1 medium tomato, seeded and chopped
- ¼ cup sliced green onions (2)
- 2 tablespoons snipped fresh cilantro
  Tortilla chips and/or vegetable dippers (such as sweet pepper wedges, zucchini slices, and jicama slices)

1. Preheat oven to 350°F. In a large bowl stir together cheeses, corn, mayonnaise dressing, green chile peppers, chipotle peppers, and garlic powder. Spread mixture in a 9-inch quiche dish, shallow 1-quart casserole, or 9-inch pie plate. Bake about 25 minutes or until heated through.
2. In a small bowl combine tomato, green onions, and cilantro. To serve, spoon tomato mixture onto cheese mixture. Serve with tortilla chips and/or vegetable dippers.

MAKES 28 SERVINGS

Per serving: 69 cal., 5 g total fat (3 g sat. fat), 12 mg chol., 137 mg sodium, 2 g carbo., 3 g pro.

HAM AND GRUYÈRE MINI TURNOVERS

Ham and Gruyère Mini Turnovers

Prep: 35 minutes **Bake:** 20 minutes
Oven: 400°F/375°F

> 1 cup finely shredded Gruyère cheese (4 ounces)
> ¾ cup chopped cooked ham
> 3 tablespoons half-and-half or light cream
> 1½ teaspoons dried sage, crushed
> Dash freshly ground black pepper
> 1 17.3-ounce package frozen puff pastry sheets (2 sheets), thawed
> 1 egg, lightly beaten
> Country Dijon mustard (optional)

1. Preheat oven to 400°F. For filling, in a medium bowl stir together cheese, ham, half-and-half, sage, and pepper.

2. On a lightly floured surface, roll out 1 pastry sheet to a 12-inch square; cut into 9 squares. Working with 1 square at a time, brush edges with egg. Place 1 tablespoon of the filling in center. Fold together opposite corners of square, forming a triangle. Press edges together with tines of a fork to seal. Place on baking sheet; brush turnovers with egg. Prick tops with fork. Repeat with remaining pastry sheet, filling, and egg.

3. Bake for 5 minutes. Reduce heat to 375°F. Bake about 15 minutes more or until puffed and golden brown. Serve warm. If desired, serve with mustard. **MAKES 18 TURNOVERS**

Per turnover: 190 cal., 13 g total fat (4 g sat. fat), 21 mg chol., 251 mg sodium, 13 g carbo., 0 g fiber, 5 g pro.

Herb and Cheese Mini Quiches

Prep: 1 hour **Bake:** 25 minutes **Oven:** 325°F

> 1 cup butter, softened
> 2 3-ounce packages cream cheese, softened
> 2 cups all-purpose flour
> ¼ cup shredded Asiago cheese (1 ounce)
> 2 eggs, lightly beaten
> ½ cup half-and-half, light cream, or milk
> ¼ cup finely shredded Gouda or Havarti cheese
> 2 tablespoons pine nuts, toasted and coarsely chopped
> 1 tablespoon snipped fresh tarragon or 2 teaspoons dried tarragon, crushed
> 1 tablespoon snipped fresh chives
> ⅛ teaspoon cracked black pepper
> Roasted red sweet pepper, finely chopped (optional)
> Snipped fresh chives (optional)

1. Preheat oven to 325°F. For pastry, in a large mixing bowl beat butter and cream cheese with an electric mixer on medium to high for 30 seconds. Beat in flour and Asiago cheese until soft dough forms. Press 1 rounded teaspoon onto bottom and up sides of 48 ungreased 1¾-inch muffin cups.

2. For filling, in a medium bowl stir together eggs, half-and-half, Gouda cheese, pine nuts, tarragon, the 1 tablespoon chives, and black pepper. Spoon about 1 heaping teaspoon of the filling into each pastry-lined muffin cup.

3. Bake for 25 to 30 minutes or until a knife inserted in centers comes out clean. Cool slightly in muffin cups. Carefully remove from muffin cups; place on a wire rack or serving platter. If desired, top with chopped roasted red pepper and additional snipped chives. Serve warm. **MAKES 48 MINI QUICHES**

Per mini quiche: 77 cal., 6 g total fat (4 g sat. fat), 25 mg chol., 53 mg sodium, 4 g carbo., 0 g fiber, 1 g pro.

CURRY-COCONUT SHRIMP WITH
MANGO DIPPING SAUCE

TAPENADE SPIRALS

Curry-Coconut Shrimp with Mango Dipping Sauce

Prep: 30 minutes **Bake:** 3 minutes per batch
Oven: 200°F

    24 fresh or frozen jumbo shrimp in shells
     1 teaspoon curry powder
     2 cups shredded coconut
    ½ cup chopped cashews
    ⅓ cup all-purpose flour
    ½ teaspoon salt
    ¼ teaspoon black pepper
     2 eggs, lightly beaten
     1 tablespoon lime juice
        Vegetable oil for deep-fat frying
     1 recipe Mango Dipping Sauce

1. Thaw shrimp, if frozen. Peel and devein shrimp, leaving tails intact. Rinse shrimp and pat dry with paper towels. Sprinkle shrimp with ½ teaspoon of the curry powder.

2. In a food processor combine coconut and cashews. Cover and pulse until finely chopped. Place mixture in a shallow bowl.

3. In another shallow bowl combine flour, the remaining ½ teaspoon curry powder, the salt, and pepper. In another shallow bowl combine eggs and lime juice.

4. Dip shrimp, 1 at a time, in the flour mixture, shaking off excess. Dip shrimp in egg mixture, then in coconut mixture to coat. Pat coconut mixture in place as necessary to adhere.

5. In a large saucepan heat 1½ inches of vegetable oil to 350°F. Cook shrimp, 4 to 6 at a time, in hot oil about 3 minutes or until golden brown. Drain on paper towels. Keep warm on a baking sheet in a 200°F oven while frying remaining shrimp. Carefully skim and discard any coconut that falls in oil between batches.

6. Serve warm shrimp with Mango Dipping Sauce. **MAKES 10 TO 12 SERVINGS**

Mango Dipping Sauce In a small bowl combine ½ cup mango chutney (snip any large pieces), ½ cup sour cream, and ½ teaspoon curry powder. Makes 1 cup.

Per serving: 148 cal., 11 g total fat (4 g sat. fat), 48 mg chol., 125 mg sodium, 7 g carbo., 1 g fiber, 5 g pro.

Tapenade Spirals

Prep: 20 minutes **Chill:** 1 to 4 hours

     1 cup pitted ripe or Greek black olives, drained
     1 tablespoon olive oil or vegetable oil
     2 teaspoons capers, drained
     2 teaspoons lemon juice or lime juice
     3 9- to 10-inch flour tortillas
    ½ of an 8-ounce tub cream cheese spread with chive and onion
        Lettuce leaves
     1 cup bottled roasted red sweet peppers, well drained and cut into thin strips
        Fresh Italian (flat-leaf) parsley sprigs (optional)

1. In a food processor combine olives, oil, capers, and lemon juice. Cover and process with several on/off turns until olives are very finely chopped.

2. Arrange tortillas on a flat surface. Spread one-third of the cream cheese spread over each tortilla; top each with one-third of the olive mixture. Place several lettuce leaves on top of the olive mixture. Arrange one-third of the pepper strips over lettuce on each tortilla. Roll up tortillas; wrap in plastic wrap. Chill for 1 to 4 hours.

3. To serve, slice each tortilla roll into 7 slices; arrange on a serving platter. If desired, garnish with parsley. **MAKES 21 SPIRALS**

Per spiral: 68 cal., 4 g total fat (2 g sat. fat), 5 mg chol., 137 mg sodium, 7 g carbo., 1 g fiber, 1 g pro.

BUFFALO-STYLE CHICKEN FINGERS

Buffalo-Style Chicken Fingers

Prep: 25 minutes **Bake:** 18 minutes
Oven: 425°F

2 cups crushed cornflakes
2 tablespoons snipped fresh parsley
½ teaspoon salt
1 pound skinless, boneless chicken breast halves
⅓ cup bottled blue cheese salad dressing
2 teaspoons water
1 to 2 teaspoons bottled hot pepper sauce
Celery sticks
Bottled blue cheese salad dressing

1. Preheat oven to 425°F. In a shallow bowl or pie plate combine crushed cornflakes, parsley, and salt. Cut chicken breasts into strips about ¾ inch wide and 3 inches long. In a large bowl combine the ⅓ cup dressing, the water, and hot pepper sauce. Add chicken; stir to coat. Roll chicken strips in crumb mixture to coat.

2. Place chicken strips in a single layer on a lightly greased 15 × 10 × 1-inch baking pan. Bake for 18 to 20 minutes or until chicken is no longer pink and crumbs are golden. Serve warm with celery and additional blue cheese dressing for dipping. **MAKES 12 SERVINGS**

Make-ahead directions Prepare as directed through Step 1. Place coated chicken strips on a foil-lined baking sheet. Freeze about 2 hours or until firm. Place frozen strips in a freezer container; cover. Freeze up to 1 month. To serve, bake as directed in Step 2.

Per serving: 184 cal., 12 g total fat (2 g sat. fat), 26 mg chol., 408 mg sodium, 9 g carbo., 0 g fiber, 11 g pro.

Hot and Sassy Chicken Wings

Prep: 25 minutes **Marinate:** 2 to 4 hours
Bake: 40 minutes **Oven:** 375°F

10 chicken wings (about 2 pounds)
1 cup white wine vinegar
¼ cup packed brown sugar
¼ cup honey
2 teaspoons garlic powder
2 to 3 teaspoons bottled hot pepper sauce
1 teaspoon salt
1 teaspoon dried thyme, crushed
½ to 1 teaspoon cayenne pepper
Nonstick cooking spray

1. Cut off and discard tips from wings. Cut wings in half at joints to make 20 pieces. Place wing pieces in a large resealable plastic bag; set aside.

2. For marinade, in a small bowl whisk together vinegar, brown sugar, honey, garlic powder, hot pepper sauce, salt, thyme, and cayenne pepper. Pour over wings in bag; seal bag. Marinate in the refrigerator for 2 to 4 hours, turning bag occasionally.

3. Preheat oven to 375°F. Line a 15 × 10 × 1-inch baking pan with foil. Lightly coat a large roasting rack with nonstick cooking spray; place rack in prepared pan. Drain chicken wings, reserving marinade. Place wings on roasting rack; set aside.

4. Transfer marinade to a medium saucepan. Bring to boiling on medium-high heat. Boil gently, uncovered, about 10 minutes or until marinade is reduced to about ½ cup and is thick and slightly syrupy, stirring occasionally.

5. Brush wings on both sides with some of the reduced marinade. Bake for 30 minutes. Turn wings over; brush with remaining marinade. Bake about 10 minutes more or until chicken is no longer pink. **MAKES 8 TO 10 APPETIZER SERVINGS**

Per serving: 205 cal., 10 g total fat (3 g sat. fat), 47 mg chol., 339 mg sodium, 16 g carbo., 0 g fiber, 11 g pro.

SLOPPY JOE MEATBALLS

SWEET AND SASSY MEATBALLS

Sloppy Joe Meatballs

Prep: 35 minutes **Bake:** 12 minutes
Cook: 5 minutes **Oven:** 350°F

 1 egg, lightly beaten
 ½ cup finely chopped onion (1 medium)
 ¼ cup fine dry bread crumbs
 ¼ teaspoon dried oregano, crushed
 ¼ teaspoon salt
 1 pound lean ground beef
 ½ cup chopped green sweet pepper
 1 tablespoon vegetable oil
 1 15-ounce can tomato sauce
 2 tablespoons packed brown sugar
 1 tablespoon yellow mustard
 1 teaspoon chili powder
 ¼ teaspoon black pepper
 ¼ teaspoon garlic salt
    Dash bottled hot pepper sauce (optional)

1. Preheat oven to 350°F. In a large bowl
combine egg, ¼ cup of the onion, the bread
crumbs, oregano, and salt. Add ground beef
and mix well. Shape into 42 meatballs about
¾ inch in diameter. Arrange in a single layer
on a 15×10×1-inch baking pan. Bake for
12 to 15 minutes or until no pink remains.
Drain off fat.
2. Meanwhile, in a large saucepan cook the
remaining ¼ cup onion and the sweet pepper
in hot oil until tender. Stir in tomato sauce,
brown sugar, mustard, chili powder, black
pepper, garlic salt, and, if desired, hot pepper
sauce. Bring to boiling; reduce heat. Simmer,
uncovered, for 5 minutes. Serve immediately.
MAKES 21 SERVINGS

Make-ahead directions Prepare meatballs
and sauce as directed. Carefully place baked
and drained meatballs in sauce; cool slightly.
Place in shallow freezer containers; cover.
Freeze for up to 1 month. To serve, thaw
meatball mixture in refrigerator overnight.
Place in a large saucepan. Cook on medium-
low heat about 10 minutes or until heated
through, stirring occasionally. Serve in a
fondue pot or slow cooker.

Per serving: 78 cal., 5 g total fat (2 g sat. fat), 26 mg
chol., 187 mg sodium, 4 g carbo., 1 g fiber, 5 g pro.

Sweet and Sassy Meatballs

Start to Finish: 30 minutes

 1 16-ounce can jellied cranberry sauce
 1 18-ounce bottle barbecue sauce
 2 1-pound packages frozen cooked
    meatballs, thawed (32 per pound)

1. For sauce, in a large skillet stir together
cranberry sauce and barbecue sauce. Cook
over medium heat until cranberry sauce is
melted, stirring occasionally.
2. Add meatballs to sauce. Cook, uncovered,
for 10 minutes or until meatballs are heated
through, stirring occasionally. Keep warm in a
chafing dish or slow cooker to serve.
MAKES 64 MEATBALLS

Make-ahead directions Prepare as
directed, in Step 1. Stir in frozen or thawed
meatballs. Cover and chill for up to 24 hours.
Heat meatballs and sauce in a large skillet on
medium heat until heated through, stirring
occasionally.

Per 4 meatballs: 60 cal., 4 g total fat (2 g sat. fat), 5 mg
chol., 177 mg sodium, 5 g carbo., 1 g fiber, 2 g pro.

Chipotle-Sauced Meatballs Prepare as
directed except substitute one 12-ounce
bottle chili sauce for the barbecue sauce and
stir in 3 to 4 tablespoons finely chopped
canned chipotle pepper in adobo sauce.

Hawaiian-Sauced Meatballs Prepare as
directed, except substitute one 8-ounce can
crushed pineapple for the cranberry sauce.

TWO-WAY TWISTS

Bacon-Tomato-Lettuce Wraps

Start to Finish: 15 minutes

- 4 slices reduced-sodium bacon
- ¼ cup light sour cream
- 2 tablespoons light mayonnaise
- 1½ teaspoons white vinegar
- 1 teaspoon sugar
- ⅛ teaspoon salt
- ⅛ teaspoon black pepper
- 1 medium tomato, seeded and chopped
- 8 leaves butterhead (Boston or Bibb) lettuce

1. Line a microwave-safe plate with a microwave-safe paper towel. Arrange bacon on the paper towel. Cover bacon with another microwave-safe paper towel. Microwave on high for 3 to 4 minutes or until bacon is crisp. Cool bacon; crumble and set aside.

2. In a small bowl combine sour cream, mayonnaise, vinegar, sugar, salt, and pepper. Gently stir in tomato and crumbled bacon.

3. To serve, spoon a scant 2 tablespoons of the bacon mixture on each lettuce leaf; roll up.

MAKES 4 (2-WRAP) SERVINGS

Per serving: 88 cal., 7 g total fat (2 g sat. fat), 12 mg chol., 228 mg sodium, 4 g carbo., 1 g fiber, 4 g pro.

Chicken Salad with Apple Slices ♡

Start to Finish: 15 minutes

- 2 tablespoons tub-style light cream cheese spread with garden vegetables
- 2 tablespoons light mayonnaise
- 1 teaspoon apple cider vinegar
- ¼ teaspoon black pepper
- 1 9-ounce package refrigerated cooked chicken breast strips, cut into bite-size pieces
- ½ cup chopped celery (1 stalk)
- ¼ cup dried cranberries
- 3 medium apples, cored and thinly sliced

1. For chicken salad, in a medium bowl stir together cream cheese, mayonnaise, vinegar, and pepper. Stir in chicken, celery, and dried cranberries. Serve salad with apple slices.

MAKES 6 SERVINGS

Per serving: 125 cal., 3 g total fat (1 g sat. fat), 27 mg chol., 201 mg sodium, 15 g carbo., 2 g fiber, 12 g pro.

Two-Way Twists

Prep: 10 minutes **Bake:** 10 minutes
Oven: 375°F

- 2 tablespoons sugar
- ¼ teaspoon ground cinnamon
- 1 11-ounce package (12) refrigerated breadsticks
- 2 tablespoons butter, melted
  Applesauce or fruit preserves

1. Preheat oven to 375°F. Grease a large baking sheet; set aside. In a small bowl stir together the sugar and cinnamon; set aside. Separate breadsticks. Brush each with melted butter; sprinkle with sugar mixture. Twist each several times. Arrange on prepared baking sheet.

2. Bake for 10 to 13 minutes or until golden. Cool on a wire rack. Serve with applesauce or preserves for dipping. **MAKES 12 TWISTS**

Per twist: 95 cal., 3 g total fat (1 g sat. fat), 5 mg chol., 199 mg sodium, 15 g carbo., 0 g fiber, 2 g pro.

TROPICAL FRUIT POPS

Melon-Berry Smoothie Pops

Prep: 20 minutes **Freeze:** 4 hours

- 1 cup frozen unsweetened whole strawberries
- 1 cup cut-up cantaloupe
- ⅓ cup orange juice
- ¼ cup fat-free milk
- 1 tablespoon honey
- 1 cup calorie-free citrus-flavor sparkling water
- 12 3-ounce frozen pop molds or 3-ounce plastic cups
- 12 wooden craft sticks or plastic spoons (optional)

1. In a blender combine strawberries, cantaloupe, orange juice, milk, and honey. Cover and blend until smooth. Stir in sparkling water.

2. Pour melon mixture into frozen pop molds; cover. (Or pour into plastic cups. Cover cups with foil. With a sharp knife make a slit in each of the foil tops. Insert sticks or spoons into the slits for handles.) Freeze about 4 hours or until firm. **MAKES 12 POPS**

Per pop: 18 cal., 0 g total fat, 0 mg chol., 5 mg sodium, 4 g carbo., 0 g fiber, 0 g pro.

Apricot-Yogurt Delight

Start to Finish: 10 minutes

- 1 cup fat-free or low-fat Greek-style plain yogurt
- ¼ cup chopped fresh or dried apricots
- 2 tablespoons low-sugar apricot preserves
- 4 teaspoons chopped walnuts, toasted

1. Divide yogurt between 2 serving bowls. Top with apricots, preserves, and walnuts. Serve immediately. **MAKES 2 SERVINGS**

Per serving: 126 cal., 3 g total fat (0 g sat. fat), 0 mg chol., 44 mg sodium, 13 g carbo., 1 g fiber, 11 g pro.

Tropical Fruit Pops

Prep: 20 minutes **Freeze:** 3 hours

- 2 cups chopped mangoes (about 2 large)
- 1 8-ounce can crushed pineapple (juice pack), undrained
- 1 medium banana, sliced
- ¼ cup frozen orange juice concentrate, thawed
- ¼ teaspoon ground ginger
- 12 to 14 frozen pop molds or 3-ounce plastic cups

1. In a blender or food processor combine mangoes, undrained pineapple, banana, orange juice concentrate, and ginger. Cover and process or blend until smooth.

2. Pour mango mixture into frozen pop molds; cover. (Or pour into plastic cups. Cover cups with foil. With a sharp knife make a slit in each of the foil tops. Insert sticks or spoons into the slits for handles.) Freeze about 3 hours or until firm. **MAKES 12 TO 14 FREEZER POPS**

Per pop: 47 cal., 0 g total fat, 0 mg chol., 1 mg sodium, 12 g carbo., 1 g fiber, 0 g pro.

MELON-BERRY SMOOTHIE POPS

Breads

CRANBERRY-PECAN MUFFINS

Cranberry-Pecan Muffins

Prep: 20 minutes **Bake:** 12 minutes
Cool: 5 minutes **Oven:** 400°F

Nonstick cooking spray
1 cup all-purpose flour
¾ cup whole wheat flour or white whole
    wheat flour
½ cup sugar
2 teaspoons baking powder
¾ teaspoon ground cinnamon
¼ teaspoon salt
1 egg
¾ cup fat-free milk
3 tablespoons canola oil
⅓ cup dried cranberries, coarsely snipped
⅓ cup chopped pecans, toasted

1. Preheat oven to 400°F. Coat twelve
2½-inch muffin cups with nonstick cooking
spray or line with paper bake cups and coat
insides of paper cups with nonstick cooking
spray; set aside. In a large bowl stir together
all-purpose flour, whole wheat flour, sugar,
baking powder, cinnamon, and salt. Make a
well in the center of the flour mixture; set aside.
2. In a medium bowl whisk together egg,
milk, and oil. Add milk mixture all at once to
flour mixture; stir just until moistened (batter
should be lumpy). Gently stir in dried
cranberries and pecans.
3. Spoon batter into prepared muffin cups,
filling each about half full. Bake for 12 to
15 minutes or until a wooden toothpick
inserted in centers comes out clean. Cool in
muffin cups on a wire rack for 5 minutes.
Remove muffins from muffin cups; serve warm.
MAKES 12 MUFFINS

Per muffin: 176 cal., 6 g total fat (1 g sat. fat), 18 mg
chol., 134 mg sodium, 27 g carbo., 1 g fiber, 4 g pro.

Jumbo Coffee Cake Muffins

Prep: 20 minutes **Bake:** 25 minutes
Cool: 15 minutes **Oven:** 350°F

Nonstick cooking spray
¼ cup packed brown sugar
¼ cup chopped nuts
2 tablespoons granulated sugar
1 teaspoon ground cinnamon
1½ cups all-purpose flour
2 teaspoons baking powder
¼ teaspoon baking soda
¼ teaspoon salt
¼ cup shortening
1 egg, lightly beaten
1 8-ounce carton sour cream
½ cup granulated sugar
½ cup milk

1. Preheat oven to 350°F. Lightly coat six
3½-inch muffin cups with nonstick cooking
spray or line with paper bake cups. Set aside.
2. In a small bowl stir together brown sugar,
nuts, the 2 tablespoons sugar, and the
cinnamon. Set aside.
3. In a medium bowl combine flour, baking
powder, baking soda, and salt. Using a pastry
blender, cut in shortening until the mixture is
crumbly. In another bowl stir together egg,
sour cream, the ½ cup sugar, and the milk. Add
egg mixture all at once to flour mixture. Stir
just until moistened (batter should be lumpy).
4. Spoon half the batter into prepared muffin
cups. Sprinkle half of the nut mixture over
batter in cups. Top with remaining batter and
the remaining nut mixture.
5. Bake about 25 minutes or until a wooden
toothpick inserted in centers comes out clean.
Cool in pan on a wire rack for 15 minutes.
Remove from muffin cups; serve warm.
MAKES 6 JUMBO MUFFINS

Tip To make standard-size muffins, use
twelve 2½-inch muffin cups; divide batter
evenly among cups. Bake in 400°F oven for
15 to 18 minutes. Cool in pan for 5 minutes.
Remove from pan and serve warm.

Per jumbo muffin: 436 cal., 21 g total fat (0 g sat. fat),
54 mg chol., 328 mg sodium, 56 g carbo., 1 g fiber, 7 g pro.

Pear-Almond Muffins ♡

Prep: 20 minutes **Bake:** 15 minutes
Cool: 5 minutes **Oven:** 400°F

Nonstick cooking spray
1 cup all-purpose flour
½ cup packed brown sugar
2 teaspoons baking powder
½ teaspoon ground ginger
¼ teaspoon salt
¾ cup whole bran cereal
¾ cup fat-free milk
¾ cup chopped, peeled pear
2 egg whites, lightly beaten
3 tablespoons canola oil
2 tablespoons finely chopped almonds
1 recipe Ginger-Cream Spread (optional)

1. Preheat oven to 400°F. Lightly coat twelve 2½-inch muffin cups with cooking spray; set aside. In a large bowl stir together flour, brown sugar, baking powder, ginger, and salt. Make a well in center of the flour mixture; set aside.
2. In a medium bowl stir together cereal and milk; let mixture stand for 5 minutes. Stir in pear, egg whites, and oil. Add cereal mixture all at once to flour mixture; stir just until moistened (batter should be lumpy).
3. Spoon batter into prepared muffin cups, filling each three-fourths full. Sprinkle with almonds. Bake 15 to 18 minutes or until a toothpick inserted near centers comes out clean. Cool in muffin cups on a wire rack for 5 minutes. Remove muffins from muffin cups; serve warm. If desired, serve with Ginger-Cream Spread. **MAKES 12 MUFFINS**

Per muffin: 154 cal., 5 g total fat (1 g sat. fat), 5 mg chol., 163 mg sodium, 24 g carbo., 2 g fiber, 4 g pro.

Ginger-Cream Spread In a small bowl stir together half of an 8-ounce tub light cream cheese, 2 teaspoons finely chopped crystallized ginger or ¼ teaspoon ground ginger, and 2 teaspoons honey.

APPLE-STREUSEL MUFFINS

Apple-Streusel Muffins ♡

Prep: 25 minutes **Bake:** 18 minutes
Cool: 5 minutes **Oven:** 375°F

Nonstick cooking spray
1 cup all-purpose flour
1 cup whole wheat flour
⅓ cup packed brown sugar
2½ teaspoons baking powder
1 teaspoon apple pie spice
¼ teaspoon salt
2 eggs, lightly beaten
1 cup buttermilk or sour milk*
2 tablespoons canola oil
¾ cup shredded, peeled apple (1 medium)
2 tablespoons finely chopped pecans
1 tablespoon flaxseed meal
1 tablespoon packed brown sugar
1 tablespoon butter

1. Preheat oven to 375°F. Coat twelve 2½-inch muffin cups with nonstick cooking spray. In a large bowl mix flours, the ⅓ cup brown sugar, the baking powder, spice, and salt. Make a well in center; set aside.
2. In a bowl combine eggs, buttermilk, and oil. Add all at once to flour mixture. Stir just until moistened (batter should be lumpy). Fold in apple. Spoon batter into prepared muffin cups, filling each about three-fourths full.
3. Combine pecans, flaxseed meal, and the 1 tablespoon brown sugar. Cut in butter until crumbly. Sprinkle over batter. Bake 18 to 20 minutes or until a toothpick inserted in centers comes out clean. Cool on a wire rack 5 minutes. Remove from muffin cups. Serve warm. **MAKES 12 MUFFINS**

*Tip To make 1 cup sour milk, place 1 tablespoon lemon juice or vinegar in a glass measuring cup. Add enough milk to equal 1 cup total liquid; stir. Let mixture stand for 5 minutes before using it in a recipe.

Per muffin: 163 cal., 6 g total fat (1 g sat. fat), 39 mg chol., 167 mg sodium, 25 g carbo., 2 g fiber, 4 g pro.

CINNAMON GRANOLA LOAF

Pear-Cheddar Quick Bread ♡

Prep: 30 minutes **Bake:** 50 minutes
Cool: 10 minutes **Stand:** 1 hour **Oven:** 350°F

- 1⅓ cups all-purpose flour
- ½ cup whole wheat pastry flour or whole wheat flour
- ¼ cup flaxseed meal or toasted wheat germ
- 2 teaspoons baking powder
- ¼ teaspoon salt
- 1½ cups shredded unpeeled pears
- ½ cup refrigerated or frozen egg product, thawed, or 2 eggs, lightly beaten
- ½ cup sugar
- ⅓ cup canola oil
- ¼ cup buttermilk or sour milk*
- ¼ cup honey
- 1 teaspoon vanilla
- ½ cup shredded white cheddar cheese (2 ounces)

1. Preheat oven to 350°F. Grease the bottom and ½ inch up the sides of one 9×5×3-inch loaf pan or two 7×3½×2-inch loaf pans; set aside. In a large bowl combine all-purpose flour, whole wheat pastry flour, flaxseed meal, baking powder, and salt. Make a well in center of the flour mixture; set aside.
2. In a medium bowl combine pears, egg product, sugar, oil, buttermilk, honey, and vanilla. Add pear mixture all at once to flour mixture. Stir just until moistened (batter should be lumpy). Fold in cheese. Spoon batter into prepared pan.
3. Bake for 50 to 55 minutes (45 to 50 minutes for the smaller pans) or until a wooden toothpick inserted near center comes out clean. Cool in pan on a wire rack for 10 minutes. Remove from pan. Cool completely on wire rack. Wrap and store overnight in the refrigerator; let stand at room temperature for 1 hour before slicing. **MAKES 1 LOAF (16 SLICES)**

*Tip To make ¼ cup sour milk, place ¾ teaspoon lemon juice or vinegar in a glass measure. Add enough milk to equal ¼ cup total liquid. Let the mixture stand for 5 minutes before using.

Per slice: 164 cal., 6 g total fat (1 g sat. fat), 4 mg chol., 107 mg sodium, 24 g carbo., 2 g fiber, 4 g pro.

Cinnamon Granola Loaf

Prep: 20 minutes **Rise:** 45 minutes
Bake: 25 minutes **Oven:** 350°F

- 1 1-pound loaf frozen sweet or white bread dough
- 3 tablespoons sugar
- 1 teaspoon ground cinnamon
- 2 tablespoons butter, softened
- ½ cup granola cereal (plain or with raisins), crushed
- ½ cup chopped almonds or pecans, toasted

1. Thaw bread according to package directions. Grease an 8×4×2-inch loaf pan; set aside. In a small bowl stir together sugar and cinnamon; set aside.
2. On a lightly floured surface, roll bread dough to a 10×8-inch rectangle. Spread with 1 tablespoon of the softened butter. Sprinkle with 2 tablespoons of the sugar mixture. Sprinkle with crushed granola and nuts to within ½ inch of the edges. Roll up tightly starting from a short side. Pinch seam to seal. Place, seam side down, in prepared pan. Cover and let rise in a warm place until nearly double in size (45 to 60 minutes).
3. Preheat oven to 350°F. Bake about 25 minutes or until bread sounds hollow when lightly tapped. Remove loaf from pan; place on wire rack. Spread with remaining 1 tablespoon butter and sprinkle with remaining 1 tablespoon sugar mixture. Let cool. **MAKES 1 LOAF (12 SLICES)**

Per slice: 172 cal., 6 g total fat (2 g sat. fat), 5 mg chol., 208 mg sodium, 25 g carbo., 1 g fiber, 4 g pro.

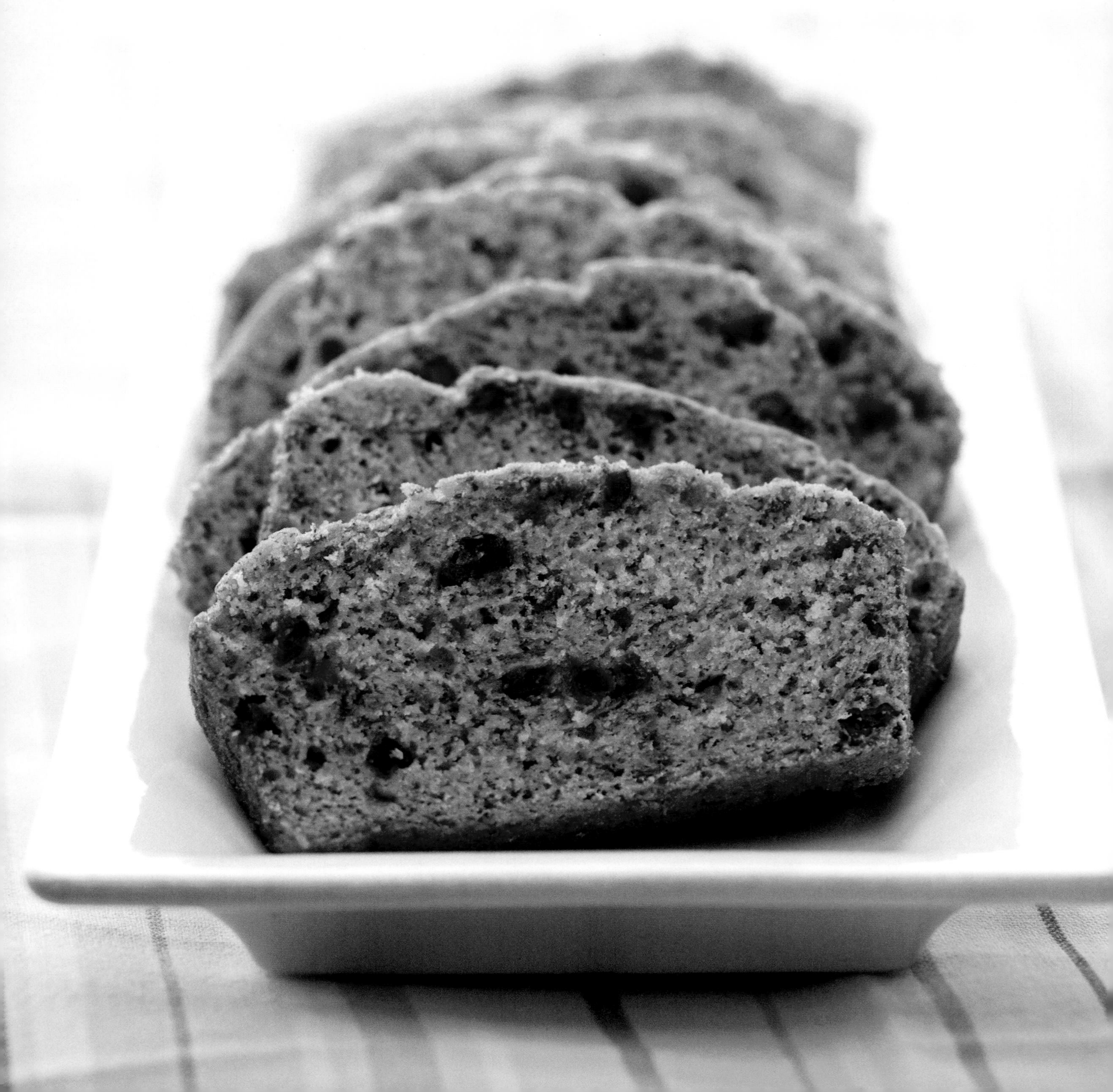

Zucchini Bread with a Twist ♡

Prep: 25 minutes **Bake:** 50 minutes
Cool: 10 minutes **Stand:** Overnight
Oven: 350°F

1¼ cups all-purpose flour
¼ cup flaxseed meal or toasted wheat germ
1½ teaspoons baking powder
1 teaspoon apple pie spice
¼ teaspoon salt
2 egg whites
1 cup finely shredded zucchini
⅔ cup sugar
¼ cup canola oil
1 teaspoon finely shredded orange peel
⅓ cup snipped dried cranberries

1. Preheat oven to 350°F. Grease bottom and ½ inch up the sides of an 8×4×2-inch loaf pan; set aside. In a large bowl stir together flour, flaxseed meal, baking powder, apple pie spice, and salt. Make a well in the center of flour mixture; set aside.
2. In a medium bowl lightly beat egg whites with a fork. Stir in zucchini, sugar, oil, and orange peel. Add zucchini mixture all at once to flour mixture. Stir just until moistened (batter should be lumpy). Fold in dried cranberries. Spoon batter into prepared pan.
3. Bake for 50 to 55 minutes or until a wooden toothpick inserted near center comes out clean. Cool in pan on a wire rack for 10 minutes. Remove bread from pan. Cool completely on wire rack. Wrap and store overnight before slicing. **MAKES 1 LOAF (12 SERVINGS)**

Per slice: 159 cal., 6 g total fat (0 g sat. fat), 0 mg chol., 105 mg sodium, 25 g carbo., 1 g fiber, 3 g pro.

BANANA BREAD

Banana Bread

Prep: 20 minutes **Bake:** 45 minutes
Cool: 2 hours **Stand:** overnight **Oven:** 350°F

Nonstick cooking spray
1 cup all-purpose flour
½ cup white whole wheat flour or whole wheat flour
2 teaspoons baking powder
½ teaspoon pumpkin pie spice
¼ teaspoon baking soda
¼ teaspoon salt
1 cup mashed bananas (2 to 3 medium)
¾ cup packed brown sugar
¼ cup fat-free milk
2 egg whites
2 tablespoons canola oil
¼ cup chopped walnuts, toasted (optional)

1. Preheat oven to 350°F. Lightly coat the bottom and ½ inch up sides of 8×4×2-inch loaf pan with cooking spray; set aside.
2. In a large bowl stir together all-purpose flour, whole wheat flour, baking powder, pumpkin pie spice, baking soda, and salt. Make a well in the center of the flour mixture; set aside.
3. In a medium bowl combine mashed bananas, brown sugar, milk, egg whites, and oil. Add banana mixture all at once to flour mixture; stir just until moistened (batter should be lumpy). If desired, fold in 2 tablespoons of the walnuts. Spoon batter into prepared loaf pan. If desired, sprinkle with the remaining 2 tablespoons walnuts.
4. Bake for 45 to 50 minutes or until a toothpick inserted near the center comes out clean. Cool in pan on a wire rack for 10 minutes. Remove bread from pan. Cool on wire rack. Wrap and store overnight before slicing.
MAKES 1 LOAF (12 SLICES)

Per slice: 143 cal., 2 g total fat (0 g sat. fat), 0 mg chol., 152 mg sodium, 28 g carbo., 1 g fiber, 3 g pro.

PEANUT BUTTER-CHOCOLATE
SWIRL BREAD

Peanut Butter-Chocolate Swirl Bread

Prep: 25 minutes **Bake:** 50 minutes
Cool: 2 hours **Oven:** 350°F

- ¾ cup packed brown sugar
- ⅓ cup creamy peanut butter
- 1½ teaspoons baking powder
- ¼ teaspoon baking soda
- ¼ teaspoon salt
- 2 egg whites
- 2 tablespoons canola oil
- 1 cup all-purpose flour
- ½ cup white whole wheat flour or whole wheat flour
- 1 cup fat-free milk
- 2 tablespoons unsweetened cocoa powder
- 1 tablespoon fat-free milk

1. Preheat oven to 350°F. Grease the bottom and ½ inch up the sides of an 8×4×2-inch loaf pan; set aside.
2. In a large bowl combine brown sugar, peanut butter, baking powder, baking soda, and salt. Beat with an electric mixer until

combined. Beat in egg whites and oil until combined. In a small bowl combine all-purpose flour and whole wheat flour. Alternately add flour mixture and the 1 cup milk to peanut butter mixture, beating on low after each addition just until combined. Transfer ½ cup of the batter to a small bowl; stir in cocoa powder and the 1 tablespoon milk.
3. Spoon half of the light-color batter evenly into prepared loaf pan. Drop all of the chocolate batter by small spoonfuls on top of batter in pan. Spoon the remaining light-color batter evenly over chocolate batter. Using a narrow metal spatula, swirl batters to create a marbled effect.
4. Bake for 50 to 55 minutes or until a wooden toothpick inserted near centers comes out clean. Cool in pan on wire rack for 10 minutes. Remove bread from pans. Cool on wire rack. Wrap and store overnight before slicing. **MAKES 1 LOAF (12 SLICES)**

Per slice: 181 cal., 6 g total fat (1 g sat. fat), 0 mg chol., 177 mg sodium, 28 g carbo., 1 g fiber, 5 g pro.

Strawberry Ripple Coffee Cake

Prep: 30 minutes **Bake:** 30 minutes
Oven: 350°F

- 1 10-ounce package frozen sweetened sliced strawberries, thawed
- 1 tablespoon cornstarch
- 2¼ cups all-purpose flour
- ¾ cup sugar
- ¾ cup cold butter, cut into pieces
- ½ teaspoon baking powder
- ½ teaspoon baking soda
- ⅛ teaspoon salt
- 1 egg
- ¾ cup buttermilk or sour milk (see tip, page 61)

1. Preheat oven to 350°F. Grease a 10×2-inch round tart pan or an 11×7×1½-inch baking pan; set aside.
2. For filling, in a small saucepan combine undrained strawberries and cornstarch. Cook and stir on medium heat until thickened and bubbly. Remove from heat. Cool slightly.
3. In a large bowl stir together flour and sugar. Using a pastry blender, cut in butter until mixture resembles coarse crumbs. Set aside ½ cup of the crumb mixture for the topping. Stir baking powder, baking soda, and salt into the remaining crumb mixture; mix well. Make a well in the center of the crumb mixture.
4. In a small bowl beat egg lightly with a fork; stir in buttermilk. Add egg mixture all at once to crumb mixture. Stir just until moistened. Remove and set aside ½ cup of the dough. Spread remaining dough into the bottom of the prepared pan. Carefully spread the strawberry filling on top of the dough in the pan. Spoon the reserved dough in small mounds on top of the filling. Sprinkle with the reserved crumb topping.
5. Bake for 30 to 35 minutes or until a wooden toothpick inserted near the center comes out clean. Cool slightly in pan on a wire rack. Remove cake from tart pan. Serve warm. **MAKES 12 SERVINGS**

Per serving: 278 cal., 13 g total fat (8 g sat. fat), 49 mg chol., 191 mg sodium, 38 g carbo., 1 g fiber, 4 g pro.

Citrus Rosemary Scones

Prep: 25 minutes **Bake:** 12 minutes
Oven: 425°F

      Nonstick cooking spray
2¾ cups all-purpose flour
⅓ cup sugar
1 tablespoon baking powder
1 tablespoon finely shredded lemon or orange peel
2 teaspoons snipped fresh rosemary or ½ teaspoon dried rosemary, crushed
¼ teaspoon salt
¼ cup butter
⅔ cup fat-free milk
1 egg, lightly beaten
1 egg white
2 teaspoons fat-free milk
      Low-sugar orange marmalade (optional)

1. Preheat oven to 425°F. Lightly coat a baking sheet with nonstick cooking spray; set aside. In a large bowl stir together flour, sugar, baking powder, lemon peel, rosemary, and salt. Using a pastry blender, cut in butter until mixture resembles coarse crumbs. Make a well in the center of flour mixture; set aside.
2. In a bowl stir together the ⅔ cup milk, the egg, and egg white. Add milk mixture all at once to flour mixture. Stir just until moistened.
3. Turn dough out onto a lightly floured surface. Knead dough by folding and gently pressing it for 10 to 12 strokes or just until dough is smooth. Pat gently into a 9-inch circle, about ½ inch thick. Cut the dough with a 2½-inch round cutter, rerolling scraps. (Or cut into 12 wedges.) Place scones on the prepared baking sheet. Brush with the 2 teaspoons milk.
4. Bake for 12 to 15 minutes or until golden brown. Serve warm. If desired, serve with orange marmalade. **MAKES 12 SCONES**

Per scone: 173 cal., 5 g total fat (3 g sat. fat), 28 mg chol., 153 mg sodium, 28 g carbo., 1 g fiber, 4 g pro.

SOUTHWESTERN DROP BISCUITS

Southwestern Drop Biscuits

Prep: 20 minutes **Bake:** 14 minutes
Oven: 425°F

1 cup all-purpose flour
¾ cup white whole wheat flour or whole wheat flour
2 teaspoons baking powder
1 to 2 teaspoons chili powder
¼ teaspoon salt
¼ teaspoon dried oregano, crushed
1 8-ounce carton light sour cream
⅓ cup fat-free milk
      Chili powder (optional)

1. Preheat oven to 425°F. Lightly grease a large baking sheet or line with parchment paper; set aside. In a medium bowl stir together all-purpose flour, whole wheat flour, baking powder, the 1 to 2 teaspoons chili powder, the salt, and oregano. Make a well in the center of the flour mixture.
2. In a small bowl whisk together sour cream and milk until smooth. Add sour cream mixture all at once to flour mixture; stir just until combined.
3. Using about ⅓ cup dough for each biscuit, drop dough into 8 mounds onto prepared baking sheet, leaving about 2 inches between mounds. If desired, sprinkle with additional chili powder.
4. Bake for 14 to 16 minutes or until golden brown. Serve warm. **MAKES 8 BISCUITS**

Per biscuit: 138 cal., 3 g total fat (2 g sat. fat), 10 mg chol., 191 mg sodium, 23 g carbo., 1 g fiber, 4 g pro.

APPLE-WALNUT SCONES

Apple-Walnut Scones

Prep: 15 minutes **Bake:** 15 minutes
Cool: 5 minutes **Oven:** 375°F

2 cups all-purpose flour
3 tablespoons sugar
1 teaspoon ground cinnamon
½ teaspoon baking powder
⅛ teaspoon salt
½ cup cold butter, cut into pieces
1 cup chopped apple
¾ cup chopped walnuts, toasted
2 eggs, lightly beaten
⅔ cup whipping cream
1 egg yolk, lightly beaten
1 tablespoon whipping cream
Sugar

1. Preheat oven to 375°F. Line a large baking sheet with parchment paper; set aside. In a large bowl combine flour, the 3 tablespoons sugar, the cinnamon, baking powder, and salt.

Using a pastry blender, cut in butter until mixture resembles coarse crumbs. Stir in apple and nuts.
2. In a small bowl combine the 2 eggs and the ⅔ cup whipping cream. Add egg mixture all at once to flour mixture. Using a fork, stir just until moistened.
3. Using a ¼-cup ice cream scoop, scoop dough and place on prepared baking sheet. Do not flatten.
4. In a small bowl combine the egg yolk and the 1 tablespoon whipping cream. Brush over the top of the scones. Sprinkle additional sugar over scones.
5. Bake for 15 to 17 minutes or until scones are lightly browned. Remove from baking sheet. Cool on a wire rack for 5 minutes; serve warm. **MAKES 16 SCONES**

Per scone: 208 cal., 14 g total fat (7 g sat. fat), 70 mg chol., 81 mg sodium, 17 g carbo., 1 g fiber, 4 g pro.

Blueberry Breakfast Scones

Prep: 30 minutes **Bake:** 15 minutes
Oven: 400°F

Nonstick cooking spray
1½ cups all-purpose flour
½ cup white whole wheat flour or whole wheat flour
¼ cup sugar
1 tablespoon baking powder
1 tablespoon finely shredded orange peel
¼ teaspoon baking soda
¼ teaspoon salt
¼ cup butter
1 egg
½ cup buttermilk
1 teaspoon vanilla
1 cup fresh or frozen blueberries
1 recipe Orange Glaze (optional)

1. Preheat oven to 400°F. Coat a baking sheet with cooking spray; set aside. In a large bowl combine all-purpose flour, whole wheat flour, sugar, baking powder, orange peel, soda, and salt. Using a pastry blender, cut in butter until mixture resembles coarse crumbs. Make a well in center of flour mixture.
2. In a small bowl whisk together egg, buttermilk, and vanilla. Add egg mixture all at once to flour mixture; stir just until moistened. Gently stir in blueberries. (Do not thaw frozen blueberries.)
3. Turn dough out onto a lightly floured surface. Knead dough by folding and gently pressing dough for 10 to 12 strokes or until nearly smooth. Transfer dough to the prepared baking sheet; pat or lightly roll dough to a 7-inch circle. Cut circle into 10 wedges. Separate wedges about 1 inch apart.
4. Bake about 15 minutes or until golden brown. Remove from baking sheet. Cool slightly on a wire rack. If desired, drizzle with Orange Glaze. Serve warm. **MAKES 10 SCONES**

Per scone: 171 cal., 5 g total fat (3 g sat. fat), 34 mg chol., 215 mg sodium, 27 g carbo., 1 g fiber, 4 g pro.

Orange Glaze In a small bowl stir together ¾ cup powdered sugar and ¼ teaspoon finely shredded orange peel. Stir in enough orange juice or fat-free milk (3 to 4 teaspoons) to make drizzling consistency.

Oatmeal Batter Bread ♡

Prep: 25 minutes **Rise:** 45 minutes
Bake: 40 minutes **Oven:** 350°F

1 cup warm milk (105°F to 115°F)
¼ cup honey or packed brown sugar
1 package active dry yeast
1¾ cups all-purpose flour
1 egg, lightly beaten
1 tablespoon vegetable oil
½ teaspoon salt
¾ cup whole wheat flour
½ cup rolled oats

1. In a large mixing bowl combine milk, honey, and yeast, stirring until yeast dissolves. Let stand for 5 minutes. Meanwhile, grease an 8×4×2-inch loaf pan; set pan aside.
2. Add flour, egg, oil, and salt to yeast mixture. Beat with an electric mixer on low until combined. Beat for 3 minutes on high, scraping sides of bowl occasionally. Using a wooden spoon, stir in whole wheat flour and oats until combined. Spoon batter into prepared loaf pan, spreading evenly. Cover; let dough rise in a warm place until double in size (about 45 minutes).
3. Preheat oven to 350°F. Bake about 40 minutes or until bread sounds hollow when lightly tapped. If necessary to prevent overbrowning, cover top of bread with foil for the last 10 to 15 minutes of baking. Immediately remove bread from pan. Cool on a wire rack.

MAKES 1 LOAF (12 SLICES)

Per slice: 166 cal., 3 g total fat (1 g sat. fat), 19 mg chol., 113 mg sodium, 31 g carbo., 2 g fiber, 5 g pro.

Apple Popovers with Maple-Spiced Butter

Prep: 15 minutes **Stand:** 30 minutes
Bake: 33 minutes **Oven:** 450°F/375°F

1¼ cups all-purpose flour
½ teaspoon salt
1⅓ cups milk
4 eggs
5 tablespoons butter, melted
2 tablespoons butter
¾ cup chopped tart apple (1 medium)
1 recipe Maple-Spiced Butter

APPLE POPOVERS WITH MAPLE-SPICED BUTTER

1. In a medium bowl whisk together flour and salt. In a second bowl whisk together milk, eggs, and the 5 tablespoons melted butter. Whisk egg mixture into flour mixture just until combined. Let stand at room temperature for 30 minutes.
2. Meanwhile, preheat oven to 450°F. Cut the 2 tablespoons butter into 12 pieces and place 1 piece in each cup of a 12-cup popover pan. Place 1 tablespoon of apple in each popover cup. Just before baking, place pan in oven and heat about 1 minute or until butter is melted and pan is hot.
3. Carefully remove pan from oven. Pour batter into cups over apples. Immediately return pan to oven. Bake for 15 minutes (do not open oven). Reduce oven to 375°F; bake for 18 to 20 minutes more or until popovers are crisp and browned.
4. Remove popovers from pan and place on wire rack. Let cool for 2 to 3 minutes. Serve hot with Maple-Spiced Butter. **MAKES 12 POPOVERS**

Maple-Spiced Butter In a small bowl stir together ½ cup butter, softened; 2 tablespoons pure maple or maple-flavor syrup; and 1 teaspoon pumpkin pie spice until smooth.

Per popover with 1 tablespoon Maple-Spiced Butter: 240 cal., 19 g total fat (11 g sat. fat), 114 mg chol., 135 mg sodium, 15 g carbo., 1 g fiber, 4 g pro.

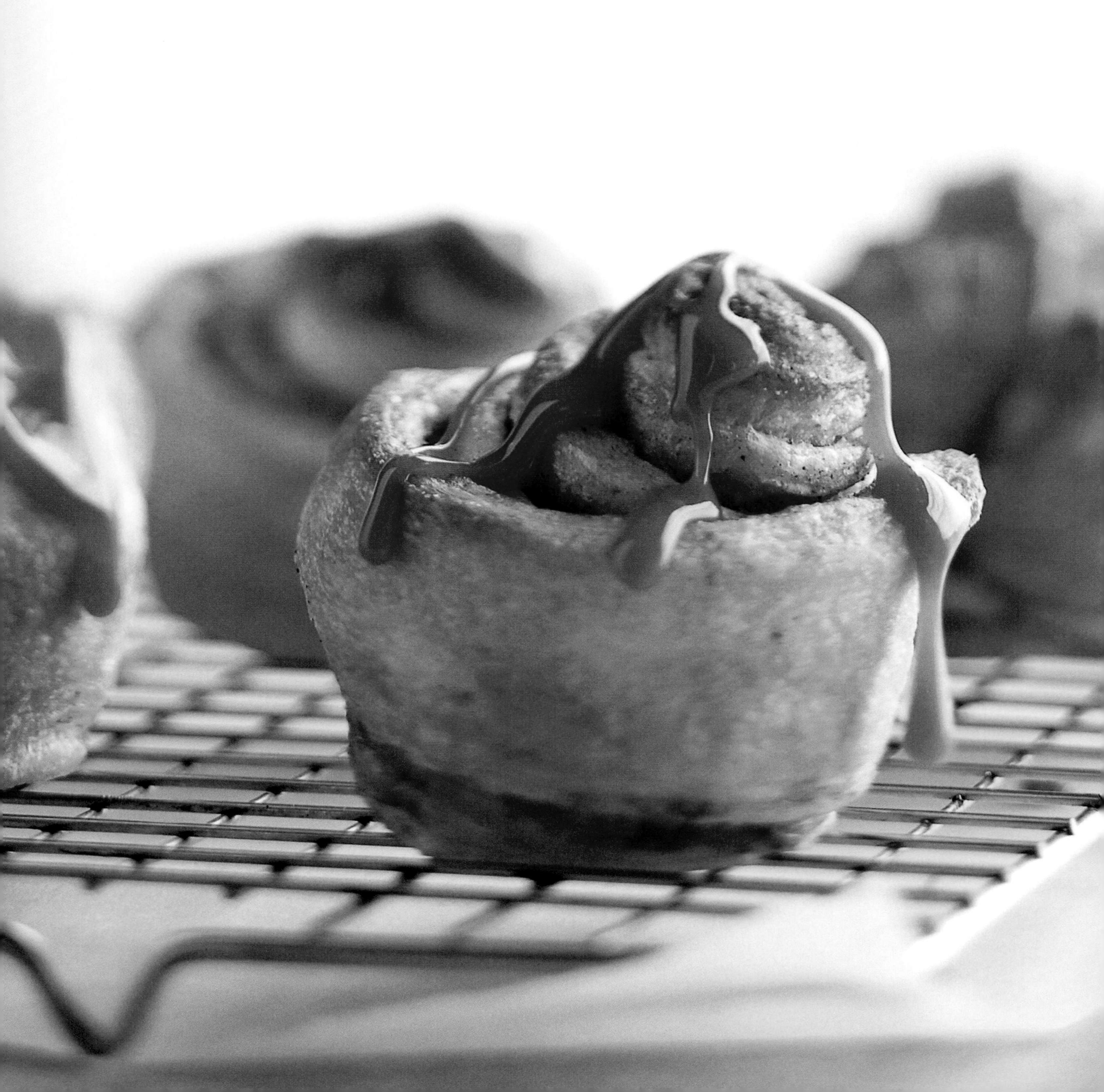

Easy Cinnamon Spirals

Prep: 25 minutes **Bake:** 12 minutes **Oven:** 375°F

Nonstick cooking spray
2 11-ounce packages (12 each) refrigerated breadsticks
⅓ cup butter, softened
¼ cup sugar
2 teaspoons ground cinnamon
½ cup caramel-flavor ice cream topping

1. Preheat oven to 375°F. Lightly coat twelve 2½-inch muffin cups with nonstick cooking spray; set aside.

2. Unroll breadstick dough and separate into 24 strips. Press each strip to flatten slightly. Press ends of 2 strips together to make 1 long strip. Repeat with remaining strips, making 12 long strips. Spread some of the butter over each long strip. In a small bowl stir together sugar and cinnamon; sprinkle over each strip. Roll each strip into a spiral, starting from a short side. Place dough spirals in prepared muffin cups, spiral sides up.

3. Bake for 12 to 15 minutes or until golden brown. Immediately remove from muffin cups; cool slightly. Drizzle with ice cream topping.

MAKES 12 ROLLS

Per roll: 245 cal., 8 g total fat (5 g sat. fat), 13 mg chol., 443 mg sodium, 40 g carbo., 1 g fiber, 4 g pro.

Dreamy Cinnamon Breakfast Rolls

Prep: 30 minutes **Rise:** 1 hour
Stand: 20 minutes **Chill:** 8 to 24 hours
Bake: 25 minutes **Oven:** 350°F

1 package 2-layer-size French vanilla cake mix
5½ to 6 cups all-purpose flour
2 packages active dry yeast
1 teaspoon salt
2½ cups warm water (120°F to 130°F)
¼ cup butter, softened
¾ cup granulated sugar
1 tablespoon ground cinnamon
1⅓ cups packed brown sugar
1 cup butter
2 tablespoons light-color corn syrup
1½ cups chopped walnuts

DREAMY CINNAMON BREAKFAST ROLLS

1. In a large mixing bowl combine dry cake mix, 2 cups of the flour, the yeast, and salt. Add the warm water; beat with an electric mixer on low until combined, scraping sides of bowl. Beat on high for 3 minutes. Using a wooden spoon, stir in as much of the remaining flour as you can.

2. Turn dough out onto a lightly floured surface. Knead in enough of the remaining flour to make a dough that is smooth and elastic (3 to 5 minutes total). Dough will still be slightly sticky. Place dough in a large greased bowl. Cover and let rise in a warm place until double in size (about 1 hour).

3. Punch dough down. Turn dough out onto a well-floured surface. Divide dough in half. Cover and let stand for 10 minutes. Roll each dough portion into a 16×9-inch rectangle.

4. Spread each dough rectangle with half of the ¼ cup butter. In a small bowl combine granulated sugar and cinnamon; sprinkle over buttered dough rectangles. Starting from a long side, roll up each dough rectangle into a spiral. Pinch seams to seal. Cut each spiral into 1-inch slices.

5. In a medium saucepan combine brown sugar, the 1 cup butter, and the corn syrup. Bring to boiling. Remove from heat. Divide mixture between two 13×9×2-inch baking pans or baking dishes.

6. Sprinkle walnuts evenly into pans or dishes. Place half of the dough slices, cut sides down, into each pan or dish. Cover; chill for 8 to 24 hours.

7. To bake, let pans or dishes of rolls stand at room temperature for 30 minutes. Preheat oven to 350°F. Bake, uncovered, about 25 minutes or until golden brown. Let cool in pans or dishes on wire racks for 10 minutes. Turn out onto foil. Serve warm or cool.

MAKES 32 ROLLS

Per roll: 298 cal., 13 g total fat (0 g sat. fat), 21 mg chol., 258 mg sodium, 43 g carbo., 1 g fiber, 4 g pro.

SEEDED PULL-APARTS

Rosemary-Chive Parker House Rolls

Prep: 30 minutes **Rise:** 1 hour 30 minutes
Bake: 12 minutes **Oven:** 375°F

 3 to 3½ cups all-purpose flour
 1 package active dry yeast
 3 tablespoons snipped fresh chives
 1 tablespoon snipped fresh rosemary
 ¾ cup water
 ¼ cup butter
 1 teaspoon sugar
 ½ teaspoon salt
 1 egg
 ¼ cup mashed potatoes
 3 tablespoons butter, melted

1. In a mixing bowl combine 1 cup of the flour, the yeast, chives, and rosemary. In a saucepan heat and stir the water, the ¼ cup butter, the sugar, and salt until warm (120°F to 130°F). Add butter mixture to flour mixture. Add egg and mashed potatoes. Beat with electric mixer on low for 30 seconds, scraping bowl constantly. Beat on high for 3 minutes. Use a wooden spoon to stir in as much of the remaining flour as possible.
2. Turn out onto a floured surface. Knead in enough remaining flour to make a moderately stiff dough that is smooth and elastic (6 to 8 minutes). Shape into a ball. Place in greased bowl, turning once. Cover; let rise in warm place until double in size (about 1 hour).
3. Punch dough down. Turn out onto lightly floured surface. Cover; let rest 10 minutes. Grease 2 large baking sheets; set aside. Roll dough until ¼ inch thick. Cut dough with a floured 2½-inch round cutter, rerolling scraps. Brush with some of the melted butter. Fold rounds in half, making the crease slightly off center. Place rolls, larger halves on top, 2 inches apart on prepared sheets. Cover; let rise until nearly double in size (30 minutes).
4. Preheat oven to 375°F. Lightly brush tops of rolls with the 3 tablespoons melted butter. Bake for 12 to 15 minutes or until golden. Serve warm. **MAKES ABOUT 30 ROLLS**

Per roll: 75 cal., 3 g total fat (2 g sat. fat), 14 mg chol., 66 mg sodium, 10 g carbo., 0 g fiber, 2 g pro.

Seeded Pull-Aparts ♡

Prep: 25 minutes **Rise:** 30 minutes
Bake: 20 minutes **Oven:** 375°F

 1 16-ounce loaf frozen whole wheat bread dough
 1 egg white
 1 tablespoon water
 3 tablespoons sesame seeds, toasted*
 2 tablespoons flaxseeds
 2 tablespoons poppy seeds
 1 tablespoon cumin seeds, toasted*

1. Thaw frozen bread dough according to package directions. Grease a 9×1½-inch round baking pan; set aside. Divide bread dough into 12 portions; roll each portion into a ball.
2. In a shallow dish lightly beat egg white and water with a fork. In a small bowl combine sesame seeds, flaxseeds, poppy seeds, and cumin seeds. Brush top of each dough ball with egg white mixture; dip in seed mixture. Place rolls in prepared pan. Cover; let rolls rise in a warm place until nearly double in size (30 to 60 minutes).
3. Preheat oven to 375°F. Bake for 20 to 25 minutes or until tops sound hollow when lightly tapped. Immediately invert rolls onto a wire rack; serve warm or at room temperature. **MAKES 12 ROLLS**

*Tip Toast sesame seeds and cumin seeds in a dry skillet over medium heat. Stir often so they don't burn.

Per roll: 137 cal., 5 g total fat (0 g sat. fat), 0 mg chol., 218 mg sodium, 20 g carbo., 3 g fiber, 6 g pro.

Chocolatey Butter-Nut Cinnamon Rolls

Prep: 30 minutes **Rise:** 30 minutes
Bake: 30 minutes **Cool:** 5 minutes **Oven:** 375°F

     2 cups powdered sugar
    ⅔ cup whipping cream
  1½ cups chopped mixed nuts
    ½ cup packed brown sugar
     1 tablespoon all-purpose flour
     1 tablespoon ground cinnamon
     2 16-ounce loaves frozen sweet roll or white
        bread dough, thawed
    ¼ cup butter, melted
  1¼ cups semisweet chocolate pieces
    ½ cup chopped mixed nuts
  1½ teaspoons shortening

1. For topping, in a medium bowl stir together powdered sugar and whipping cream until smooth. Divide mixture between two 2-quart rectangular or square baking dishes. Sprinkle 1 cup of the chopped nuts evenly over mixture in baking dishes; set aside.
2. For filling, in a small bowl stir together brown sugar, flour, and cinnamon; set aside.
3. On a lightly floured surface, roll each loaf of dough into a 12×8-inch rectangle (if dough is difficult to roll out, let it rest a few minutes and try again). Brush dough rectangles with melted butter. Sprinkle filling, ½ cup of the chocolate pieces, and the remaining ½ cup chopped nuts over each rectangle. Roll up each rectangle, starting from a long side. Pinch dough to seal seams. Slice each roll into 6 equal pieces. Arrange 6 pieces, cut sides down, in each prepared dish. Cover and let rise in a warm place until nearly double in size (30 to 45 minutes). Use a greased toothpick to break any surface bubbles.
4. Preheat oven to 375°F. Bake for 30 to 35 minutes or until sides of rolls are brown and center rolls do not appear doughy (do not underbake). If necessary to prevent overbrowning, cover with foil during the last 15 to 20 minutes of baking. Cool in dishes on wire racks for 5 minutes; remove from dishes.
5. In a small saucepan combine the remaining ¾ cup chocolate pieces and the shortening.

APRICOT LADDER LOAF

Cook and stir over low heat until chocolate is melted and smooth; drizzle over cinnamon rolls. Serve warm. **MAKES 12 ROLLS**

Per roll: 586 cal., 27 g total fat (12 g sat. fat), 72 mg chol., 176 mg sodium, 80 g carbo., 4 g fiber, 10 g pro.

Apricot Ladder Loaf

Prep: 30 minutes **Rise:** 40 minutes
Bake: 20 minutes **Oven:** 350°F

        Nonstick cooking spray
     1 16-ounce loaf frozen white or whole
        wheat bread dough, thawed
    ½ cup sugar-free apricot spread
    ½ cup chopped fresh or canned apricots

1. Coat 2 baking sheets with nonstick cooking spray. On a lightly floured surface, divide dough in half. Roll each half into a 12×7-inch rectangle. Transfer to prepared baking sheets.

2. Cut up any large pieces of fruit in the preserves. For each loaf, spoon about ¼ cup of the preserves down the center third of the dough rectangle to within 1 inch of the ends. Sprinkle ¼ cup of the fruit over the preserves. On the long sides, make 2-inch-long cuts from the edges toward the center at 1-inch intervals. Starting at one end, alternately fold opposite strips of dough, at an angle, across filling. Slightly press the ends together in the center to seal. Cover; let rise in a warm place until nearly double in size (about 40 minutes).
3. Preheat oven to 350°F. Bake about 20 minutes or until golden. Remove from baking sheets. Cool slightly on wire racks; serve warm. **MAKES 2 LOAVES (24 SLICES)**

Per slice: 54 cal., 0 g total fat, 0 mg chol., 44 mg sodium, 10 g carbo., 0 g fiber, 1 g pro.

CHAPTER 4

Soups, Salads & Sandwiches

VEGETABLE BEEF STEW

Three-Pepper Beef Stew

Prep: 35 minutes **Cook:** 1 hour 30 minutes

    1 tablespoon canola oil
    4 medium carrots, cut into 1-inch pieces
    2 stalks celery, cut into 1-inch pieces
    1 cup chopped onion (1 large)
    6 cloves garlic, minced, or 1 tablespoon
       minced garlic
    2 pounds beef chuck roast, trimmed of fat
       and cut into 1-inch cubes
 1¾ cups dry red wine or one 14-ounce can
       lower-sodium beef broth
    1 14-ounce can lower-sodium beef broth
    2 tablespoons tomato paste
    1 tablespoon Worcestershire sauce
    2 to 3 teaspoons bottled cayenne pepper
       sauce
  ¼ to ½ teaspoon crushed red pepper
    2 large potatoes, unpeeled, cut into 1-inch
       pieces
    2 medium red sweet peppers, cut into
       1-inch pieces
    2 tablespoons cold water
    1 tablespoon cornstarch

1. In a 4- to 6-quart Dutch oven heat oil on medium heat. Add carrots, celery, onion, and garlic; cook about 5 minutes or until onion is tender, stirring occasionally. Add beef; cook about 15 minutes or until browned, stirring occasionally. Drain off fat.

2. Stir in wine, beef broth, tomato paste, Worcestershire sauce, pepper sauce, and crushed red pepper. Bring to boiling; reduce heat. Simmer, covered, for 1 hour, stirring occasionally.

3. Add potatoes and sweet peppers. Return to boiling; reduce heat. Simmer, covered, for 15 to 20 minutes or until meat and potatoes are tender.

4. In a small bowl stir together the cold water and cornstarch. Stir into beef mixture. Cook and stir until thickened and bubbly. Cook and stir for 2 minutes more. **MAKES 6 SERVINGS**

Per serving: 401 cal., 10 g total fat (3 g sat. fat), 82 mg chol., 358 mg sodium, 25 g carbo., 4 g fiber, 36 g pro.

Vegetable Beef Stew ♡

Prep: 25 minutes **Cook:** 8 to 10 hours (low) or 4 to 5 hours (high); plus 15 minutes (high)

    1 1½-pound boneless beef chuck pot roast
    1 pound butternut squash, peeled, seeded,
       and cut into 1-inch pieces (about 2½ cups)
    2 small onions, cut into wedges
    2 cloves garlic, minced
    1 14-ounce can lower-sodium beef broth
    1 8-ounce can tomato sauce
    2 tablespoons Worcestershire sauce
    1 teaspoon dry mustard
  ¼ teaspoon black pepper
  ⅛ teaspoon ground allspice
    2 tablespoons cold water
    4 teaspoons cornstarch
    1 9-ounce package frozen Italian green
       beans

1. Trim fat from meat. Cut meat into 1-inch pieces. Place meat in a 3½- to 4½-quart slow cooker. Add butternut squash, onions, and garlic. Stir in beef broth, tomato sauce, Worcestershire sauce, dry mustard, pepper, and allspice.

2. Cover and cook on low-heat setting for 8 to 10 hours or on high-heat setting for 4 to 5 hours.

3. If using low-heat setting, turn to high-heat setting. In a small bowl combine the cold water and cornstarch. Stir cornstarch mixture and green beans into mixture in slow cooker. Cover and cook about 15 minutes more or until thickened. **MAKES 6 SERVINGS**

Per serving: 220 cal., 5 g total fat (1 g sat. fat), 67 mg chol., 465 mg sodium, 18 g carbo., 3 g fiber, 27 g pro.

Chipotle Chili with Hominy and Beans ♥

Start to Finish: 25 minutes

Nonstick cooking spray
8 ounces extra-lean ground beef or uncooked ground chicken or turkey breast
1 cup chopped onion (1 large)
1½ teaspoons ground cumin
½ teaspoon dried oregano, crushed
1 to 2 teaspoons chopped canned chipotle chile peppers in adobo sauce*
2 14.5-ounce cans no-salt-added stewed tomatoes, undrained
1 15-ounce can red beans, rinsed and drained
1 15-ounce can yellow hominy, rinsed and drained
¾ chopped green or red sweet pepper (1 medium)
½ cup water
6 tablespoons reduced-fat shredded cheddar cheese (optional)

1. Lightly coat an unheated large saucepan with nonstick cooking spray. Preheat on medium heat. Add ground beef and onion; cook until browned. If necessary, drain off fat.
2. Stir in cumin and oregano; cook for 1 minute more. Add chipotle peppers, undrained tomatoes, red beans, hominy, sweet pepper, and the water. Bring to boiling; reduce heat. Simmer, covered, for 5 minutes. If desired, sprinkle servings with cheese.

MAKES 6 SERVINGS

*Tip Because chile peppers contain volatile oils that can burn your skin and eyes, avoid direct contact with them as much as possible. When working with chile peppers, wear plastic or rubber gloves. If your bare hands do touch the peppers, wash your hands and nails well with soap and warm water.

Per serving: 257 cal., 7 g total fat (3 g sat. fat), 26 mg chol., 477 mg sodium, 35 g carbo., 9 g fiber, 13 g pro.

Meatballs and Vegetable Soup with Pasta

Prep: 20 minutes **Cook:** 10 minutes

3 14-ounce cans beef broth
1 12- to 16-ounce package frozen cooked meatballs
1 15- to 16-ounce can Great Northern beans or cannellini beans (white kidney beans), rinsed and drained
1 14.5-ounce can diced tomatoes with basil, garlic, and oregano
1 10-ounce package frozen mixed vegetables
1 cup dried small pasta (such as macaroni, small shell, mini penne, or rotini)
Crusty bread (optional)
Shredded Parmesan cheese (optional)

1. In a 4-quart pot stir together beef broth, meatballs, beans, undrained tomatoes, and vegetables. Bring to boiling. Stir in pasta. Return to boiling; reduce heat. Simmer, uncovered, about 10 minutes or until pasta is tender. If desired, serve with bread and sprinkle servings with Parmesan cheese.

MAKES 6 TO 8 SERVINGS

Per serving: 319 cal., 5 g total fat (2 g sat. fat), 32 mg chol., 1,552 mg sodium, 45 g carbo., 7 g fiber, 24 g pro.

Beef and Vegetable Soup with Pasta
Prepare as above, except substitute one 17-ounce package refrigerated cooked beef tips with gravy for the frozen cooked meatballs.

ASIAN PORK SOUP

Italian Pork and Pepper Soup

Prep: 20 minutes **Cook:** 6 to 8 hours (low) or 3 to 4 hours (high); plus 15 minutes (high)

1½ pounds boneless pork shoulder
  2 14-ounce cans beef broth
  1 14.5-ounce can diced tomatoes with basil, oregano, and garlic
  1 cup bottled roasted red sweet peppers, drained and cut into bite-size strips
  ½ cup chopped onion (1 medium)
  2 tablespoons balsamic vinegar
  ¼ teaspoon black pepper
  2 cups sliced zucchini
    Shredded Parmesan cheese (optional)

1. Trim fat from meat. Cut meat into 1-inch pieces. In a 3½- or 4-quart slow cooker combine meat, beef broth, undrained tomatoes, roasted sweet peppers, onion, vinegar, and pepper.
2. Cover and cook on low-heat setting for 6 to 8 hours or on high-heat setting for 3 to 4 hours.
3. If using low-heat setting, turn to high-heat setting. Stir in zucchini. Cover and cook about 15 minutes more or until zucchini is crisp-tender. If desired, sprinkle servings with Parmesan cheese. **MAKES 6 SERVINGS**

Stovetop method Trim fat from 1½ pounds boneless pork shoulder. Cut meat into 1-inch pieces. In a 4-quart Dutch oven brown meat, half at a time, in 2 tablespoons hot vegetable oil. With second batch of meat, add onion and cook until onion is crisp-tender. Return all meat to the pan. Stir in beef broth, undrained tomatoes, roasted peppers, balsamic vinegar, and black pepper. Bring to boiling; reduce heat. Simmer, covered, for 50 minutes. Add 2 cups sliced zucchini; return to boiling. Reduce heat; cook, covered, about 15 minutes more or until zucchini and pork are tender. If desired, sprinkle servings with Parmesan cheese.

Per serving: 217 cal., 7 g total fat (2 g sat. fat), 73 mg chol., 943 mg sodium, 12 g carbo., 1 g fiber, 25 g pro.

Asian Pork Soup

Start to Finish: 25 minutes

  1 tablespoon canola oil
12 ounces lean boneless pork, cut into thin bite-size strips
  2 cups sliced fresh shiitake mushrooms
  2 cloves garlic, minced
  3 14-ounce cans reduced-sodium chicken broth
  2 tablespoons dry sherry
  2 tablespoons reduced-sodium soy sauce
  2 teaspoons grated fresh ginger or ½ teaspoon ground ginger
  ¼ teaspoon crushed red pepper
  2 cups shredded napa cabbage
  2 tablespoons thinly sliced green onion (1)
    Fresh cilantro sprigs (optional)

1. In a large saucepan heat oil on medium heat. Add pork; cook and stir for 2 to 3 minutes or until slightly pink in center. Remove from pan; set aside. Add mushrooms and garlic to saucepan; cook until tender.
2. Stir in chicken broth, sherry, soy sauce, ginger, and crushed red pepper. Bring to boiling. Stir in pork, napa cabbage, and green onion; heat through. If desired, garnish servings with cilantro. **MAKES 6 SERVINGS**

Per serving: 160 cal., 6 g total fat (1 g sat. fat), 31 mg chol., 691 mg sodium, 10 g carbo., 1 g fiber, 16 g pro.

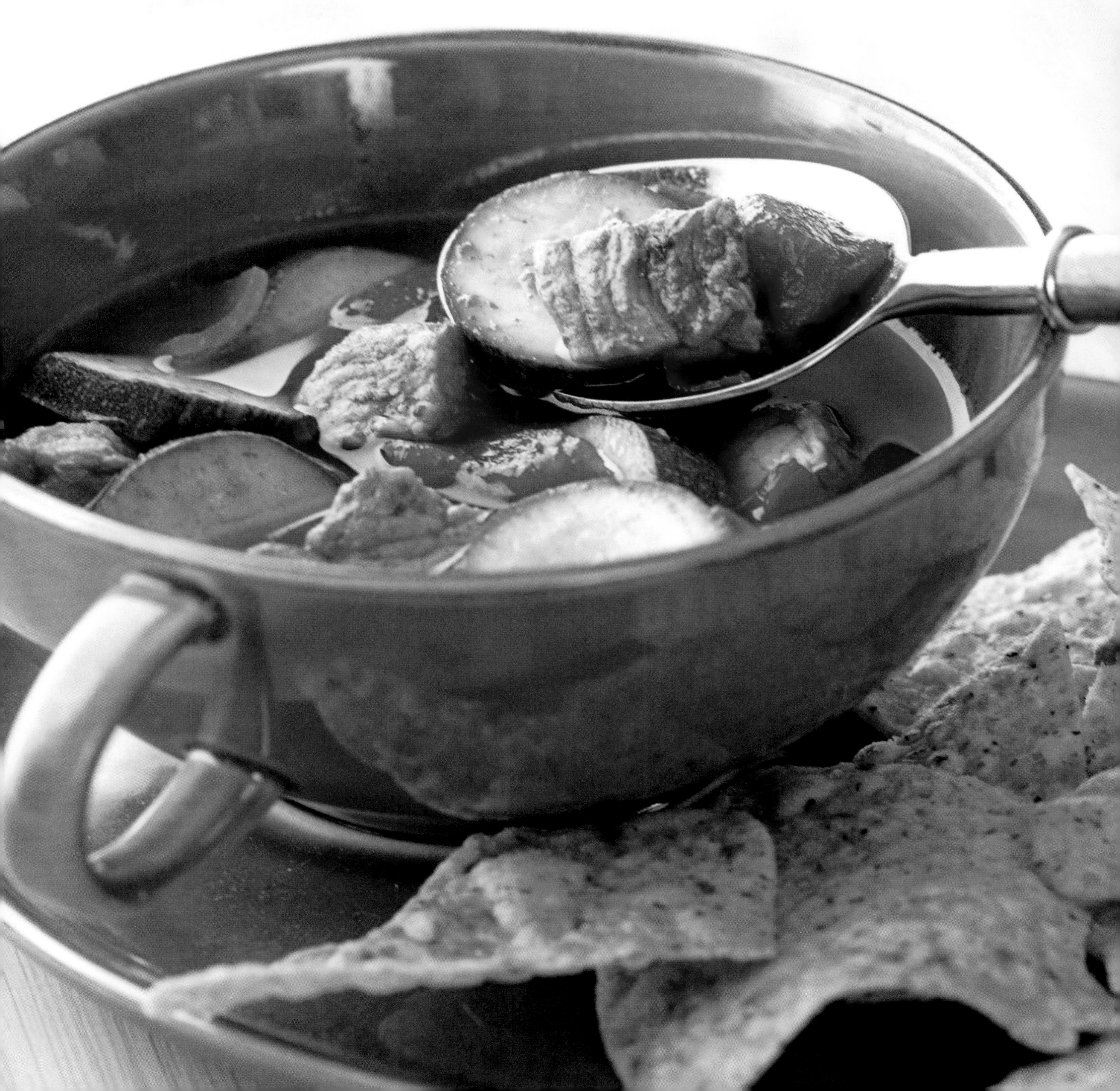

KALE, LENTIL, AND CHICKEN SOUP

*Note If you wish to substitute brown or yellow lentils for the red lentils, you will need to increase the cooking time. Check package directions for cooking times and add the lentils in Step 2.

Per serving: 199 cal., 5 g total fat (1 g sat. fat), 31 mg chol., 833 mg sodium, 20 g carbo., 5 g fiber, 18 g pro.

Thai Coconut Shrimp Soup

Start to Finish: 25 minutes

- 12 ounces fresh or frozen peeled and deveined medium shrimp
- 3 cups low-sodium chicken broth
- 1 14-ounce can unsweetened lite coconut milk
- 1 tablespoon fish sauce (nam pla)
- 2 teaspoons grated fresh ginger
- 1 teaspoon red curry paste
- 1 clove garlic, minced
- ½ teaspoon kosher salt
- 1 cup green beans cut into 1-inch pieces (4 ounces)
- ¼ cup thinly sliced green onions (2)
  Lime wedges

1. Thaw shrimp, if frozen. Rinse shrimp and pat dry with paper towels; set aside.
2. In a large saucepan combine chicken broth, coconut milk, fish sauce, ginger, curry paste, garlic, and salt. Bring to boiling. Add green beans. Return to boiling; reduce heat. Simmer for 2 minutes.
3. Add shrimp to soup. Return to boiling; reduce heat. Cook about 5 minutes or until shrimp are opaque. Top servings with green onions and serve with lime wedges.

MAKES 5 (1-CUP) SERVINGS

Per cup: 160 cal., 7 g total fat (4 g sat. fat), 103 mg chol., 656 mg sodium, 9 g carbo., 1 g fiber, 18 g pro.

Kale, Lentil, and Chicken Soup ♡

Start to Finish: 35 minutes

- 1 tablespoon olive oil
- 1 cup chopped onion (1 large)
- 1 cup coarsely chopped carrots (2 medium)
- 2 cloves garlic, minced
- 6 cups reduced-sodium chicken broth
- 1 tablespoon snipped fresh basil or 1 teaspoon dried basil, crushed
- 4 cups coarsely chopped kale (about 8 ounces)
- ½ teaspoon salt
- ⅛ teaspoon black pepper
- 1½ cups cubed cooked chicken (about 8 ounces)
- 1 medium tomato, seeded and chopped
- ½ cup dry red lentils*

1. In a large saucepan heat oil on medium-low heat. Add onion, carrots, and garlic. Cover and cook for 5 to 7 minutes or until vegetables are nearly tender, stirring occasionally.
2. Add chicken broth and dried basil (if using) to vegetable mixture. Bring to boiling; reduce heat. Simmer, covered, for 10 minutes. Stir in kale, salt, and pepper. Return to boiling; reduce heat. Simmer, covered, for 10 minutes.
3. Stir in cooked chicken, tomato, red lentils, and fresh basil (if using). Simmer, covered, for 5 to 10 minutes more or until kale and lentils are tender. MAKES 6 SERVINGS

MANGO-STEAK SALAD WITH LIME DRESSING

Mango-Steak Salad with Lime Dressing ♡

Prep: 25 minutes **Grill:** 17 minutes

- 12 ounces beef flank steak or boneless beef top sirloin steak, cut 1 inch thick
- ⅛ teaspoon salt
- ⅛ teaspoon black pepper
- ⅓ cup lime juice
- 2 tablespoons olive oil
- 2 tablespoons snipped fresh cilantro
- 1 tablespoon honey
- 2 cloves garlic, minced
- 8 cups torn romaine
- 5 ounces jicama, peeled and cut into thin bite-size strips (1 cup)
- 1 medium mango, seeded, peeled, and sliced
- 1 small red onion, cut into thin wedges

1. Trim fat from steak. If using flank steak, score both sides of steak in a diamond pattern by making shallow diagonal cuts at 1-inch intervals. Sprinkle steak with salt and pepper.

2. For a charcoal grill, place steak on the rack of an uncovered grill directly over medium coals. Grill until medium doneness (160°F), turning once halfway through grilling time. Allow 17 to 21 minutes for flank steak or 18 to 22 minutes for top sirloin steak. (For a gas grill, preheat grill. Reduce heat to medium. Place steak on grill rack over heat. Cover and grill as above.) Thinly slice steak diagonally across the grain.

3. Meanwhile, for dressing, in a small bowl whisk together lime juice, olive oil, cilantro, honey, and garlic.

4. To serve, divide romaine among 6 serving plates. Top with steak slices, jicama, mango, and red onion. Drizzle dressing over salads.

MAKES 6 SERVINGS

Per serving: 195 cal., 9 g total fat (2 g sat. fat), 23 mg chol., 87 mg sodium, 17 g carbo., 3 g fiber, 14 g pro.

SAGE-WHITE BEAN SOUP

Sage-White Bean Soup ♡

Prep: 25 minutes **Stand:** 1 hour **Cook:** 1 hour

- 1 pound dry Great Northern or navy beans
- 8 cups water
- 1 tablespoon olive oil
- 1 cup chopped onion (1 large)
- 12 cloves garlic, minced
- 4 14-ounce cans reduced-sodium chicken broth
- 2 tablespoons snipped fresh sage or 2 teaspoons dried sage, crushed
- ½ teaspoon salt
- ½ teaspoon black pepper
- 1 recipe Sage French Bread Toasts (optional)
  Fresh sage leaves (optional)

1. Rinse beans. In a 4-quart pot combine beans and the 8 cups water. Bring to boiling; reduce heat. Simmer, uncovered, for 2 minutes. Remove from heat. Cover; let stand for 1 hour. (Or let the uncooked beans and water soak overnight.) Drain and rinse beans; set aside.

2. In the same pot heat olive oil on medium heat. Add onion; cook until tender. Add garlic; cook and stir for 1 minute. Stir in beans and chicken broth. Bring to boiling; reduce heat. Simmer, covered, for 1 to 1½ hours or until beans are tender.

3. Stir in snipped sage, salt, and pepper. If desired, top each serving with Sage French Bread Toasts and fresh sage leaves.

MAKES 8 SERVINGS

Sage French Bread Toasts Preheat oven to 425°F. Brush a little olive oil onto eight ½-inch slices baguette-style French bread. Rub each slice with a cut garlic clove; sprinkle with snipped fresh or crushed dried sage. Bake for 5 to 7 minutes or until light brown.

Per serving: 236 cal., 2 g total fat (0 g sat. fat), 0 mg chol., 630 mg sodium, 40 g carbo., 12 g fiber, 15 g pro.

SUPER-CRUNCHY SUPPER SALAD

Super-Crunchy Supper Salad

Start to Finish: 35 minutes

    3 tablespoons apple juice
    3 tablespoons canola oil
    1 tablespoon red or white wine vinegar or
      cider vinegar
    4 to 6 cups torn mixed salad greens
    2 medium apples or pears, cored and cut
      into wedges
    8 ounces lean cooked beef, ham, chicken
      breast, or turkey breast, cut into thin bite-
      size strips (about 1½ cups)
    2 medium carrots, cut into thin bite-size strips
    1 cup thinly sliced, halved yellow summer
      squash

1. For dressing, in a screw-top jar combine apple juice, oil, and vinegar. Cover and shake well.
2. Divide salad greens among 4 plates. Top with apples, beef, carrots, and squash. Drizzle dressing over salads. **MAKES 4 SERVINGS**

Per serving: 272 cal., 15 g total fat (3 g sat. fat), 50 mg chol., 67 mg sodium, 16 g carbo., 4 g fiber, 20 g pro.

Teriyaki Beef and Watercress Salad

Prep: 20 minutes **Marinate:** 20 minutes
Grill: 14 minutes

    1 pound boneless beef top sirloin steak,
      1 inch thick
    3 tablespoons light teriyaki sauce
    3 tablespoons reduced-sodium soy sauce
    2 tablespoons salad oil
 1½ tablespoons rice wine vinegar
    1 teaspoon sugar
   ½ teaspoon grated fresh ginger
   ¼ teaspoon salt
    4 cups watercress, tough stems removed
   ½ of a seedless cucumber, thinly sliced
    4 red radishes, thinly sliced
    2 teaspoons black sesame seeds

1. Place steak in a resealable plastic bag set in a bowl. Add teriyaki sauce and the 2 tablespoons soy sauce to the bag. Seal bag; turn to coat steak. Marinate in the refrigerator for 20 minutes.
2. For a charcoal grill, grill steaks on the rack of an uncovered grill directly over medium coals to desired doneness, turning once halfway through grilling. Allow 14 to 18 minutes for medium rare (145°F) and 18 to 22 minutes for medium (160°F). (For a gas grill, preheat grill. Reduce heat to medium. Place steaks on the grill rack over heat. Cover and grill as directed.)
3. For dressing, in a small bowl whisk together salad oil, vinegar, sugar, ginger, salt, and the remaining 1 tablespoon soy sauce.
4. For salad, in a large bowl combine watercress, cucumber, and radishes. Slice steak; add to salad. Drizzle with dressing; toss to coat. Sprinkle with sesame seeds.

MAKES 4 SERVINGS

Per serving: 318 cal., 21 g total fat (6 g sat. fat), 52 mg chol., 844 mg sodium, 6 g carbo., 1 g fiber, 26 g pro.

Sautéed Pork and Pear Salad

Start to Finish: 30 minutes

12 ounces boneless pork top loin roast or pork tenderloin, trimmed and cut into thin bite-size strips
½ teaspoon dried sage, crushed
¼ teaspoon salt
¼ teaspoon black pepper
    Nonstick cooking spray
¼ cup coarsely chopped hazelnuts (filberts) or almonds
⅓ cup pear nectar
1 tablespoon olive oil
2 teaspoons Dijon mustard or chipotle chile pepper-style mustard
6 cups torn mixed salad greens
2 medium pears, cored and sliced

1. Sprinkle pork strips with sage, salt, and pepper. Coat an unheated large nonstick skillet with nonstick cooking spray. Preheat on medium-high heat. Add pork to hot skillet. Cook and stir for 2 to 3 minutes or until pork is slightly pink in the center. Add nuts. Cook and stir for 30 seconds more. Remove pork mixture. Cover and keep warm.
2. For dressing, carefully add pear nectar, olive oil, and mustard to hot skillet. Cook and stir just until blended, scraping up any crusty browned bits from bottom of skillet.
3. Divide salad greens and pear slices among 4 plates. Top with pork mixture; drizzle with warm dressing. Serve immediately. **MAKES 4 SERVINGS**

Per serving: 278 cal., 13 g total fat (2 g sat. fat), 47 mg chol., 256 mg sodium, 20 g carbo., 5 g fiber, 21 g pro.

GREEN CHILE AND CHICKEN TACO SALAD

Green Chile and Chicken Taco Salad

Start to Finish: 30 minutes

2 tablespoons olive oil
½ cup finely chopped onion (1 medium)
2 cloves garlic, minced
2 4-ounce cans chopped green chile peppers, drained
2 tablespoons all-purpose flour
3 cups chopped or shredded cooked chicken (about 1 pound)
1 cup reduced-sodium chicken broth
1 tablespoon lime juice
1 teaspoon ground cumin
¾ teaspoon kosher salt
½ teaspoon chili powder
    Lettuce leaves or tortilla chips

1. In a large pot heat oil on medium-high heat. Add onion and garlic. Cook and stir until onion is tender.
2. Stir in chile peppers and flour. Add chicken, chicken broth, lime juice, cumin, salt, and chili powder. Bring to boiling; reduce heat. Cook and stir until thickened and bubbly. Cook and stir for 1 minute more. Serve over lettuce or tortilla chips. **MAKES 4 SERVINGS**

Per serving: 280 cal., 13 g total fat (3 g sat. fat), 82 mg chol., 950 mg sodium, 15 g carbo., 3 g fiber, 26 g pro.

SEAFOOD SALAD WITH
GINGER-CREAM DRESSING

Seafood Salad with Ginger-Cream Dressing ♡

Start to Finish: 25 minutes

1 pound fresh or frozen sea scallops, cooked and chilled*
8 ounces fresh or frozen peeled and deveined shrimp, cooked and chilled**
6 cups fresh spinach leaves or torn mixed salad greens
2 large mangoes or small papayas, seeded, peeled, and cut into chunks
1 recipe Ginger-Cream Dressing
2 tablespoons cashew halves or sliced almonds, toasted (optional)

1. Halve any large scallops. In a large salad bowl combine scallops, shrimp, spinach, and mangoes. Drizzle Ginger-Cream Dressing over scallop mixture; toss gently to coat.
2. To serve, divide the scallop mixture among 6 plates. If desired, sprinkle with cashews.
MAKES 6 SERVINGS

Ginger-Cream Dressing In a small bowl stir together ⅓ cup light dairy sour cream, 2 teaspoons grated fresh ginger or ½ teaspoon ground ginger, 1 teaspoon white wine vinegar, ½ teaspoon finely shredded orange peel, 1 teaspoon orange juice, and dash cayenne pepper. Makes about ½ cup.

*Tip To cook scallops, add ½ cup water to a large skillet. Bring to boiling. Add scallops. Return to boiling; reduce heat. Simmer,

covered, for 4 to 6 minutes or until scallops turn opaque. Drain and chill.

**Tip If desired, leave the tails on the shrimp. To cook shrimp, in a medium saucepan bring 2 cups water to boiling. Add shrimp; return to boiling. Cook, uncovered, for 1 to 3 minutes or until shrimp turn opaque. Rinse under cold running water; drain and chill.

Per serving: 174 cal., 3 g total fat (1 g sat. fat), 86 mg chol., 184 mg sodium, 16 g carbo., 2 g fiber, 22 g pro.

Balsamic Chicken over Greens

Prep: 15 minutes **Marinate:** 1 to 4 hours
Broil: 12 minutes

4 skinless, boneless chicken breast halves (about 1 pound)
¾ cup bottled reduced-calorie balsamic vinaigrette salad dressing
3 cloves garlic, minced
¼ teaspoon crushed red pepper
8 cups torn mixed salad greens

1. Place chicken breast halves in a resealable plastic bag set in a shallow dish. For marinade, stir together ⅓ cup of the vinaigrette, the garlic, and crushed red pepper. Pour marinade over the chicken. Seal bag; turn to coat chicken. Marinate in the refrigerator for 1 to 4 hours, turning bag occasionally.
2. Preheat broiler. Drain chicken, reserving marinade. Place chicken on the unheated rack of a broiler pan. Broil 4 to 5 inches from heat for 12 to 15 minutes or until chicken is no longer pink (170°F), turning once and brushing with reserved marinade halfway through broiling. Discard any remaining marinade.
3. Divide greens among 4 plates. Slice chicken; arrange chicken on greens. Serve with the remaining vinaigrette. **MAKES 4 SERVINGS**

Per serving: 203 cal., 7 g total fat (1 g sat. fat), 66 mg chol., 703 mg sodium, 6 g carbo., 1 g fiber, 28 g pro.

BALSAMIC CHICKEN OVER GREENS

DILLED TUNA POTATO SALAD

Salad Niçoise on Flatbread ♡

Start to Finish: 25 minutes

- 4 ounces fresh green beans, trimmed (if desired) and cut into 1-inch pieces (about 1 cup)
- 1 12-ounce can chunk white or light tuna (water pack), drained and flaked
- 1 cup halved cherry tomatoes
- ⅓ cup chopped pitted niçoise or kalamata olives
- ¼ cup finely chopped sweet onion (such as Vidalia, Walla Walla, or Maui)
- 2 tablespoons snipped fresh mint
- 1 tablespoon lemon juice
- 2 teaspoons olive oil
- ⅛ teaspoon black pepper
- 3 cups packaged mesclun mix
- 3 large pita breads, halved crosswise
- 6 cherry tomatoes (optional)
- 6 pitted niçoise or kalamata olives (optional)
- 6 mint leaves (optional)
- 6 short wooden skewers (optional)

1. In a covered medium saucepan cook green beans in boiling water about 4 minutes or until crisp-tender. Drain; rinse under cold water. Drain again.

2. Place green beans in a large bowl. Stir in tuna, the 1 cup cherry tomatoes, the ⅓ cup olives, onion, and the 2 tablespoons mint. Add lemon juice, olive oil, and pepper; toss to combine. Stir in mesclun.

3. Fill each pita half with about ½ cup of the tuna mixture. If desired, thread a whole cherry tomato, a whole olive, and a mint leaf on the skewers; serve skewers with sandwiches.

MAKES 6 SANDWICHES

Per sandwich: 210 cal., 5 g total fat (1 g sat. fat), 24 mg chol., 527 mg sodium, 23 g carbo., 3 g fiber, 17 g pro.

Dilled Tuna Potato Salad ♡

Prep: 25 minutes **Chill:** 4 to 6 hours

- 3 medium red potatoes (about 1 pound)
- ½ cup light mayonnaise dressing or salad dressing
- ½ cup plain fat-free yogurt
- 1 tablespoon snipped fresh dill or 1 teaspoon dried dill
- 1 tablespoon fat-free milk
- ½ teaspoon finely shredded lemon peel
- ¼ teaspoon salt
- 1 clove garlic, minced
- 1 cup chopped cucumber
- ¼ cup sliced green onions (2)
- ¼ cup coarsely chopped radishes
- 1 9-ounce can chunk white tuna (water pack), drained and broken into chunks
- 2 hard-cooked eggs, chopped
- 12 leaves savoy cabbage or Chinese (napa) cabbage

1. Scrub potatoes. Cut into ½-inch cubes. In a covered medium saucepan cook potatoes in a small amount of boiling water for 10 to 12 minutes or just until tender. Drain; let cool.

2. Meanwhile, in a large bowl stir together mayonnaise dressing, yogurt, dill, milk, lemon peel, salt, and garlic. Stir in cucumber, green onions, and radishes. Add cooked potatoes, tuna, and chopped eggs; toss gently to coat. Cover and chill for 4 to 6 hours.

3. To serve, line 6 bowls with cabbage leaves. Gently stir tuna mixture; spoon on top of cabbage. **MAKES 6 SERVINGS**

Per serving: 243 cal., 10 g total fat (2 g sat. fat), 96 mg chol., 461 mg sodium, 22 g carbo., 5 g fiber, 18 g pro.

SALMON PENNE SALAD WITH RASPBERRY VINAIGRETTE

Raspberry Vinaigrette In a small bowl whisk together ¼ cup raspberry vinegar; 2 tablespoons olive oil; 1 tablespoon honey mustard; 2 teaspoons sugar; 1 clove garlic, minced; and ¼ teaspoon black pepper. Cover and chill until serving time.

Per serving: 368 cal., 14 g total fat (2 g sat. fat), 33 mg chol., 42 mg sodium, 41 g carbo., 4 g fiber, 18 g pro.

Wheat Berry Tabbouleh ♡

Start to Finish: 25 minutes

2⅔ cups cooked wheat berries*
 ¾ cup chopped tomato (1 large)
 ¾ cup chopped cucumber
 ½ cup snipped fresh parsley
 ¼ cup thinly sliced green onions (2)
 1 tablespoon snipped fresh mint
 3 tablespoons vegetable oil
 3 tablespoons lemon juice
 ¼ teaspoon salt
 4 lettuce leaves
   Lemon slices (optional)

1. In a large bowl combine cooked wheat berries, tomato, cucumber, parsley, green onions, and mint.
2. For dressing, in a screw-top jar combine oil, lemon juice, and salt. Cover and shake well. Drizzle dressing over wheat berry mixture; toss to coat. Serve immediately or cover and chill for up to 4 hours. Serve in a lettuce-lined bowl** and, if desired, garnish with lemon slices. **MAKES ABOUT 4½ CUPS (5 SIDE-DISH SERVINGS)**

*Tip To cook wheat berries, bring one 14-ounce can vegetable or chicken broth and ¼ cup water to boiling. Add 1 cup wheat berries. Return to boiling; reduce heat. Simmer, covered, for 45 to 60 minutes or until tender; drain. Cover and chill for up to 3 days.

**Tip For a light meal or starter course, spoon tabbouleh into seeded avocado halves.

Per serving: 148 cal., 9 g total fat (1 g sat. fat), 0 mg chol., 295 mg sodium, 17 g carbo., 2 g fiber, 3 g pro.

Salmon Penne Salad with Raspberry Vinaigrette

Prep: 30 minutes **Broil:** 4 to 6 minutes per ½-inch thickness **Chill:** 2 to 4 hours

 1 8- to 10-ounce fresh or frozen skinless, boneless salmon fillet or other fish fillet
 1 recipe Raspberry Vinaigrette
 6 ounces dried penne pasta (about 2 cups)
 1 cup bias-sliced fresh asparagus
 1 cup fresh red raspberries or sliced fresh strawberries
   Lettuce leaves (optional)
 ¼ cup sliced green onions (2)

1. Thaw fish, if frozen. Rinse fish; pat dry with paper towels. Measure the thickness of the fish. Remove 2 teaspoons of the Raspberry Vinaigrette; brush onto fish. Cover and chill the remaining vinaigrette until ready to use.

2. Preheat broiler. Place fish on the greased unheated rack of a broiler pan; tuck under any thin edges. Broil 4 inches from heat until fish begins to flake easily when tested with a fork, allowing 4 to 6 minutes per ½-inch thickness and turning once if fish is more than 1 inch thick.
3. Meanwhile, cook pasta according to package directions, adding asparagus the last 2 minutes. Drain; rinse with cold water. Drain again. Return pasta to pan. Add reserved vinaigrette; toss gently to coat.
4. Flake cooked salmon. Add salmon to pasta; toss gently. Cover and chill 2 to 4 hours.
5. To serve, add berries to pasta mixture; toss gently to mix. If desired, serve on lettuce-lined plates. Top with onions. **MAKES 4 SERVINGS**

CHIPOTLE BBQ SANDWICHES

VINAIGRETTE-DRESSED STEAK SANDWICHES

Chipotle BBQ Sandwiches

Prep: 25 minutes **Marinate:** 4 to 6 hours
Grill: 17 minutes

- 1 8-ounce can tomato sauce
- 3 tablespoons tomato paste
- 1 tablespoon Dijon mustard
- 1 tablespoon Worcestershire sauce
- 2 teaspoons honey
- 1 teaspoon finely chopped chipotle chile peppers in adobo sauce (see note, page 85)
- 1 clove garlic, minced
- 1 12-ounce beef flank steak
- 1 medium green sweet pepper, quartered
- 4 ½-inch slices sweet onion
     Nonstick cooking spray
- 4 ciabatta rolls, split and toasted

1. For marinade, combine tomato sauce, tomato paste, 2 tablespoons *water*, mustard, Worcestershire sauce, honey, chile peppers, and garlic. Score both sides of steak in a diamond pattern. Place steak in a large resealable plastic bag. Pour marinade over steak. Seal bag; turn to coat. Marinate steak in refrigerator for 4 to 6 hours, turning occasionally.
2. Drain steak, reserving marinade. Lightly coat sweet pepper and onion with cooking spray. For a charcoal grill, place steak, sweet peppers, and onion on rack of uncovered grill directly over medium coals. Grill steak for 17 to 21 minutes or until medium doneness (160°F) and vegetables for 8 to 12 minutes or until tender, turning steak and vegetables once. (For a gas grill, preheat grill. Reduce heat to medium. Place steak, sweet pepper quarters, and onion slices on grill rack over heat. Cover; grill as above.)
3. Meanwhile, for BBQ sauce, pour reserved marinade into a small saucepan. Bring to boiling; reduce heat. Simmer, uncovered, about 5 minutes or until desired consistency.
4. Thinly slice steak across the grain. Thinly slice sweet pepper lengthwise. Place steak, sweet pepper, and onion on the bottom halves of the rolls. Add BBQ sauce and add ciabatta roll tops. **MAKES 4 SANDWICHES**

Per sandwich: 378 cal., 9 g total fat (3 g sat. fat), 35 mg chol., 1,030 mg sodium, 47 g carbo., 4 g fiber, 25 g pro.

Vinaigrette-Dressed Steak Sandwich

Prep: 35 minutes **Marinate:** 1 hour

- 12 ounces boneless beef top sirloin steak, cut ½ inch thick
- ½ cup reduced-fat, reduced-calorie bottled balsamic-, raspberry-, or Italian-flavor vinaigrette
- ½ teaspoon crushed red pepper
- 1 clove garlic, minced
- ¼ cup light mayonnaise dressing
- 1 small red onion, thinly sliced
- 2 teaspoons vegetable oil
- 4 hoagie rolls (about 2 ounces each), split and toasted
- 1¼ cups small lettuce leaves
- ⅔ cup fresh basil leaves, thinly sliced

1. If desired, partially freeze steak for easier slicing. Trim fat from steak. Thinly slice steak across the grain into bite-size strips. In a medium bowl combine vinaigrette, red pepper, and garlic. In a small bowl combine 1 tablespoon of the vinaigrette mixture and the mayonnaise dressing. Cover and chill.
2. Add steak strips to the remaining vinaigrette mixture; stir to coat evenly. Cover and marinate in the refrigerator for 1 hour. Drain steak strips, discarding marinade.
3. In a large nonstick skillet cook steak strips and onion in hot oil on medium-high heat for 2 to 3 minutes or until meat is brown and onion is crisp-tender.
4. To assemble, spread mayonnaise dressing-vinaigrette mixture evenly onto 1 side of each bread slice. Top with lettuce and basil. With a slotted spoon, divide steak and onion mixture among the bread slices.
MAKES 4 SANDWICHES

Per sandwich: 397 cal., 12 g total fat (2 g sat. fat), 55 mg chol., 500 mg sodium, 48 g carbo., 3 g fiber, 23 g pro.

ROAST BEEF-MANGO PANINI

are toasted. Carefully remove top skillet, which may be hot. Turn sandwiches and top again with the skillet. Cook for 7 to 10 minutes more or until rolls are toasted and cheese melts.) **MAKES 4 SANDWICHES**

Per serving: 381 cal., 5 g total fat (3 g sat. fat), 35 mg chol., 1,042 mg sodium, 61 g carbo., 2 g fiber, 20 g pro.

Turkey-Sweet Pepper Panini Prepare as directed, except substitute thinly sliced turkey breast for the roast beef and ½ cup bottled roasted red sweet peppers, drained and cut into strips, for the mango.

Per sandwich: 306 cal., 6 g total fat (2 g sat. fat), 42 mg chol., 1,277 mg sodium, 47 g carbo., 3 g fiber, 17 g pro.

Salami and Brie Panini

Start to Finish: 20 minutes

- 3 teaspoons olive oil
- 1 Granny Smith apple, cored
- 1 loaf ciabatta bread, cut into ½-inch slices, or 4 ciabatta rolls
- 4 ounces Brie, sliced
- 12 thin slices hard salami (about 4 ounces)

1. Brush a grill pan or a very large skillet with 1 teaspoon of the olive oil. Preheat pan on medium heat. Cut apple into thin rings; place in pan. Cook for 2 to 3 minutes or just until tender; remove from pan.

2. If using rolls, split in half horizontally. Place cheese on 4 of the bread slices or bottom halves of rolls. Top with salami, apple rings, and remaining bread or roll tops. Brush both sides of each sandwich with the remaining 2 teaspoons olive oil.

3. Place sandwiches on grill pan. Cook on medium heat until bread is toasted, turning once. Serve hot. **MAKES 4 SANDWICHES**

Per sandwich: 475 cal., 22 g total fat (10 g sat. fat), 59 mg chol., 1,306 mg sodium, 48 g carbo., 3 g fiber, 22 g pro.

Roast Beef-Mango Panini

Prep: 20 minutes **Cook:** 4 minutes per batch

- 4 6-inch whole wheat hoagie buns, split
  Olive oil nonstick cooking spray
- 10 ounces thinly sliced cooked roast beef
- ½ cup fresh basil leaves or fresh baby spinach
- 12 refrigerated mango slices, well drained
- 1 teaspoon freshly ground black pepper
- ¼ cup semisoft goat cheese (chèvre) or 4 ounces provolone cheese, sliced

1. Lightly coat outsides of hoagie buns with nonstick cooking spray. Turn roll bottoms coated sides down; divide roast beef among roll bottoms. Top each with some of the basil and 3 mango slices. Sprinkle with pepper.

Turn the bun tops coated sides down; spread each with goat cheese. Place on sandwiches, cheese sides down.

2. Preheat an electric sandwich press, panini griddle, or covered indoor grill according to manufacturer's directions. (Or coat an unheated grill pan or large skillet with nonstick cooking spray. Preheat on low to medium-low heat for 1 to 2 minutes.) Add sandwiches in batches, if necessary. If using sandwich press, panini griddle, or covered indoor grill, close lid and grill for 4 to 5 minutes or until rolls are toasted and cheese melts. (If using grill pan or skillet, place a heavy skillet with a can of vegetables on sandwiches. Cook on medium-low heat for 7 to 10 minutes or until bottoms

SALAMI AND BRIE PANINI

Mushroom and Ham Fold-Overs

Prep: 25 minutes **Bake:** 8 minutes
Oven: 375°F

- 1 tablespoon olive oil
- 2 cups sliced fresh mushrooms
- 1 cup chopped red or green sweet pepper (1 large)
- 2 teaspoons snipped fresh oregano or ½ teaspoon dried oregano, crushed
- 1 8-ounce can pizza sauce
- 4 oval multigrain wraps
- 6 ounces thinly sliced low-sodium cooked ham, coarsely chopped
- ½ cup shredded reduced-fat cheddar cheese or reduced-fat mozzarella cheese (2 ounces)

1. Preheat oven to 375°F. In a large skillet heat olive oil on medium heat. Add mushrooms and sweet pepper; cook for 5 to 10 minutes or until vegetables are tender, stirring occasionally. Stir in oregano.

2. Meanwhile, spread some of the pizza sauce on one side of each wrap, leaving a ½-inch border around the edge. Divide ham among wraps, arranging it on half of each wrap. Top ham with mushroom mixture. Sprinkle with cheese. Fold wraps in half. Place on a large baking sheet. Bake for 8 to 10 minutes or until heated through.

MAKES 4 SERVINGS

Per serving: 284 cal., 13 g total fat (4 g sat. fat), 34 mg chol., 1,232 mg sodium, 26 g carbo., 11 g fiber, 25 g pro.

Red, White, and Green Panini

Prep: 25 minutes **Grill:** 6 minutes per batch

- 1 recipe Red Onion Relish
- 1 16-ounce loaf unsliced ciabatta or Italian bread
- 2 tablespoons olive oil
- ¼ cup mayonnaise
- 1 tablespoon purchased basil pesto
- 6 ounces thinly sliced provolone cheese
- 4 ounces thinly sliced coppacola or cooked ham
- 4 ounces thinly sliced salami
- 2 cups fresh spinach or arugula

RED, WHITE, AND GREEN PANINI

1. Prepare Red Onion Relish; set aside. Cut bread in half horizontally. Brush the outside of the loaf with olive oil. Place the bottom half of the loaf on a piece of waxed paper, cut side up. Set top aside. In a small bowl stir together mayonnaise and pesto; set aside.

2. Preheat an electric sandwich press, a covered indoor grill, a grill pan, or a skillet. To assemble sandwiches, place half of the provolone cheese on the bottom half of the bread loaf. Spread mayonnaise mixture over cheese. Layer with coppacola, salami, Red Onion Relish, spinach, and the remaining cheese. Replace top of loaf. Cut loaf crosswise into 4 sandwiches.

3. Place sandwiches (half at a time, if necessary) in the sandwich press or indoor grill; cover and cook about 6 minutes or until cheese melts and bread is toasted. (If using a grill pan or skillet, place a heavy skillet with a

can of vegetables on sandwiches. Cook on medium-low heat about 2 minutes or until bread is toasted. Carefully remove top skillet, which may be hot. Turn sandwiches, top again with the skillet, and grill until remaining side is toasted.) **MAKES 4 SANDWICHES**

Red Onion Relish In a medium bowl combine 1 medium red onion, halved and thinly sliced (1 cup); 2 tablespoons olive oil; 1 tablespoon red wine vinegar; and 1 teaspoon snipped fresh oregano. Season with salt and black pepper. Cover and let stand at room temperature for up to 2 hours. Drain before using. Makes about 1 cup.

Per sandwich: 869 cal., 54 g total fat (16 g sat. fat), 77 mg chol., 2,114 mg sodium, 63 g carbo., 4 g fiber, 32 g pro.

GRILLED CHICKEN SANDWICHES

Grilled Chicken Sandwiches ♡

Prep: 20 minutes **Grill:** 12 minutes

- ¼ cup light mayonnaise or salad dressing
- ½ teaspoon finely shredded lime peel or lemon peel
- 1 medium zucchini or yellow summer squash, cut lengthwise into ¼-inch slices
- 3 tablespoons Worcestershire-style marinade for chicken
- 4 small skinless, boneless chicken breast halves (1 to 1¼ pounds)
- 4 whole wheat hamburger buns, split and toasted
- 1 medium tomato, thinly sliced

1. For lime dressing, in a small bowl combine mayonnaise and lime peel. Cover and chill until serving time.

2. Brush zucchini slices with 1 tablespoon of the Worcestershire-style marinade; set aside. Brush all sides of the chicken with the remaining 2 tablespoons Worcestershire-style marinade.

3. For a charcoal grill, place chicken on the rack of an uncovered grill directly over medium coals. Grill for 12 to 15 minutes or until no longer pink (170°F), turning once halfway through grilling. Add zucchini slices to grill for the last 6 minutes of grilling time for chicken, turning once and grilling until zucchini slices are softened and lightly browned. (For a gas grill, preheat grill. Reduce heat to medium. Place chicken on the grill rack. Cover and grill as above, adding zucchini as directed.)

4. To serve, spread lime dressing on cut sides of toasted buns. If desired, halve zucchini slices crosswise. Place chicken, tomato slices, and zucchini slices on bun bottoms; add bun tops. **MAKES 4 SANDWICHES**

Per sandwich: 298 cal., 7 g total fat (1 g sat. fat), 71 mg chol., 587 mg sodium, 27 g carbo., 3 g fiber, 31 g pro.

Greek Fusion Burgers ♡

Prep: 25 minutes **Grill:** 10 minutes

- 1 pound uncooked ground turkey breast
- 2 teaspoons finely chopped canned chipotle chile peppers in adobo sauce (see note, page 85)
- 1 teaspoon dried oregano, crushed
- ¼ cup light tub-style cream cheese, softened
- ¼ cup shredded reduced-fat cheddar cheese (1 ounce)
- 1 tablespoon finely chopped green onion
- ⅛ teaspoon salt
- 2 large whole wheat pita bread rounds, halved crosswise
- 2 small tomatoes, sliced
- ½ of a medium cucumber, cut into thin bite-size strips

1. In a medium bowl combine turkey, 1 teaspoon of the chile peppers, and the oregano. Shape mixture into four ½-inch-thick oval patties.

2. For a charcoal grill, grill patties on the rack of an uncovered grill directly over medium heat for 10 to 13 minutes or until done (165°F), turning once halfway through grilling. (For a gas grill, preheat grill. Reduce heat to medium. Place patties on grill rack over heat. Cover and grill as above.)

3. Meanwhile, in a small bowl combine the remaining 1 teaspoon chile pepper, the cream cheese, cheddar cheese, green onion, and salt.

4. Open cut sides of halved pita bread rounds to make pockets. Spread cream cheese mixture into pockets. Add cucumber, grilled patties, and tomato slices. **MAKES 4 BURGERS**

Per burger: 272 cal., 6 g total fat (3 g sat. fat), 58 mg chol., 473 mg sodium, 22 g carbo., 3 g fiber, 33 g pro.

TUNA SALAD POCKETS

Roasted Veggie Pitas

Prep: 25 minutes **Roast:** 8 minutes
Oven: 450°F

- 1 small zucchini (6 ounces), thinly sliced lengthwise
- 1 small yellow summer squash (6 ounces), thinly sliced lengthwise
- 1 medium onion, thinly sliced (½ cup)
- ½ cup sliced fresh mushrooms
- ½ of a red sweet pepper, cut into thin strips
- 2 tablespoons olive oil
- ½ teaspoon salt
- ¼ teaspoon black pepper
- 2 large pita bread rounds, halved
- 4 teaspoons bottled vinaigrette or Italian salad dressing
- 3 ounces smoked provolone or mozzarella cheese, shredded (¾ cup)

1. Preheat oven to 450°F. Place zucchini, summer squash, onion, mushrooms, and sweet pepper in a large bowl. Add oil, salt, and black pepper; toss to coat. Spread mixture evenly in a 15×10×1-inch baking pan. Roast, uncovered, for 8 to 10 minutes or until vegetables are tender.
2. Divide roasted vegetables among pita bread halves; drizzle with salad dressing. Top with shredded cheese. If desired, place the filled pitas on a baking sheet and bake in the 450°F oven for 2 to 3 minutes or until cheese melts. **MAKES 4 SERVINGS**

Per serving: 270 cal., 16 g total fat (5 g sat. fat), 15 mg chol., 669 mg sodium, 24 g carbo., 2 g fiber, 10 g pro.

Avocado Veggie Pitas Prepare as above, except omit salad dressing. In a small bowl mash 1 halved, seeded, and peeled avocado with 1 tablespoon lime juice and ¼ teaspoon salt. Spread avocado mixture in pita bread rounds before filling with vegetables.

Tuna Salad Pockets

Start to Finish: 20 minutes

- 1 12-ounce can solid white tuna (water pack), drained and broken into chunks
- ¼ cup finely chopped red onion
- ¼ cup thinly sliced celery
- ¼ cup shredded carrot
- 1 tablespoon capers, rinsed and drained
- 2 tablespoons olive oil
- 2 tablespoons lime juice
- 1 tablespoon Dijon mustard
- 1 tablespoon champagne vinegar or white wine vinegar
- 1½ cups torn mixed salad greens
- 2 large whole wheat pita bread rounds

1. In a medium bowl combine tuna, onion, celery, carrot, and capers; set aside. For vinaigrette, in a screw-top jar combine olive oil, lime juice, mustard, and vinegar. Cover and shake well to combine. Pour vinaigrette over tuna mixture; toss gently to combine. Add greens; toss gently to combine.
2. Cut pita rounds in half crosswise; open pita halves to make pockets. Fill pockets with tuna mixture. **MAKES 4 SANDWICHES**

Per sandwich: 272 cal., 10 g total fat (2 g sat. fat), 36 mg chol., 659 mg sodium, 22 g carbo., 3 g fiber, 24 g pro.

CHAPTER 5

Pasta, Grains & Beans

THREE-CHEESE ZITI AND SMOKED CHICKEN BAKE

Three-Cheese Ziti and Smoked Chicken Bake

Prep: 25 minutes **Bake:** 25 minutes
Stand: 10 minutes **Oven:** 375°F

    Butter
12 ounces dried cut ziti
 3 tablespoons butter or margarine
 2 cloves garlic, minced
 3 tablespoons all-purpose flour
 ¼ teaspoon salt
 ¼ teaspoon ground white pepper
3½ cups milk
 8 ounces Asiago cheese, finely shredded
    (1½ cups)
 4 ounces fontina cheese, finely shredded
    (1 cup)
 2 ounces blue cheese, crumbled (½ cup)
 2 cups chopped smoked chicken or
    shredded purchased roasted chicken

 ⅓ cup panko (Japanese-style) bread crumbs
    or fine dry bread crumbs
 2 teaspoons white truffle oil or melted butter

1. Preheat oven to 375°F. Butter a 2-quart baking dish; set aside. Cook pasta according to package directions. Drain pasta; return to hot saucepan. Cover and keep warm.
2. Meanwhile, in a medium saucepan melt the 3 tablespoons butter over medium heat. Add garlic; cook for 30 seconds. Stir in flour, salt, and white pepper. Add milk all at once. Cook and stir until thickened and bubbly. Add Asiago, fontina, and blue cheeses, stirring until melted. Add chicken, stirring to combine.
3. Pour cheese mixture over cooked ziti; gently toss to coat. Transfer mixture to the prepared baking dish. In a small bowl combine panko crumbs and truffle oil. Sprinkle crumb mixture evenly over mixture in baking dish.
4. Bake about 25 minutes or until bubbly and lightly browned. Let stand for 10 minutes before serving. **MAKES 6 SERVINGS**

Per serving: 753 cal., 39 g total fat (22 g sat. fat), 141 mg chol., 953 mg sodium, 56 g carbo., 2 g fiber, 43 g pro.

Peanut Noodles with Chicken and Carrots

Start to Finish: 30 minutes

 1 8-ounce package soba (buckwheat
    noodles)
1½ cups shredded cooked chicken
    (8 ounces)
 1 cup shredded carrots (2 medium)
 1 red sweet pepper, cut into thin strips
 ½ cup thinly sliced green onions (4)
 3 tablespoons snipped fresh mint or cilantro
 ½ cup smooth peanut butter
 ⅓ cup reduced-sodium chicken broth
 2 tablespoons rice wine vinegar
 2 tablespoons reduced-sodium soy sauce
 2 teaspoons Asian hot chili sauce
 1 teaspoon grated fresh ginger
 ¼ cup coarsely chopped peanuts
    Fresh mint or cilantro (optional)

1. Cook soba noodles according to package directions. Rinse with cold water; drain.
2. In a large bowl gently toss together noodles, chicken, carrots, sweet pepper, green onions, and the 3 tablespoons mint.
3. For dressing, in a medium bowl whisk together peanut butter, chicken broth, vinegar, soy sauce, chili sauce, and ginger until smooth. If dressing is too thick, whisk in a little additional chicken broth.
4. Add enough dressing to noodle mixture to coat. Sprinkle with peanuts. Pass remaining dressing. If desired, garnish with additional mint. **MAKES 4 SERVINGS**

Per serving: 560 cal., 24.5 g total fat (5.5 g sat. fat), 41 mg chol., 783 mg sodium, 60 g carbo., 8 g fiber, 30 g pro.

Penne with Broccoli Rabe and Pancetta

Start to Finish: 30 minutes

- 12 ounces broccoli rabe or 1½ cups broccoli florets
- 8 cups dried whole wheat or multigrain penne pasta (8 ounces)
- ½ cup chopped onion (1 medium)
- 2 ounces chopped pancetta or bacon
- 2 cloves garlic, minced
- 1⅓ cups chopped, seeded plum tomatoes (4 medium)
- ⅓ cup dry white wine or chicken broth
  Salt and freshly ground black pepper
- ¼ cup finely shredded Asiago cheese (1 ounce)

1. Thoroughly wash broccoli rabe; drain well. If using broccoli rabe, remove and discard large leaves; cut into 4-inch lengths. Set aside.

2. In a large saucepan cook pasta in a large amount of lightly salted boiling water for 9 minutes. Add broccoli rabe. Cook about 3 minutes more or until pasta is tender; drain well. Return pasta mixture to saucepan; cover and keep warm.

3. Meanwhile, in a medium saucepan cook onion, pancetta, and garlic on medium heat for 3 to 5 minutes or until pancetta is crisp and onion is tender, stirring occasionally. Reduce heat to low. Add tomatoes and wine; cook for 2 minutes more, stirring frequently.

4. Add tomato mixture to pasta mixture; toss gently to combine. Season with salt and pepper. Transfer to a serving dish. Sprinkle with cheese. **MAKES 4 TO 6 SERVINGS**

Per serving: 348 cal., 8 g total fat (3 g sat. fat), 18 mg chol., 462 mg sodium, 51 g carbo., 8 g fiber, 16 g pro.

Mexican Chorizo Noodle Bowl

Start to Finish: 40 minutes

- 1 pound uncooked chorizo or hot Italian sausage
- 2 cloves garlic, minced
- 3 14-ounce cans chicken or vegetable broth
- 2 cups salsa
- 1 to 2 canned chipotle chiles in adobo sauce, finely chopped (see tip, page 129)
- 1 teaspoon dried oregano, crushed
- 1 teaspoon ground cumin
- 10 ounces dried vermicelli or dried angel hair pasta
- 1 cup chopped zucchini
- ⅔ cup finely grated queso anejito, mozzarella cheese, or farmer's cheese
- ¼ cup snipped fresh cilantro or Italian (flat-leaf) parsley
  Fresh cilantro sprigs (optional)

1. Remove casing from sausage, if present. In a 4-quart pot cook chorizo and garlic until meat is brown. Drain off fat.

2. Stir chicken broth, salsa, chipotle peppers, oregano, and cumin into sausage mixture in pot. Bring to boiling; reduce heat. Simmer, covered, for 15 minutes.

3. Add pasta and zucchini to sausage mixture in pot. Simmer, uncovered, for 2 to 3 minutes or until pasta is tender, stirring occasionally. Remove pot from heat; stir in ⅓ cup of the cheese and the ¼ cup cilantro. Spoon mixture into serving bowls. Sprinkle with remaining cheese. If desired, garnish with cilantro sprigs. **MAKES 6 SERVINGS**

Per serving: 621 cal., 36 g total fat (14 g sat. fat), 82 mg chol., 2,129 mg sodium, 43 g carbo., 3 g fiber, 30 g pro.

RAVIOLI WITH SWEET PEPPERS

Fresh Herb Pasta Primavera ♡

Start to Finish: 35 minutes

- 8 ounces dried multigrain or whole grain penne or mostaccioli
- 3 cups assorted fresh vegetables (such as red sweet pepper strips, trimmed sugar snap peas, 2-inch-long pieces trimmed asparagus, and/or quartered-lengthwise packaged peeled baby carrots)
- 1 cup halved cherry tomatoes
- ½ cup reduced-sodium chicken broth
- 3 tablespoons all-purpose flour
- ½ teaspoon salt
- 1¼ cups low-fat milk
- ¼ cup dry sherry or reduced-sodium chicken broth
- ¾ cup finely shredded Parmesan or Asiago cheese (3 ounces)
- ½ cup lightly packed fresh basil, coarsely chopped
- 4 teaspoons snipped fresh thyme or oregano
- ⅓ cup sliced green onions (optional)

1. In a 4-quart Dutch oven cook pasta according to package directions; add the 3 cups assorted vegetables for the last 2 minutes of cooking. Drain well. Return to hot Dutch oven. Add cherry tomatoes.

2. In a medium saucepan whisk together chicken broth, flour, and salt until smooth. Stir in milk and sherry. Cook and stir until thickened and bubbly; cook and stir for 2 minutes more. Remove from heat; stir in Parmesan cheese, basil, and thyme.

3. Add herb sauce to pasta mixture; toss gently to coat. Divide among 6 serving plates. If desired, sprinkle with green onions.

MAKES 6 SERVINGS

Per serving: 253 cal., 5 g total fat (3 g sat. fat), 12 mg chol., 496 mg sodium, 41 g carbo., 6 g fiber, 13 g pro.

Ravioli with Sweet Peppers

Start to Finish: 25 minutes

- 1 9-ounce package refrigerated whole wheat four-cheese ravioli
- 1 tablespoon olive oil
- 2 medium red and/or green sweet peppers, seeded and cut into thin strips
- 1 cup thinly sliced carrots (2 medium)
- ½ cup chopped onion (1 medium)
- 2 cloves garlic, minced
- 1 14.5-ounce can diced tomatoes, undrained
- 3 tablespoons snipped fresh basil or 2 teaspoons dried basil, crushed
  Black pepper
  Small basil leaves (optional)

1. Cook pasta according to package directions, except omit any oil or salt; drain. Return pasta to hot saucepan. Cover and keep warm.

2. Meanwhile, in a large nonstick skillet heat oil on medium-high heat. Add sweet peppers, carrots, onion, and garlic; cook and stir about 5 minutes or until vegetables are tender. Stir in undrained tomatoes and the 3 tablespoons snipped basil. Cook and stir about 2 minutes more or until heated through. Season with black pepper.

3. Add vegetable mixture to the cooked pasta; toss gently to combine. If desired, sprinkle with small basil leaves. **MAKES 4 SERVINGS**

Per serving: 287 cal., 10 g total fat (4 g sat. fat), 43 mg chol., 617 mg sodium, 38 g carbo., 6 g fiber, 11 g pro.

Broccoli-Spinach Lasagna ♡

Prep: 35 minutes **Bake:** 55 minutes
Stand: 10 minutes **Oven:** 375°F

- 9 dried whole grain lasagna noodles
  Nonstick cooking spray
- ½ cup chopped onion (1 medium)
- 4 cloves garlic, minced
- 1 14-ounce package frozen broccoli florets
- 1 cup vegetable broth
- 1 tablespoon snipped fresh rosemary or
  1 teaspoon dried rosemary, crushed
- 2 10-ounce packages frozen chopped
  spinach, thawed and well drained
- 1 26- to 28-ounce jar meatless tomato
  pasta sauce
- 2 cups shredded part-skim mozzarella
  cheese (8 ounces)

1. Preheat oven to 375°F. Cook lasagna
noodles according to package directions.
Drain noodles; rinse with cold water and drain
well. Set aside.
2. Meanwhile, lightly coat an unheated large
skillet with cooking spray. Cook onion and
garlic on medium heat for 3 minutes, stirring
occasionally. Stir in broccoli, broth, and
rosemary. Bring to boiling; reduce heat.
Simmer, covered, for 1 minute. Uncover and
stir in spinach; remove from heat.
3. Lightly coat a 3-quart rectangular baking
dish with nonstick cooking spray. Spread
½ cup of the pasta sauce evenly in bottom of
dish. Arrange 3 of the lasagna noodles on the
sauce. Layer with half of the spinach mixture;
sprinkle with ½ cup of the mozzarella cheese.
Spoon ¾ cup of the pasta sauce on the
cheese. Top with 3 more noodles, the
remaining spinach mixture, ½ cup mozzarella
cheese, and ¾ cup of the pasta sauce. Top
with the remaining 3 noodles. Spoon the
remaining pasta sauce on the noodles. Sprinkle
with the remaining 1 cup mozzarella cheese.
4. Bake, covered, for 40 minutes. Uncover;
bake about 15 minutes more or until heated
through. Let stand for 10 minutes. If desired,
garnish with *fresh rosemary.* **MAKES 8 SERVINGS**

Per serving: 249 cal., 6 g total fat (3 g sat. fat), 18 mg
chol., 696 mg sodium, 33 g carbo., 9 g fiber, 16 g pro.

PASTA WITH SWISS CHARD

Pasta with Swiss Chard ♡

Start to Finish: 35 minutes

- 8 ounces dried whole grain bowtie or
  mostaccioli pasta
- 12 ounces fresh Swiss chard or spinach
- 1 tablespoon olive oil
- 4 cloves garlic, minced
- ⅔ cup light ricotta cheese
- ¼ cup fat-free milk
- ¼ cup snipped fresh basil or 2 teaspoons
  dried basil, crushed
- ¼ teaspoon salt
- ¼ teaspoon black pepper
- ⅛ teaspoon ground nutmeg
- 2 medium tomatoes, seeded and chopped
- ¼ cup shredded Parmesan cheese

1. Cook pasta according to package
directions, except omit any oil or salt. Drain
well. Return pasta to hot saucepan. Cover
and keep warm.

2. Meanwhile, cut out and discard center ribs
from Swiss chard or remove stems from
spinach. Coarsely chop greens; set aside. In
a large nonstick skillet heat oil on medium
heat. Add garlic; cook for 15 seconds. Add
Swiss chard. Cook on medium-low heat
about 3 minutes or until greens are wilted and
tender, stirring frequently. Stir in ricotta
cheese, milk, basil, salt, pepper, and nutmeg.
Cook and stir for 3 to 5 minutes more or until
heated through.
3. Add the ricotta mixture and tomatoes to
cooked pasta; toss gently to combine.
Sprinkle servings with Parmesan cheese.
MAKES 4 SERVINGS

Per serving: 307 cal., 8 g total fat (2 g sat. fat), 14 mg
chol., 435 mg sodium, 51 g carbo., 8 g fiber, 14 g pro.

GARDEN VEGETABLES LASAGNA

Garden Vegetables Lasagna ♡

Prep: 45 minutes **Bake:** 45 minutes
Stand: 10 minutes **Oven:** 375°F

Nonstick cooking spray
9 dried whole grain or regular lasagna noodles
3 cups packaged broccoli florets
2 red sweet peppers, seeded and cut into bite-size strips
2 medium zucchini and/or yellow summer squash, sliced (about 2½ cups)
2 15-ounce cartons light ricotta cheese
½ cup snipped fresh basil or 1 tablespoon dried basil, crushed
1 tablespoon snipped fresh thyme or 1 teaspoon dried thyme, crushed
3 cloves garlic, minced
½ teaspoon salt
¼ teaspoon black pepper
¼ teaspoon bottled hot pepper sauce
2 cups shredded reduced-fat mozzarella cheese (8 ounces)
¼ cup shredded fresh basil (optional)

1. Preheat oven to 375°F. Lightly coat a 3-quart rectangular baking dish with nonstick cooking spray; set aside. In a 4-quart pot cook lasagna noodles in a large amount of boiling water for 10 to 12 minutes or until tender but still firm; drain. Rinse with cold water; drain again.

2. Place a steamer basket in the 4-quart pot. Add water to just below the bottom of the basket. Bring to boiling. Add broccoli, sweet peppers, and zucchini; cover and reduce heat. Steam for 6 to 8 minutes or until vegetables are crisp-tender. Remove from heat.

3. In a bowl combine ricotta cheese, the ½ cup snipped basil, the thyme, garlic, salt, black pepper, and hot pepper sauce. Layer 3 of the cooked noodles in the prepared baking dish. Spread with one-third of the ricotta cheese mixture. Top with one-third of the vegetable mixture and ⅔ cup of the mozzarella cheese. Repeat layers twice.

4. Bake, covered, for 45 to 55 minutes or until heated through. Uncover; let stand for 10 minutes before serving. If desired, sprinkle with the shredded basil. **MAKES 8 SERVINGS**

Per serving: 296 cal., 9 g total fat (5 g sat. fat), 41 mg chol., 426 mg sodium, 31 g carbo., 6 g fiber, 20 g pro.

Artichoke-Basil Lasagna

Prep: 45 minutes **Bake:** 40 minutes
Stand: 15 minutes **Oven:** 350°F

9 dried whole grain lasagna noodles
1 tablespoon olive oil
2 8- or 9-ounce packages frozen artichoke hearts, thawed and well drained
¼ cup pine nuts
4 cloves garlic, minced
1 15-ounce carton light ricotta cheese
1½ cups reduced-fat shredded Italian-blend cheese or part-skim mozzarella cheese (6 ounces)
1 cup snipped fresh basil or 4 teaspoons dried basil, crushed
1 egg
¼ teaspoon salt
1 cup reduced-sodium chicken broth
¼ cup all-purpose flour
2 cups fat-free milk
Chopped fresh tomato (optional)
Italian (flat-leaf) parsley (optional)

1. Preheat oven to 350°F. Cook lasagna noodles according to package directions. Drain noodles; rinse with cold water and drain well. Set aside.

2. In a large skillet heat oil on medium heat. Add artichokes, pine nuts, and garlic; cook about 5 minutes or until artichokes, nuts, and garlic start to brown, stirring frequently. Transfer to a large bowl. Stir in ricotta cheese, ½ cup of the Italian-blend cheese, ½ cup of the fresh basil or 1 tablespoon of the dried basil, the egg, and salt.

3. For sauce, in a medium saucepan whisk together chicken broth and flour until smooth. Stir in milk. Cook and stir on medium heat until sauce is slightly thickened and bubbly. Remove from heat. Stir in the remaining ½ cup fresh basil or 1 teaspoon dried basil.

4. Pour 1 cup of the sauce into a 3-quart rectangular baking dish. Top with 3 of the lasagna noodles. Dollop with one-third of the ricotta mixture (about 1⅓ cups); carefully spread evenly over the noodles. Top with one-third of the remaining sauce (about ⅔ cup). Sprinkle with ⅓ cup of the remaining Italian-blend cheese. Repeat layers twice more, beginning with the lasagna noodles and ending with the Italian-blend cheese.

5. Bake, uncovered, about 40 minutes or until heated through and top is lightly browned. Let stand for 15 minutes before serving. If desired, top with chopped tomato and parsley. **MAKES 8 SERVINGS**

Per serving: 330 cal., 12 g total fat (5 g sat. fat), 52 mg chol., 431 mg sodium, 35 g carbo., 8 g fiber, 21 g pro.

NUTTY GORONZOLA ROLL-UPS

THREE-CHEESE MANICOTTI

Nutty Gorgonzola Roll-Ups

Prep: 40 minutes **Bake:** 40 minutes
Oven: 375°F

- 8 dried lasagna noodles
- 12 ounces cream cheese, softened
- 2 cups shredded Italian-style cheese blend (8 ounces)
- 1 cup crumbled Gorgonzola or other blue cheese (4 ounces)
- 1 cup chopped walnuts, toasted
- 2 tablespoons snipped fresh basil or 2 teaspoons dried basil, crushed
- 1 26-ounce jar tomato-basil pasta sauce
   Freshly ground black pepper (optional)
   Shredded fresh basil (optional)
- 6 cups shredded fresh spinach

1. Preheat oven to 375°F. Cook lasagna noodles according to package directions; drain. Rinse with cold water; drain again. Place noodles in a single layer on a sheet of foil; set aside.

2. Meanwhile, in a large bowl combine cream cheese, Italian cheese, Gorgonzola cheese, ³/₄ cup of the walnuts, and the snipped fresh or dried basil. Spread cheese mixture evenly over lasagna noodles. Roll up each noodle into a spiral.

3. Place lasagna rolls, seam sides down, in an ungreased 2-quart rectangular baking dish. Top with pasta sauce. Bake, covered, about 40 minutes or until heated through.

4. Sprinkle with the remaining ¼ cup walnuts. If desired, sprinkle with pepper and shredded fresh basil. Serve lasagna rolls on spinach, spooning sauce in dish over rolls.

MAKES 8 SERVINGS

Per serving: 513 cal., 37 g total fat (17 g sat. fat), 77 mg chol., 813 mg sodium, 28 g carbo., 4 g fiber, 21 g pro.

Three-Cheese Manicotti ♥

Prep: 30 minutes **Bake:** 35 minutes
Stand: 10 minutes **Oven:** 350°F

- 20 dried manicotti shells
- 2½ cups low-fat ricotta cheese (24 ounces)
- 2 cups shredded part-skim mozzarella cheese (4 ounces)
- ½ cup refrigerated or frozen egg product, thawed, or 2 eggs
- ⅓ cup grated Romano or Asiago cheese
- ¼ cup snipped fresh parsley
- ¼ teaspoon black pepper
- 4 cups purchased light tomato basil pasta sauce
   Snipped fresh parsley (optional)

1. Cook manicotti shells according to package directions; set aside. For filling, in a large bowl combine ricotta cheese, 1 cup of the mozzarella cheese, the eggs, Romano cheese, ¼ cup parsley, and the black pepper.

2. Preheat oven to 350°F. Spread 1 cup of the pasta sauce in the bottom of a 3-quart rectangular baking dish. Spoon about 3 tablespoons of the filling into each cooked shell. Arrange in prepared baking dish. Spoon remaining pasta sauce evenly over filled shells in baking dish.

3. Bake for 35 to 40 minutes or until heated through. Sprinkle with the remaining 1 cup mozzarella cheese. Bake about 5 minutes more or until cheese is melted. Let stand on a wire rack for 10 minutes before serving. If desired, sprinkle with additional parsley.

MAKES 10 TO 12 SERVINGS

Per serving: 293 cal., 8 g total fat (4 g sat. fat), 36 mg chol., 640 mg sodium, 37 g carbo., 3 g fiber, 20 g pro.

CHEESY TURKEY AND SPINACH PIE

Spaghetti Pie ♡

Prep: 35 minutes **Bake:** 25 minutes
Stand: 15 minutes **Oven:** 350°F

    Nonstick cooking spray
 4 ounces dried spaghetti
 2 egg whites, lightly beaten
 ⅓ cup grated Parmesan cheese
 1 tablespoon olive oil
 2 egg whites, lightly beaten
 1 12-ounce container (1¼ cups) low-fat
    cottage cheese, drained
 8 ounces uncooked ground turkey breast
 1 cup sliced fresh mushrooms
 ½ cup chopped onion (1 medium)
 ½ cup chopped green or red sweet pepper
 2 cloves garlic, minced
 1 8-ounce can no-salt-added tomato sauce
 1½ teaspoons dried Italian seasoning,
    crushed
 ⅛ teaspoon salt
 ½ cup shredded part-skim mozzarella cheese
    (2 ounces)

1. Preheat oven to 350°F. Coat a 9-inch pie plate with nonstick cooking spray; set aside. For crust, cook spaghetti according to package directions, except omit the vegetable oil and salt. Meanwhile, in a bowl stir together 2 egg whites, the Parmesan cheese, and olive oil. Drain spaghetti well; add to egg white mixture; toss to coat. Press spaghetti mixture evenly into the bottom and up the sides of the prepared pie plate; set aside.
2. In a small bowl stir together 2 egg whites and cottage cheese. Spread the cottage cheese mixture over the crust. Set aside.
3. In a large skillet cook turkey, mushrooms, onion, sweet pepper, and garlic until meat is browned. Drain off fat. Stir tomato sauce, Italian seasoning, and salt into meat mixture in skillet. Spoon over cottage cheese mixture in crust.
4. Bake about 20 minutes or until heated through. Sprinkle with mozzarella cheese. Bake about 5 minutes more or until the cheese is melted. Let stand for 15 minutes before serving. Cut into wedges to serve.
MAKES 6 SERVINGS

Per serving: 256 cal., 7 g total fat (3 g sat. fat), 27 mg chol., 479 mg sodium, 23 g carbo., 2 g fiber, 26 g pro.

Cheesy Turkey and Spinach Pie

Prep: 30 minutes **Bake:** 45 minutes
Stand: 10 minutes **Oven:** 350°F

    Nonstick cooking spray
 4 ounces dried fine noodles (1¾ cups)
 3 eggs
 1 8-ounce package cream cheese, softened,
    or mascarpone cheese
 ⅓ cup sour cream
 ⅓ cup mayonnaise
 ¼ cup snipped fresh basil or 1 tablespoon
    dried basil, crushed
 ½ teaspoon garlic salt
 ¼ teaspoon crushed red pepper
 2 cups chopped cooked turkey (10 ounces)
 1 10-ounce package frozen chopped
    spinach, thawed and well drained
 1 cup shredded Monterey Jack cheese
    (4 ounces)
 ⅓ cup chopped roasted red sweet pepper

1. Preheat oven to 350°F. Coat a 9-inch deep-dish pie plate or a 2-quart square baking dish with cooking spray. Place on a baking sheet; set aside. Cook noodles according to package directions; drain well.
2. Meanwhile, in a large bowl whisk together eggs, cream cheese, sour cream, mayonnaise, basil, garlic salt, and crushed red pepper until well combined. Stir in cooked noodles, turkey, spinach, Monterey Jack cheese, and roasted red pepper. Spread mixture in prepared plate or dish (if using pie plate, it will be very full).
3. Bake, uncovered, for 45 to 50 minutes or until edges are slightly puffed and golden. Let stand on a wire rack for 10 minutes before serving. **MAKES 6 TO 8 SERVINGS**

Per serving: 520 cal., 37 g total fat (17 g sat. fat), 225 mg chol., 481 mg sodium, 18 g carbo., 3 g fiber, 29 g pro.

My dear granddaughter, you are

Always in My

Heart

My Dear Granddaughter, You are always in my Heart

Genuine Diamond Bracelet
Lavishly Plated with Sterling Silver and 24K Gold

RESERVATION APPLICATION
SEND NO MONEY NOW

THE
BRADFORD EXCHANGE
— JEWELRY —

345 Milwaukee Avenue · Niles, IL 60714-1393

YES. Please reserve the *"Always in My Heart"* Granddaughter Diamond Bracelet for me as described in this announcement.

Please Respond Promptly

ORDER PROMPTLY FOR CHRISTMAS DELIVERY

us $9.98 shipping and service. Sales subject to duct availability and order acceptance.

Signature _____

Mrs. Mr. Ms. _____
                    Name (Please Print Clearly)

Address _____

City _____ State _____ Zip _____

E-Mail (optional) _____

01-10488-001-B61801

Grain-Vegetable Medley ♡

Prep: 20 minutes **Cook:** 10 minutes
Stand: 5 minutes

  1 14-ounce can reduced-sodium chicken
      broth
  ¼ cup water
1½ cups fresh green beans, trimmed and cut
      into 2-inch-long pieces
  ⅔ cup quick-cooking barley
  2 tablespoons lemon juice
  1 tablespoon olive oil
  ⅛ teaspoon salt
  ⅛ teaspoon black pepper
  ½ cup whole wheat couscous
  4 cups coarsely shredded fresh spinach
  ¼ cup sliced green onions (2)
1½ teaspoons snipped fresh thyme or
      ½ teaspoon dried thyme, crushed
      Lemon wedges (optional)

1. In a large saucepan bring chicken broth
and the water to boiling; stir in green beans
and uncooked barley. Return to boiling;
reduce heat. Simmer, covered, for 10 to
12 minutes or until barley is tender.
2. Meanwhile, in a small bowl whisk together
lemon juice, olive oil, salt, and pepper.
3. Stir uncooked couscous into barley
mixture. Stir in lemon juice mixture, spinach,
green onions, and thyme. Remove from heat.
Cover and let stand for 5 minutes. To serve,
fluff with a fork. If desired, serve with lemon
wedges. **MAKES 4 SERVINGS**

Per serving: 274 cal., 5 g total fat (1 g sat. fat), 0 mg
chol., 340 mg sodium, 51 g carbo., 11 g fiber, 11 g pro.

Southwest Quinoa Pilaf ♡

Start to Finish: 40 minutes

  1 tablespoon olive oil
1½ cups chopped onion
  6 cloves garlic, minced
1¼ cups quinoa
  ½ teaspoon ground cumin
  1 14-ounce can reduced-sodium chicken
      broth or vegetable broth
1¼ cups water
  1 recipe Black Bean, Corn, and Jicama
      Salsa
  2 tablespoons snipped fresh cilantro
      Fresh cilantro sprigs (optional)

1. In a 4-quart Dutch oven heat oil on
medium heat. Add onion and garlic; cook until
tender, stirring occasionally. Rinse and drain
quinoa. Add quinoa and cumin to onion and
garlic in Dutch oven; cook and stir about
3 minutes or until quinoa is lightly browned.
2. Add broth and the water to quinoa mixture.
Bring to boiling; reduce heat. Simmer, covered,
for 15 to 20 minutes or until all of the liquid is
absorbed and quinoa is tender. Divide quinoa
mixture among 6 plates. Top with Black Bean,
Corn, and Jicama Salsa. Sprinkle with
snipped cilantro. If desired, garnish with
cilantro sprigs. **MAKES 6 SERVINGS**

Black Bean, Corn, and Jicama Salsa In a
large bowl toss together one 15-ounce can
black beans, rinsed and drained; 1 cup frozen
whole kernel corn, thawed; 1 large tomato,
chopped; ½ cup peeled, chopped jicama;
¼ cup thinly sliced green onions; 1 fresh
jalapeño, halved, seeded, and finely
chopped;* 2 tablespoons lime juice; and
¼ teaspoon salt. Makes 4 cups.

***Tip** Because chile peppers contain volatile
oils that can burn your skin and eyes, avoid
direct contact with them as much as possible.
When working with chile peppers, wear
plastic or rubber gloves. If your bare hands do
touch the peppers, wash your hands and
nails well with soap and warm water.

Per serving: 261 cal., 5 g total fat (1 g sat. fat), 0 mg
chol., 443 mg sodium, 48 g carbo., 7 g fiber, 12 g pro.

SANTA FE RICE AND BEANS

Red Lentil Rice

Start to Finish: 35 minutes

- 1 tablespoon olive oil
- ½ cup chopped onion (1 medium)
- 2 cloves garlic, minced
- 1 teaspoon cumin seeds, crushed
- ½ teaspoon salt
- ⅛ teaspoon cayenne pepper
- 1⅓ cups basmati rice or long grain rice
- 2 14-ounce cans chicken broth
- ½ cup water
- 1 cup frozen peas
- ½ cup dry red lentils, rinsed
- ¼ cup snipped fresh mint
- 1 teaspoon garam masala
- 1 recipe Yogurt Raita

1. In a 4-quart pot heat olive oil on medium heat. Add onion, garlic, cumin seeds, salt, and cayenne pepper. Cook and stir for 2 minutes. Add rice; cook and stir 1 minute more. Remove from heat. Carefully add broth and the water; bring to boiling. Reduce heat; simmer, covered, for 10 minutes.

2. Stir in peas and lentils; return to boiling. Reduce heat; simmer, covered, for 8 to 10 minutes or just until lentils are tender. Remove from heat; stir in mint and garam masala. Let stand, covered, for 5 minutes before serving. Serve with Yogurt Raita.

MAKES 6 SERVINGS

Yogurt Raita In a medium bowl combine one 6-ounce carton plain yogurt; ¾ cup seeded, chopped cucumber; ½ cup seeded, chopped tomato; 1 tablespoon snipped fresh mint; ⅛ teaspoon salt; and a dash black pepper.

Per serving: 274 cal., 3 g total fat (1 g sat. fat), 3 mg chol., 827 mg sodium, 50 g carbo., 4 g fiber, 10 g pro.

Santa Fe Rice and Beans ♡

Start to Finish: 20 minutes

- 1 tablespoon olive oil
- 1 12-ounce package fresh green beans and carrots*
- 12 ounces smoked turkey sausage, halved lengthwise and sliced
- 1 14.5-ounce can no-salt-added diced tomatoes, undrained
- 1 15-ounce can black beans, rinsed and drained
- 1 8.5-ounce pouch cooked whole grain Santa Fe rice medley

1. In a very large skillet heat oil over medium heat. Add green beans and carrots; cook for 5 to 6 minutes or until crisp-tender, stirring occasionally. Add sausage and undrained tomatoes to skillet; bring to boiling. Add black beans and rice; heat through.

MAKES 6 SERVINGS

*Tip If you can't find the packaged green beans and carrots, use 4 cups fresh green beans, trimmed, and 1 cup shredded carrots (2 medium).

Per serving: 245 cal., 8 g total fat (2 g sat. fat), 38 mg chol., 890 mg sodium, 29 g carbo., 8 g fiber, 16 g pro.

RED LENTIL RICE

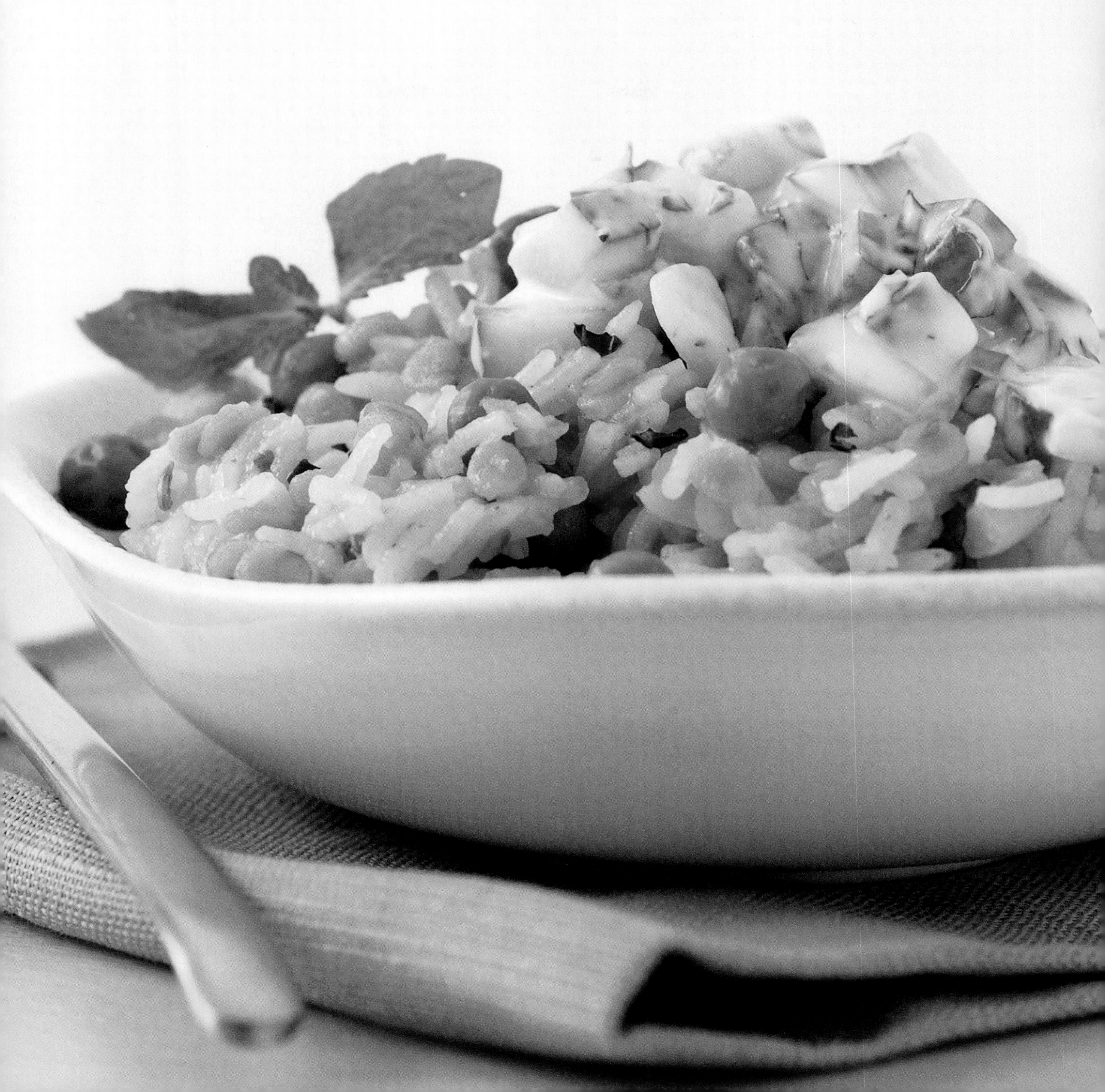

Summer Vegetable Pilaf ♡

Prep: 25 minutes **Cook:** 20 minutes
Stand: 5 minutes

- 1 14.5-ounce can vegetable broth
- ½ cup chopped onion (1 medium)
- ½ cup dry lentils, rinsed and drained
- ½ cup uncooked long grain white rice
- ¼ cup water
- 1 teaspoon finely shredded lemon peel
- 1½ cups small fresh broccoli florets, sliced zucchini or yellow summer squash, and/or fresh snow or sugar snap pea pods
- 1 medium carrot, cut into thin strips
- 2 teaspoons olive oil
- ½ small eggplant, peeled and diced
- 2 cloves garlic, minced
- 3 plum tomatoes, chopped
- ¼ cup snipped fresh basil
- ¼ cup finely shredded Asiago or Parmesan cheese (1 ounce)

1. In a 3-quart saucepan combine broth, onion, lentils, rice, the water, and lemon peel. Bring to boiling; reduce heat. Simmer, covered, for 20 minutes, adding broccoli and carrot during the last 3 to 5 minutes of cooking.
2. Meanwhile, in a large skillet heat oil on medium heat. Add eggplant and garlic; cook about 5 minutes or until the eggplant is soft, stirring occasionally.
3. Remove lentil mixture from heat. Let stand, covered, for 5 minutes. Carefully stir in the eggplant mixture, tomatoes, and basil. To serve, sprinkle with cheese. **MAKES 4 SERVINGS**

Per serving: 275 cal., 6 g total fat (2 g sat. fat), 8 mg chol., 495 mg sodium, 44 g carbo., 11 g fiber, 12 g pro.

VEGETABLE TWO-GRAIN CASSEROLE

Vegetable Two-Grain Casserole ♡

Prep: 20 minutes **Bake:** 1 hour
Stand: 5 minutes **Oven:** 350°F

- 1 15-ounce can red kidney or black beans, rinsed and drained
- 1 14.5- to 18.5-ounce can ready-to-serve lentil soup
- 1 cup shredded smoked cheddar cheese or Gouda cheese (4 ounces)
- 1 cup fresh shiitake or cremini mushrooms, stems removed and halved
- 1 cup frozen whole kernel corn
- ½ cup shredded carrot (1 medium)
- ½ cup regular barley
- ⅓ cup bulgur
- ¼ cup chopped onion
- ½ teaspoon dried thyme, crushed
- 1 cup chicken or vegetable broth

1. Preheat oven to 350°F. Lightly grease a 2-quart square baking dish. In the prepared baking dish combine beans, soup, ½ cup of the cheese, the mushrooms, corn, carrot, barley, bulgur, onion, thyme, ½ teaspoon *black pepper,* and ¼ teaspoon *salt.* Stir in the broth
2. Bake, covered, about 1 hour or until barley and bulgur are tender, stirring twice. Top with the remaining ½ cup cheese. Let stand, covered, about 5 minutes or until cheese is melted. If desired serve with toasted *pita wedges.* **MAKES 5 SERVINGS**

Per serving: 204 cal., 5 g total fat (3 g sat. fat), 10 mg chol., 828 mg sodium, 55 g carbo., 13 g fiber, 17 g pro.

BROWN RICE-SPINACH CUSTARDS

Couscous Cakes with Salsa ♡

Prep: 20 minutes **Cook:** 4 minutes
Stand: 20 minutes **Oven:** 200°F

  ½ cup whole wheat couscous
  2 tablespoons whole wheat flour
  ¼ teaspoon baking soda
  ⅛ teaspoon salt
  1 egg
  ¾ cup buttermilk or sour fat-free milk*
  1 tablespoon canola oil
  1 recipe Black Bean Salsa
     Nonstick cooking spray

1. In a medium bowl combine uncooked couscous, whole wheat flour, baking soda, and salt. In a small bowl beat egg with a fork. Stir in buttermilk and oil. Stir buttermilk mixture into couscous mixture. Let stand for 20 minutes (batter will thicken as it stands).
2. Meanwhile, prepare Black Bean Salsa; set aside. Preheat oven to 200°F.
3. Lightly coat an unheated griddle or large nonstick skillet with cooking spray. Preheat on medium heat. For each cake, spoon 2 slightly rounded tablespoons of batter onto hot griddle; quickly spread to 3½-inch rounds. Cook 2 minutes per side or until browned, turning when bottoms are lightly browned and edges are slightly dry. Keep warm in oven while cooking remaining cakes. Serve Black Bean Salsa over cakes. **MAKES 4 SERVINGS**

Black Bean Salsa In a medium bowl stir together ¾ cup frozen whole kernel corn, thawed; ½ of a 15-ounce can black beans (¾ cup), rinsed and drained; ¾ cup purchased fresh salsa;* ½ cup chopped, peeled jicama; 1 tablespoon snipped fresh cilantro; 1 tablespoon lime juice; and ½ teaspoon ground cumin. Makes 2 cups.

*Tip To make ¾ cup sour fat-free milk, place 2 teaspoons lemon juice or vinegar in a glass measuring cup. Add enough fat-free milk to equal ¾ cup total liquid; stir. Let stand for 5 minutes before using.

Per serving: 270 cal., 6 g total fat (1 g sat. fat), 55 mg chol., 639 mg sodium, 46 g carbo., 8 g fiber, 13 g pro.

Brown Rice-Spinach Custards ♡

Prep: 25 minutes **Bake:** 25 minutes
Oven: 350°F

  1 tablespoon olive oil
  ½ cup chopped onion (1 medium)
  4 eggs
  ½ cup low-fat cottage cheese
  3 ounces reduced-fat feta cheese, crumbled
  1 tablespoon snipped fresh dill or
     ½ teaspoon dried dill
  ½ teaspoon salt
  2 10-ounce packages frozen chopped spinach, thawed and well drained
  2 cups cooked brown rice
  1 tablespoon lemon juice
     Fresh lemon peel strips (optional)

1. Preheat oven to 350°F. In a small skillet heat oil on medium heat. Add onion; cook until tender, stirring occasionally. Cool slightly.
2. In a large bowl beat eggs with a fork. Stir in cottage cheese, feta cheese, dill, salt, and cooked onion. Add spinach, cooked brown rice, and lemon juice, stirring until well mixed. Place six 8- to 10-ounce ramekins or custard cups in a 15×10×1-inch baking pan. Divide rice mixture among the dishes.
3. Bake for 25 to 30 minutes or until a knife inserted near the centers of custards comes out clean. If desired, garnish with lemon peel.
MAKES 6 SERVINGS

Per serving: 213 cal., 8 g total fat (3 g sat. fat), 146 mg chol., 648 mg sodium, 20 g carbo., 4 g fiber, 14 g pro.

CONFETTI BARLEY SALAD

Tabbouleh with Edamame and Feta

Start to Finish: 25 minutes

2½ cups water
1¼ cups bulgur
¼ cup lemon juice
3 tablespoons purchased basil pesto
2 cups fresh or thawed frozen shelled sweet soybeans (edamame)
2 cups cherry tomatoes, cut up
⅓ cup crumbled reduced-fat feta cheese
⅓ cup thinly sliced green onions
2 tablespoons snipped fresh parsley
¼ teaspoon black pepper
Fresh parsley sprigs (optional)

1. In a medium saucepan bring the water to boiling; add uncooked bulgur. Return to boiling; reduce heat. Simmer, covered, about 15 minutes or until most of the liquid is absorbed. Remove from heat. Transfer to a large bowl.

2. In a small bowl whisk together lemon juice and pesto. Add to bulgur along with soybeans, cherry tomatoes, feta cheese, green onions, the snipped parsley, and pepper. Toss gently to combine. If desired, garnish with parsley sprigs. **MAKES 6 SERVINGS**

Per serving: 266 cal., 10 g total fat (1 g sat. fat), 3 mg chol., 181 mg sodium, 34 g carbo., 9 g fiber, 14 g pro.

Confetti Barley Salad ♡

Prep: 15 minutes **Cook:** 45 minutes

5 cups water
1 cup pearl barley
2 cups frozen succotash, thawed
¼ cup white wine vinegar
3 tablespoons olive oil
1 tablespoon Dijon mustard
2 teaspoons snipped fresh oregano or ½ teaspoon dried oregano, crushed
2 cloves garlic, minced
½ teaspoon salt
¼ teaspoon black pepper
1 cup finely chopped red sweet pepper
⅓ cup sliced pitted ripe olives
Fresh herb sprigs (optional)

1. In a large saucepan bring the water to boiling. Stir in barley; reduce heat. Simmer, covered, for 45 to 50 minutes or just until barley is tender, adding succotash for the last 10 minutes of cooking; drain. Rinse with cold water; drain again.

2. Meanwhile, for dressing, in a screw-top jar combine vinegar, oil, mustard, oregano, garlic, salt, and black pepper. Cover and shake well.

3. In a large bowl stir together the barley mixture, sweet pepper, and olives. Shake dressing; pour over barley mixture; toss gently to coat. Serve immediately or cover and refrigerate for up to 24 hours. If desired, garnish with fresh herb sprigs. **MAKES 6 SERVINGS**

Per serving: 247 cal., 8 g total fat (1 g sat. fat), 0 mg chol., 363 mg sodium, 38 g carbo., 5 g fiber, 6 g pro.

CHILI-STYLE VEGETABLE PASTA

Chili-Style Vegetable Pasta ♡

Prep: 20 minutes **Cook:** 5 to 6 hours (low) or 2½ to 3 hours (high)

- 2 14.5-ounce cans no-salt-added diced tomatoes, undrained
- 1 15-ounce can garbanzo beans (chickpeas), rinsed and drained
- 1 15-ounce can red kidney beans, rinsed and drained
- 1 8-ounce can tomato sauce
- 1 cup finely chopped onion (1 large)
- 1 cup chopped green or yellow sweet pepper
- 2 to 3 teaspoons chili powder
- 2 cloves garlic, minced
- ½ teaspoon dried oregano, crushed
- ⅛ teaspoon cayenne pepper
- 8 ounces dried whole wheat wagon wheel pasta and/or vegetable wagon wheel pasta (2 cups)
- ½ cup shredded reduced-fat cheddar cheese (2 ounces)

1. In a 3½- or 4-quart slow cooker combine undrained tomatoes, garbanzo beans, kidney beans, tomato sauce, onion, sweet pepper, chili powder, garlic, oregano, and cayenne pepper. Cover and cook on low-heat setting for 5 to 6 hours or on high-heat setting for 2½ to 3 hours.

2. To serve, cook pasta according to package directions; drain. Serve bean mixture over hot cooked pasta. Sprinkle with cheese.

MAKES 6 SERVINGS

Per serving: 327 cal., 4 g total fat (1 g sat. fat), 7 mg chol., 693 mg sodium, 63 g carbo., 12 g fiber, 18 g pro.

Cannellini Bean Burgers

Prep: 25 minutes **Cook:** 10 minutes

- 1 15- to 16-ounce can cannellini beans (white kidney beans), rinsed and drained
- ¾ cup soft whole wheat bread crumbs (1 slice)
- ½ cup chopped onion (1 medium)
- ¼ cup walnut pieces, toasted if desired
- 2 tablespoons coarsely chopped fresh basil or 1 teaspoon dried basil, crushed
- 2 cloves garlic, quartered
- 1 tablespoon olive oil
- 4 whole grain hamburger buns, split and toasted
- 2 tablespoons bottled light ranch salad dressing
- 2 cups fresh spinach leaves
- ½ of a medium tomato, sliced

1. In a food processor combine cannellini beans, ¼ cup of the bread crumbs, the onion, walnuts, basil, and garlic. Cover and process until mixture is coarsely chopped and holds together.

2. Shape the bean mixture into four ½-inch-thick patties. Place the remaining ½ cup bread crumbs in a shallow dish. Carefully brush both sides of each patty with oil. Dip patties in bread crumbs, turning to coat.

3. Preheat a grill pan or large skillet on medium heat. Add patties to pan or skillet. Cook for 10 to 12 minutes or until heated through, turning patties once. (Reduce heat to medium-low if patties brown too quickly.)

4. Spread cut sides of bun bottoms with salad dressing. Top with patties, spinach, tomato slices, and bun tops. **MAKES 4 BURGERS**

Per burger: 299 cal., 11 g total fat (1 g sat. fat), 2 mg chol., 497 mg sodium, 44 g carbo., 9 g fiber, 13 g pro.

GREEK GARBANZO SALAD

Italian Beans and Pesto Lettuce Wraps

Prep: 15 minutes **Cook:** 15 minutes
Chill: Up to 3 days

  1 14-ounce can reduced-sodium chicken
     broth or vegetable broth
  ¾ cup bulgur
  ¾ cup chopped red sweet pepper (1 medium)
  ⅓ cup refrigerated basil pesto
  ¼ cup thinly sliced green onions (2)
  2 tablespoons balsamic vinegar
  2 cups cooked or canned red kidney beans,
     pinto beans, Christmas lima beans, and/or
     other white beans*
     Black pepper
 12 Bibb lettuce leaves

1. In a large saucepan combine broth and
bulgur. Bring to boiling; reduce heat. Simmer,
covered, about 15 minutes or until bulgur is
tender. Remove from heat.
2. Stir in sweet pepper, pesto, green onions,
and balsamic vinegar. Stir in beans. Season
with black pepper. Transfer to an airtight storage
container. Cover and chill for up to 3 days.
3. To serve, spoon bean mixture evenly into
lettuce leaves. Roll up. **MAKES 6 SERVINGS**

*Tip To cook dried beans, rinse ¾ cup dried
beans. In a large saucepan combine rinsed
beans and 5 cups water. Bring to boiling;
reduce heat. Simmer, uncovered, for
2 minutes. Remove from heat. Cover and let
stand for 1 hour. Drain; rinse beans and
return to saucepan. Add 5 cups fresh water.
Bring to boiling; reduce heat. Simmer,
covered, for 1¼ to 1½ hours or until beans
are tender; drain.

Per serving: 251 cal., 10 g total fat (0 g sat. fat), 2 mg
chol., 267 mg sodium, 33 g carbo., 8 g fiber, 10 g pro.

Greek Garbanzo Salad

Prep: 25 minutes **Chill:** 4 to 24 hours

  1 15-ounce can garbanzo beans
     (chickpeas), rinsed and drained
  2 medium tomatoes, cut into chunks
  1 large cucumber, seeded and chopped
     (about 2 cups)
  1 cup coarsely chopped green sweet
     pepper
  ½ cup thinly sliced red onion
  2 tablespoons olive oil
  2 tablespoons red wine vinegar
  1 tablespoon snipped fresh mint
  1 tablespoon lemon juice
  2 cloves garlic, minced
  ½ cup crumbled reduced-fat feta cheese
     (2 ounces)
     Salt and black pepper
  2 cups packaged mixed salad greens

1. In a large bowl combine garbanzo beans,
tomatoes, cucumber, sweet pepper, and red
onion. Stir gently to mix.
2. In a small bowl whisk together oil, red wine
vinegar, mint, lemon juice, and garlic. Pour
over garbanzo bean mixture; toss to coat.
Cover and chill for 4 to 24 hours.
3. Stir in feta cheese. Season with salt and
black pepper. Serve over mixed greens.

MAKES 4 SERVINGS

Per serving: 200 cal., 10 g total fat (3 g sat. fat), 5 mg
chol., 694 mg sodium, 25 g carbo., 7 g fiber, 11 g pro.

CHAPTER 6

Meat

143

SOUTHWEST STEAK WITH MANGO SALAD

Southwest Steak with Mango Salad

Prep: 20 minutes **Broil:** 17 minutes
Stand: 10 minutes

    1   teaspoon ground cumin
    1   teaspoon dried oregano, crushed
 1½   teaspoons kosher salt
    ½   teaspoon chili powder
    1   clove garlic, minced
    1   1-pound flank steak
    1   teaspoon finely shredded orange peel
    3   tablespoons orange juice
    3   tablespoons champagne vinegar
    2   tablespoons snipped fresh cilantro
    2   teaspoons honey
    ⅓   cup canola oil
    5   cups mixed baby salad greens
    ½   of a mango, peeled and cut into 1-inch
        chunks
    1   avocado, seeded, peeled, and sliced

1. In a small bowl combine cumin, oregano, ½ teaspoon of the salt, the chili powder, and garlic. Set spice mixture aside.
2. Preheat broiler. Sprinkle both sides of steak with ½ teaspoon salt. Place steak on the unheated rack of a broiler pan. Broil 3 to 4 inches from the heat for 17 to 21 minutes or until medium doneness (160°F), turning once. Sprinkle the spice mixture over steak. Use the back of a spoon to spread evenly. Let stand for 10 minutes.

3. Meanwhile, for dressing, in a medium bowl combine orange peel, orange juice, vinegar, cilantro, honey, and the remaining ½ teaspoon salt. Add oil in a slow stream, whisking constantly until thickened. Set aside.
4. In a large salad bowl toss together salad greens and mango. Add 3 to 4 tablespoons dressing; toss to coat. Thinly slice steak across the grain. Arrange steak, salad, and avocado on plates. Pass remaining dressing. **MAKES 4 SERVINGS**

Per serving: 480 cal., 36.5 g total fat (7 g sat. fat), 56 mg chol., 598 mg sodium, 16 g carbo., 3 g fiber, 24 g pro.

Cilantro-Lime Flank Steak ♡

Prep: 15 minutes **Marinate:** 1 to 2 hours
Grill: 17 minutes

    1   1-pound beef flank steak
    ¼   cup water
    ¼   cup lime juice
    6   cloves garlic, minced
    2   tablespoons snipped fresh cilantro
    2   teaspoons snipped fresh oregano or
        ½ teaspoon dried oregano, crushed
    ¼   teaspoon ground chipotle chile pepper or
        chili powder
    ¼   teaspoon salt
    ⅛   teaspoon black pepper
    1   cup Avocado-Poblano Pico de Gallo
        Lime wedges (optional)
        Fresh cilantro (optional)

1. Trim fat from steak. Score both sides of steak in a diamond pattern by making shallow diagonal cuts at 1-inch intervals. Place steak in a resealable plastic bag set in a shallow dish.
2. For marinade, in a small bowl stir together the water, lime juice, garlic, cilantro, oregano, and chipotle chile pepper. Pour marinade over steak in bag. Seal bag; turn to coat steak. Marinate in the refrigerator for 1 to 2 hours, turning bag occasionally.
3. Drain steak, reserving marinade. Sprinkle steak with salt and pepper. Place steak on the rack of an uncovered grill directly over medium coals. Grill for 17 to 21 minutes or until medium doneness (160°F), turning once

and brushing with the reserved marinade halfway through grilling. Discard any remaining marinade. (For a gas grill, preheat grill. Reduce heat to medium. Place steak on grill rack over heat. Cover and grill as above.)
4. To serve, thinly slice beef across the grain; divide among 4 dinner plates. Top with Avocado-Poblano Pico de Gallo. If desired, garnish with lime wedges and additional cilantro. **MAKES 4 SERVINGS**

Avocado-Poblano Pico de Gallo Preheat broiler. Place 1 fresh poblano chile pepper or green sweet pepper and 1 yellow or red sweet pepper on a foil-lined baking sheet. Broil 4 inches from the heat for 7 to 10 minutes or until skins are bubbly and blackened, turning occasionally. Carefully bring the foil up and around the peppers to enclose. Let stand about 15 minutes or until cool enough to handle. Pull the skins off gently and slowly using a paring knife.* Discard skins. Remove pepper stems, seeds, and membranes; chop the peppers. In a medium bowl combine chopped peppers; 1 medium tomato, chopped; ⅓ cup chopped red onion; 2 tablespoons snipped fresh cilantro; ½ teaspoon finely shredded lime peel; 1 tablespoon lime juice; and ¼ teaspoon salt. Gently toss to combine. Stir in 1 small avocado, halved, seeded, peeled, and chopped. Makes about 3¼ cups.

*Tip Because chile peppers contain volatile oils that can burn your skin and eyes, avoid direct contact with them as much as possible. When working with chile peppers, wear plastic or rubber gloves. If your bare hands do touch the peppers, wash your hands and nails well with soap and warm water.

Per serving: 203 cal., 9 g total fat (3 g sat. fat), 47 mg chol., 250 mg sodium, 5 g carbo., 1 g fiber, 26 g pro.

BISTRO BEEF STEAK WITH
WILD MUSHROOM RAGOÛT

Dijon-Pepper Steak

Prep: 20 minutes **Cook:** 7 to 8 hours (low) or 3½ to 4 hours (high)

- 2 pounds boneless beef sirloin steak, cut 1 inch thick
- 1 to 1½ teaspoons cracked black pepper
- 1 tablespoon canola oil
- 2 cups packaged whole trimmed baby carrots
- 1 medium onion, sliced
- 1 10.75-ounce can reduced-fat and reduced-sodium condensed cream of celery soup
- 2 tablespoons Dijon mustard
- 3 cups hot cooked multigrain penne pasta (optional)
  Snipped fresh parsley

1. Trim fat from meat. Cut meat into 6 serving-size pieces. Sprinkle cracked pepper evenly over meat; press in with your fingers. In a large skillet heat oil on medium-high heat. Brown meat, half at a time, in the hot oil. Drain off fat. Set aside.

2. Place carrots and onion in a 3½- or 4-quart slow cooker. Add meat. In a medium bowl stir together soup and mustard. Pour over meat and vegetables in cooker.

3. Cover and cook on low-heat setting for 7 to 8 hours or on high-heat setting for 3½ to 4 hours. If desired, use a fork to slightly break up steak pieces and serve over hot cooked pasta. Garnish with parsley. **MAKES 6 SERVINGS**

Per serving: 275 cal., 9 g total fat (3 g sat. fat), 65 mg chol., 410 mg sodium, 10 g carbo., 1 g fiber, 34 g pro.

Bistro Beef Steak with Wild Mushroom Ragoût

Prep: 25 minutes **Broil:** 9 minutes

- 5 cloves garlic, minced
- 2 teaspoons herbes de Provence
- ½ teaspoon black pepper
- ¼ teaspoon salt
- 3 8-ounce boneless beef top loin steaks, cut ¾ inch thick
- 1 tablespoon olive oil
- ⅓ cup finely chopped shallots
- 8 ounces assorted wild mushrooms (oyster, cremini, and/or shiitake), sliced*

- ¼ cup dry sherry (optional)
- 1 14-ounce can lower-sodium beef broth
- 1 tablespoon cornstarch

1. Preheat broiler. In a small bowl combine 3 of the minced garlic cloves, 1 teaspoon of the herbes de Provence, the pepper, and salt. Trim fat from beef steaks. Sprinkle herb mixture over all sides of the steaks; rub in with your fingers. Place steaks on the unheated rack of broiler pan. Broil 3 to 4 inches from the heat for 9 to 11 minutes for medium-rare to medium doneness (145°F to 160°F), turning once halfway through broiling.

2. Meanwhile, for mushroom ragoût, in a large nonstick skillet heat oil on medium-high heat. Add shallots and the remaining 2 minced garlic cloves; cook until shallots are tender. Add mushrooms; cook until mushrooms are tender and any liquid evaporates, stirring occasionally. Remove from heat. If desired, stir in sherry. Return to heat. Bring to boiling. Cook, uncovered, for 30 to 60 seconds or until liquid evaporates. In a bowl stir together broth, cornstarch, and the remaining 1 teaspoon herbes de Provence. Stir into mixture in skillet. Cook and stir on medium heat until bubbly. Cook and stir for 2 minutes more.

3. Cut each steak in half and serve with the mushroom ragoût. **MAKES 6 SERVINGS**

*Tip Stem the oyster and shiitake mushrooms before slicing.

Per serving: 206 cal., 8 g total fat (2 g sat. fat), 66 mg chol., 291 mg sodium, 4 g carbo., 1 g fiber, 27 g pro.

BEEF AND CHIPOTLE BURRITOS

Beef and Chipotle Burritos

Prep: 35 minutes
Cook: 8 to 10 hours (high) or 4 to 5 hours (low)

  1 recipe Pico de Gallo Salsa
1½ pounds boneless beef round steak, cut ¾ inch thick
  2 14.5-ounce cans no-salt-added diced tomatoes, undrained
⅓ cup chopped onion (1 small)
  2 canned chipotle peppers in adobo sauce, finely chopped (see tip, page 144)
  3 cloves garlic, minced
  1 teaspoon dried oregano, crushed
¼ teaspoon ground cumin
  8 7- to 8-inch whole wheat flour tortillas, warmed
½ cup shredded reduced-fat cheddar cheese (2 ounces)

1. Prepare Pico de Gallo Salsa. Trim fat from meat. Cut meat into 6 serving-size pieces. Place meat in a 3½- or 4-quart slow cooker. Add undrained tomatoes, onion, chipotle peppers, garlic, oregano, and cumin.
2. Cover and cook on low-heat setting for 8 to 10 hours or on high-heat setting for 4 to 5 hours.
3. Using a slotted spoon, transfer meat and tomatoes to a large bowl; reserve cooking liquid in slow cooker. Using 2 forks, pull meat apart into shreds. Stir enough of the reserved cooking liquid into meat to moisten.
4. To serve, spoon meat mixture just below centers of tortillas. Top with cheese and Pico de Gallo Salsa. Roll up tortillas.
MAKES 8 SERVINGS

Pico de Gallo Salsa In a small bowl combine 1 cup finely chopped tomatoes; 2 tablespoons finely chopped onion; 2 tablespoons snipped fresh cilantro; and 1 fresh serrano chile pepper, seeded and finely chopped (see tip, page 144). Stir in ½ cup chopped, peeled jicama and ¼ cup radishes cut into thin bite-size strips. Cover; chill for several hours.

Per serving: 308 cal., 9 g total fat (3 g sat. fat), 62 mg chol., 482 mg sodium, 24 g carbo., 12 g fiber, 30 g pro.

Ginger Beef Stir-Fry ♡

Start to Finish: 35 minutes

½ cup lower-sodium beef broth
  3 tablespoons reduced-sodium soy sauce
2½ teaspoons cornstarch
  2 to 3 teaspoons finely chopped fresh ginger
     Nonstick cooking spray
1½ cups sliced fresh mushrooms
½ cup thinly bias-sliced carrot (1 medium)
  3 cups small broccoli florets
  1 small red sweet pepper, seeded and cut into ¼-inch-wide strips (1 cup)
  1 tablespoon vegetable oil
  8 ounces beef top round steak, cut into thin bite-size strips
  2 green onions, bias-sliced into 2-inch lengths
  2 cups hot cooked brown rice

1. For sauce, in a bowl stir together broth, soy sauce, cornstarch, and ginger; set aside.
2. Lightly coat an unheated wok or large nonstick skillet with nonstick cooking spray. Preheat on medium-high heat. Add mushrooms and carrot; stir-fry 2 minutes. Add broccoli and sweet pepper; stir-fry about 2 minutes more or until vegetables are crisp-tender. Remove vegetables from wok.
3. Carefully add oil to wok. Add beef; stir-fry for 2 to 3 minutes or until desired doneness. Push beef from center of wok. Stir sauce. Add sauce to center of wok. Cook and stir until thickened and bubbly. Return vegetables to wok. Add onions. Stir all ingredients together; heat through. Serve over hot cooked rice. **MAKES 4 SERVINGS**

Per serving: 274 cal., 7 g total fat (1 g sat. fat), 32 mg chol., 552 mg sodium, 34 g carbo., 5 g fiber, 20 g pro.

WINE-BALSAMIC GLAZED STEAK

Salsa Swiss Steak

Prep: 20 minutes **Cook:** 9 to 10 hours (low) or 4½ to 5 hours (high)

2 pounds boneless beef round steak, cut 1 inch thick
1 to 2 large red or green sweet peppers, cut into bite-size strips
1 medium onion, sliced
1 10.75-ounce can condensed cream of mushroom soup
1 cup bottled salsa
2 tablespoons all-purpose flour
1 teaspoon dry mustard
1 recipe Quick Corn Bread or mashed potatoes (optional)

1. Trim fat from meat. Cut meat into 6 serving-size pieces. In a 3½- or 4-quart slow cooker place meat, sweet peppers, and onion. In a medium bowl stir together soup, salsa, flour, and mustard. Pour over meat and vegetables in cooker.
2. Cover and cook on low-heat setting for 9 to 10 hours or on high-heat setting for 4½ to 5 hours. If desired, serve with Quick Corn Bread or mashed potatoes.

MAKES 6 SERVINGS

Per serving: 251 cal., 6 g total fat (2 g sat. fat), 65 mg chol., 574 mg sodium, 10 g carbo., 1 g fiber, 37 g pro.

Quick Corn Bread Preheat oven to 400°F. In a medium bowl combine 1 cup all-purpose flour, ¾ cup cornmeal, 2 tablespoons sugar, 2½ teaspoons baking powder, and ¾ teaspoons salt; set aside. Melt 1 tablespoon butter in a 10-inch cast-iron skillet or 9×1½-inch round baking pan. Place pan in preheated oven about 3 minutes or until butter melts. Swirl butter in pan to coat bottom and sides. In a small bowl combine 2 lightly beaten eggs, 1 cup milk, and ¼ cup melted butter. Add egg mixture all at once to flour mixture. Stir just until moistened. Pour batter into hot pan. Bake for 15 to 20 minutes or until a wooden toothpick inserted near center comes out clean. Cool slightly on wire rack; serve warm.

Wine-Balsamic Glazed Steak

Start to Finish: 30 minutes

2 boneless beef top sirloin steaks, cut ½ to ¾ inch thick (8 to 10 ounces per steak)
4 teaspoons olive oil
2 cups sliced fresh mushrooms
4 cloves garlic, minced
¼ teaspoon crushed red pepper
½ cup dry red wine or low-calorie cranberry juice*
¼ cup balsamic vinegar
2 tablespoons reduced-sodium soy sauce
2 teaspoons honey

1. Trim fat from steaks; cut each steak into 2 equal portions to make 4 total portions. In a very large skillet heat oil on medium-high heat. Add steaks. Reduce heat to medium; cook for 10 to 13 minutes or to desired doneness (145°F for medium rare or 160°F for medium), turning steaks occasionally. If meat browns too quickly, reduce heat to medium-low. Transfer meat to a serving platter; keep warm.
2. Add mushrooms, garlic, and red pepper to skillet; cook and stir for 2 minutes. Remove skillet from heat. Carefully add wine. Return to heat. Boil gently, uncovered, for 3 to 5 minutes or until most of the liquid is evaporated. Add vinegar, soy sauce, and honey; return to simmering. Cook and stir about 2 minutes or until slightly thickened. Spoon over steaks. **MAKES 4 SERVINGS**

***Tip** If using the cranberry juice option, omit the honey.

Per serving: 267 cal., 9 g total fat (2 g sat. fat), 48 mg chol., 336 mg sodium, 11 g carbo., 1 g fiber, 28 g pro.

SKILLET TOSTADAS

Skillet Tostadas

Start to Finish: 25 minutes

- 8 ounces ground beef, ground pork, uncooked ground chicken, or uncooked ground turkey
- ½ cup chopped onion (1 medium)
- 1 15-ounce can light red kidney beans, black beans, or pinto beans, rinsed and drained
- 1 11-ounce can condensed nacho cheese soup
- ⅓ cup bottled salsa
- 8 tostada shells
- 1 cup shredded taco cheese (4 ounces)
  Shredded lettuce
  Chopped tomatoes
  Sour cream or guacamole (optional)

1. In a large skillet cook ground beef and onion until meat is brown and onion is tender. Drain off fat. Stir in beans, nacho cheese soup, and salsa. Heat through.

2. Divide beef-salsa mixture among tostada shells. Top with cheese, lettuce, and tomatoes. If desired, serve with sour cream or guacamole. **MAKES 4 SERVINGS**

Per serving: 576 cal., 33 g total fat (15 g sat. fat), 81 mg chol., 1,277 mg sodium, 42 g carbo., 11 g fiber, 26 g pro.

Skillet Tacos Prepare as above, except divide beef-salsa mixture among 8 corn taco shells, warmed according to package directions.

Bloody Mary Pot Roast

Prep: 20 minutes **Cook:** 10 to 12 hours (low) or 5 to 6 hours (high)

- 1 3- to 3½-pound boneless beef chuck pot roast
- 2 tablespoons vegetable oil (optional)
- ¾ cup hot-style tomato juice
- ¼ cup water
- 1 teaspoon Worcestershire sauce
- 2 cloves garlic, minced
- 2 tablespoons cold water
- 4 teaspoons cornstarch
- 1 tablespoon prepared horseradish
  Salt and black pepper

1. Trim fat from meat. If necessary, cut meat to fit in a 3½- or 4-quart slow cooker. If desired, in a large skillet heat oil on medium-high heat. Brown meat on all sides in hot oil. Drain off fat. Transfer meat to the cooker.

2. In a small bowl combine tomato juice, the ¼ cup water, the Worcestershire sauce, and garlic; pour over meat in cooker.

3. Cover and cook on low-heat setting for 10 to 12 hours or on high-heat setting for 5 to 6 hours.

4. Transfer meat to a cutting board, reserving cooking liquid. Slice meat; transfer to serving platter and cover to keep warm.

5. For gravy, pour reserved cooking liquid into a glass measuring cup; skim off fat. Measure 1½ cups of the reserved cooking liquid. In a small saucepan combine the 2 tablespoons cold water and the cornstarch; stir in the 1½ cups reserved cooking liquid. Cook and stir on medium heat until thickened and bubbly. Cook and stir for 2 minutes more. Stir in horseradish. Season to taste with salt and pepper. Serve the gravy with the sliced meat.

MAKES 10 SERVINGS

Per serving: 180 cal., 5 g total fat (2 g sat. fat), 81 mg chol., 255 mg sodium, 2 g carbo., 0 g fiber, 29 g pro.

INDIAN BEEF PATTIES WITH CUCUMBER-YOGURT SAUCE

Italian Shepherd's Pie ♡

Prep: 30 minutes **Bake:** 25 minutes
Stand: 15 minutes **Oven:** 375°F

¾ cup shredded reduced-fat Italian-blend cheeses or reduced-fat mozzarella cheese (3 ounces)
2 cups mashed potatoes or refrigerated mashed potatoes
8 ounces lean ground beef
4 ounces uncooked turkey Italian sausage links, casings removed
½ cup chopped onion (1 medium)
2 cups sliced zucchini or yellow summer squash
1 14.5-ounce can diced tomatoes, undrained
½ of a 6-ounce can (⅓ cup) tomato paste
¼ teaspoon black pepper
  Paprika (optional)

1. Preheat oven to 375°F. Stir ½ cup of the cheese into mashed potatoes; set mixture aside.
2. In a large skillet combine ground beef, sausage, and onion; cook until meat is brown and onion is tender. Drain off fat. Stir zucchini, undrained tomatoes, tomato paste, and pepper into meat mixture in skillet. Bring to boiling.
3. Divide meat mixture among six 10-ounce individual casserole dishes or ramekins. Spoon mashed potato mixture into mounds on top of hot meat mixture in dishes. Sprinkle with the remaining ¼ cup cheese. If desired, sprinkle with paprika.
4. Place dishes in a 15×10×1-inch baking pan. Bake, uncovered, about 25 minutes or until hot and bubbly. Let stand for 15 minutes before serving. **MAKES 6 SERVINGS**

Per serving: 224 cal., 8 g total fat (4 g sat. fat), 42 mg chol., 641 mg sodium, 22 g carbo., 4 g fiber, 18 g pro.

Indian Beef Patties with Cucumber-Yogurt Sauce

Prep: 15 minutes **Grill:** 14 minutes

1 cup plain low-fat yogurt
⅔ cup chopped, seeded cucumber
½ cup finely chopped onion (1 medium)
1 jalapeño, seeded and finely chopped*
2 tablespoons snipped fresh mint or 1 teaspoon dried mint, crushed
1 teaspoon ground cumin
1 teaspoon bottled minced garlic (2 cloves) or ¼ teaspoon garlic powder
½ teaspoon salt
1 pound lean ground beef
  Indian flatbread (optional)

1. For sauce, in a small bowl stir together yogurt and cucumber. Cover and chill until ready to serve.
2. In a medium bowl combine onion, jalapeño, mint, cumin, garlic, and salt. Add ground beef; mix well. Form meat mixture into four ¾-inch-thick patties.
3. Place patties on the rack of an uncovered grill directly over medium coals. Grill for 14 to 18 minutes or until patties are done (160°F),** turning once. If desired, serve the patties on flatbread. Spoon sauce over patties. **MAKES 4 SERVINGS**

*Tip Because chile peppers contain volatile oils that can burn your skin and eyes, avoid direct contact with them as much as possible. When working with chile peppers, wear plastic or rubber gloves. If your bare hands do touch the peppers, wash your hands and nails well with soap and warm water.

**Tip The internal color of a burger is not a reliable doneness indicator. A beef or pork patty cooked to 160°F is safe, regardless of color. To measure the doneness of a patty, insert an instant-read thermometer through the side of the patty to a depth of 2 to 3 inches.

Per serving: 241 cal., 12 g total fat (5 g sat. fat), 75 mg chol., 377 mg sodium, 8 g carbo., 1 g fiber, 24 g pro.

SIMPLE BEEF AND NOODLES

Herb-Garlic Beef Roast with Potatoes and Carrots

Start to Finish: 20 minutes

    1   17-ounce package refrigerated cooked
        beef roast au jus
    1   pound small round red potatoes,
        quartered
    3   medium carrots, cut into ¾-inch pieces
    1   tablespoon canola oil
        Freshly ground black pepper
    3   tablespoons snipped fresh Italian (flat-leaf)
        parsley
    3   to 6 cloves garlic, minced
    1   tablespoon finely shredded lemon peel

1. In a large skillet cook beef roast, covered, on medium heat for 10 minutes. Uncover and simmer for 5 minutes more or until juices are slightly reduced.

2. Meanwhile, in a microwave-safe dish combine potatoes and carrots. Drizzle with oil and sprinkle with pepper; toss to coat. Tightly cover with lid or plastic wrap. Microwave on high about 10 minutes or until tender.

3. For herb-garlic mixture, in a small bowl combine parsley, garlic, and lemon peel. To serve, stir vegetables into skillet with beef and juices. Divide among serving dishes. Sprinkle with herb-garlic mixture. **MAKES 4 SERVINGS**

Per serving: 311 cal., 12 g total fat (5 g sat. fat), 64 mg chol., 465 mg sodium, 28 g carbo., 4 g fiber, 25 g pro.

Simple Beef and Noodles

Prep: 15 minutes **Cook:** 20 minutes

    1   17-ounce package refrigerated cooked
         beef tips with gravy
    ½   teaspoon dried basil, crushed
    ¼   teaspoon black pepper
    1   10.75-ounce can condensed golden
         mushroom soup
    ½   cup beef broth
    1½   cups sliced fresh mushrooms
    1   cup packaged peeled baby carrots, halved
         lengthwise
    ⅓   cup thinly sliced onion (1 small)
    1   12-ounce package frozen egg noodles

1. In a large saucepan combine beef tips with gravy, basil, and pepper. Stir in soup and broth. Bring to boiling. Add mushrooms, carrots, and onion. Return to boiling; reduce heat to low. Simmer, covered, for 20 to 25 minutes or until vegetables are tender, stirring frequently.

2. Meanwhile, cook noodles according to package directions; drain. Serve meat mixture over noodles. **MAKES 4 TO 6 SERVINGS**

Per serving: 458 cal., 12 g total fat (4 g sat. fat), 150 mg chol., 1,349 mg sodium, 61 g carbo., 4 g fiber, 27 g pro.

Veal Scaloppine ♡

Start to Finish: 35 minutes

- 12 ounces boneless veal leg round steak or veal leg sirloin steak, cut ¼ inch thick and trimmed of fat
- ¼ teaspoon salt
- ¼ teaspoon black pepper
- ½ cup chopped onion (1 medium)
- ¼ cup water
- 2 cloves garlic, minced
- 1 14.5-ounce can no-salt-added diced tomatoes, undrained
- 3 tablespoons dry white wine or reduced-sodium chicken broth
- 1 tablespoon snipped fresh oregano or 1 teaspoon dried oregano, crushed
- 1 tablespoon capers, rinsed and drained (optional)
  Nonstick cooking spray
- 2 cups hot cooked whole wheat pasta

1. Cut meat into 8 pieces. Place each piece of meat between 2 pieces of plastic wrap. Working from center to edges, pound with flat side of a meat mallet to about an ⅛-inch thickness. Remove plastic wrap. Sprinkle meat with salt and ⅛ teaspoon of the pepper. Set aside.

2. For sauce, in a medium saucepan combine onion, the water, and garlic. Cover and cook until onion is tender. Stir in undrained tomatoes, wine, oregano, capers (if desired), and the remaining ⅛ teaspoon pepper. Bring to boiling; reduce heat. Simmer, uncovered, about 15 minutes or until desired consistency. Keep warm.

3. Meanwhile, lightly coat an unheated large skillet with nonstick cooking spray. Preheat on medium-high heat. Cook veal, half at a time, for 2 to 4 minutes or until desired doneness, turning once. Transfer veal to a serving platter. Keep warm.

4. To serve, spoon sauce over veal. Serve with pasta. **MAKES 4 SERVINGS**

Per serving: 219 cal., 2 g total fat (1 g sat. fat), 66 mg chol., 244 mg sodium, 26 g carbo., 4 g fiber, 23 g pro.

Veal Chops with Pesto-Stuffed Mushrooms

Prep: 15 minutes **Marinate:** 2 to 6 hours
Grill: 11 minutes

- ¼ cup dry white wine or chicken broth
- 1 tablespoon snipped fresh sage
- 1 tablespoon olive oil
- 1 tablespoon Worcestershire-style marinade for chicken
- 3 cloves garlic, minced
- ¼ teaspoon black pepper
- 4 bone-in veal loin chops, cut ¾ inch thick (about 2½ pounds)
- 8 large fresh mushrooms (2 to 2½ inches in diameter), stems removed
- 3 tablespoons purchased refrigerated reduced-fat basil pesto

1. For marinade, in a bowl combine wine, sage, oil, Worcestershire sauce, garlic, and pepper. Place meat and mushrooms in a resealable plastic bag set in a shallow dish.

Pour marinade into bag. Seal bag; turn to coat meat. Marinate in the refrigerator for 2 to 6 hours, turning bag occasionally.

2. For a charcoal grill, place chops on rack of an uncovered grill directly over medium coals. Grill 11 to 13 minutes for medium doneness, turning once halfway through grilling. Place mushrooms, stemmed sides down, on grill rack. Grill for 4 minutes. Turn mushrooms stemmed sides up; spoon pesto on mushrooms. Grill about 4 minutes more or until hot. (For a gas grill, preheat grill. Reduce heat to medium. Place chops, then mushrooms on grill rack over heat. Cover and grill as above.)

3. Serve chops with mushrooms. If desired, garnish with parsley. **MAKES 4 SERVINGS**

Per serving: 286 cal., 12 g total fat (3 g sat. fat), 134 mg chol., 294 mg sodium, 5 g carbo., 1 g fiber, 36 g pro.

PORK CHOPS PRIMAVERA

Margarita-Glazed Pork Chops

Prep: 10 minutes **Grill:** 7 minutes

4 boneless pork top loin chops, cut ¾ inch thick (1 to 1½ pounds)
⅓ cup low-sugar orange marmalade
1 fresh jalapeño, seeded and finely chopped*
2 tablespoons tequila or lime juice
½ teaspoon grated fresh ginger or ¼ teaspoon ground ginger
¼ cup snipped fresh cilantro

1. Trim fat from pork. For glaze, in a small bowl stir together orange marmalade, jalapeño, tequila, and ginger.
2. For a charcoal grill, place chops on the rack of an uncovered grill directly over medium coals. Grill for 7 to 9 minutes or until no pink remains (160°F) and juices run clear, turning once halfway through grilling and spooning glaze over chops frequently during the last 2 minutes of grilling. (For a gas grill, preheat grill. Reduce heat to medium. Place chops on grill rack over heat. Cover and grill as above.) To serve, sprinkle pork chops with cilantro. **MAKES 4 SERVINGS**

*Tip Because chile peppers contain volatile oils that can burn your skin and eyes, avoid direct contact with them as much as possible. When working with chile peppers, wear plastic or rubber gloves. If your bare hands do touch the peppers, wash your hands and nails well with soap and warm water.

Per serving: 184 cal., 3 g total fat (1 g sat. fat), 62 mg chol., 211 mg sodium, 8 g carbo., 0 g fiber, 26 g pro.

Pork Chops Primavera ♡

Start to Finish: 30 minutes

12 ounces fresh young green beans, trimmed
2 tablespoons water
2 slices turkey bacon, cut into 1-inch pieces
4 bone-in pork loin or rib chops, cut ½ inch thick
1 tablespoon reduced-sodium soy sauce
2 teaspoons canola oil
3 tablespoons apple butter
¼ cup water
1 cup red and/or yellow cherry or grape tomatoes

1. In a 2-quart microwave-safe dish combine green beans and the 2 tablespoons water. Microwave, covered, on high for 4 minutes, stirring once. Drain and set aside.
2. In a very large skillet cook bacon until crisp. Remove bacon from skillet; set aside.
3. Meanwhile, trim fat from chops. Brush chops with soy sauce. Add oil to skillet; heat on medium heat. Add chops to skillet; cook until brown on both sides. Add apple butter and the ¼ cup water. Simmer, covered, for 5 minutes. Add green beans, bacon, and tomatoes. Cook, uncovered, for 3 to 5 minutes or until apple butter mixture is thickened. **MAKES 4 SERVINGS**

Per serving: 307 cal., 7 g total fat (3 g sat. fat), 83 mg chol., 309 mg sodium, 26 g carbo., 4 g fiber, 33 g pro.

Mediterranean Pork Chops

Prep: 10 minutes **Roast:** 35 minutes
Oven: 425°F/350°F

- 4 boneless or bone-in pork loin chops, cut
  ½ inch thick (1 to 1½ pounds)
- ¼ teaspoon salt
- ¼ teaspoon freshly ground black pepper
- 1 tablespoon finely snipped fresh rosemary
  or 1 teaspoon dried rosemary, crushed
- 3 cloves garlic, minced

1. Preheat oven to 425°F. Sprinkle all sides of chops with salt and pepper; set aside. In a small bowl combine rosemary and garlic. Sprinkle rosemary mixture evenly over all sides of the chops; rub in with your fingers.
2. Place chops on a rack in a shallow roasting pan. Roast chops for 10 minutes. Reduce oven temperature to 350°F and continue roasting about 25 minutes or until no pink remains (160°F) and juices run clear. **MAKES 4 SERVINGS**

Per serving: 161 cal., 5 g total fat (2 g sat. fat), 62 mg chol., 192 mg sodium, 1 g carbo., 0 g fiber, 25 g pro.

Cranberry Pork Loin Chops

Start to Finish: 30 minutes

  Nonstick cooking spray
- 4 boneless pork loin chops, cut ½ inch thick
  (about 1¼ pounds)
- ⅛ teaspoon black pepper
- ½ cup canned whole cranberry sauce
- 2 tablespoons frozen orange juice
  concentrate, thawed
- 1 tablespoon honey
- ¼ teaspoon ground ginger
- ⅛ teaspoon ground nutmeg

1. Lightly coat an unheated large nonstick skillet with nonstick cooking spray. Preheat on medium-high heat. Sprinkle all sides of the · chops with pepper. Add chops to hot skillet; reduce heat to medium and cook for 8 to 10 minutes or until done (160°F), turning once. Remove chops from skillet; cover to keep warm.
2. Meanwhile, for sauce, in a small bowl combine cranberry sauce, orange juice concentrate, honey, ginger, and nutmeg. Add cranberry mixture to same skillet. Cook, uncovered, for

1 to 2 minutes or until sauce thickens slightly. Serve sauce over pork. **MAKES 4 SERVINGS**

Per serving: 285 cal., 7 g total fat (2 g sat. fat), 89 mg chol., 172 mg sodium, 21 g carbo., 1 g fiber, 31 g pro.

Pork Medallions with Lemon-Pecan Spinach

Start to Finish: 40 minutes

- 1 pound pork tenderloin, cut crosswise into
  8 slices
- ¼ teaspoon salt
- ¼ teaspoon coarsely ground black pepper
- 1 tablespoon canola oil
- 2 tablespoons lemon juice
- ⅛ teaspoon bottled hot pepper sauce
- 1 10-ounce package frozen chopped
  spinach, thawed and well drained
- ¼ cup sliced green onions (2)
- 2 tablespoons chopped pecans
- 1 tablespoon snipped fresh parsley
- ⅛ teaspoon salt

1. If necessary, press each pork tenderloin slice to 1-inch thickness. Sprinkle pork slices lightly with the ¼ teaspoon salt and the pepper. In a large skillet heat oil on medium-high heat. Add pork slices; cook for 6 to 8 minutes or until slightly pink in the center (160°F), turning once halfway through cooking. Remove pork slices from skillet, reserving drippings in the skillet. Cover pork and keep warm.
2. Stir lemon juice and hot pepper sauce into reserved drippings in skillet. Stir in spinach, green onions, pecans, parsley, and the ⅛ teaspoon salt; cook on low heat until spinach mixture is heated through. Place spinach mixture on serving plate; arrange pork slices on top. If desired, garnish with lemon slices. **MAKES 4 SERVINGS**

Per serving: 213 cal., 10 g total fat (2 g sat. fat), 73 mg chol., 318 mg sodium, 5 g carbo., 3 g fiber, 27 g pro.

CRANBERRY PORK ROAST

Thai Pork Stir-Fry

Start to Finish: 30 minutes

- 2 tablespoons olive oil
- 1 tablespoon reduced-sodium soy sauce
- ½ teaspoon garlic powder
- ½ teaspoon finely chopped fresh ginger or ¼ teaspoon ground ginger
- ½ teaspoon black pepper
- ½ teaspoon ground cardamom
- ½ teaspoon chili powder
- 1½ pounds pork loin, cut into bite-size strips
- 2 cups broccoli florets
- 1 cup thinly sliced carrots (2)
- 1 cup cauliflower florets
- 2 tablespoons white vinegar
- 1 tablespoon curry powder
- 2 cups hot cooked brown rice

1. In a very large skillet combine olive oil, soy sauce, garlic powder, ginger, pepper, cardamom, and chili powder. Add half of the pork; stir-fry pork on medium-high heat for 3 minutes. Using a slotted spoon, remove pork from skillet. Repeat with the remaining half of the pork. Return all of the pork to the skillet.

2. Add broccoli, carrots, cauliflower, vinegar, and curry powder to pork mixture. Bring to boiling; reduce heat. Simmer, covered, for 3 to 5 minutes or until vegetables are crisp-tender, stirring occasionally.

3. Serve pork and vegetables over brown rice.

MAKES 6 SERVINGS

Per serving: 301 cal., 11 g total fat (3 g sat. fat), 71 mg chol., 206 mg sodium, 21 g carbo., 3 g fiber, 28 g pro.

Cranberry Pork Roast

Prep: 25 minutes **Cook:** 6 to 7 hours (low) or 3 to 3½ hours (high) plus 10 minutes

- 1 3-pound boneless pork top loin roast (double loin, tied)
  Salt and black pepper
- 1 tablespoon vegetable oil
- 1 16-ounce can whole cranberry sauce
- ½ cup cranberry juice
- ¼ cup sugar
- 1 teaspoon dry mustard
- ¼ teaspoon ground cloves
- 2 tablespoons cornstarch
- 2 tablespoons cold water
  Hot cooked rice pilaf, rice, or noodles (optional)

1. Trim fat from roast. Sprinkle roast with salt and pepper. In a large skillet heat oil on medium heat. Cook pork in hot oil until well browned on all sides. Place pork in a 4- to 5-quart slow cooker. In a medium bowl combine cranberry sauce, cranberry juice, sugar, mustard, and cloves. Pour over roast. Cover and cook on low-heat setting for 6 to 7 hours or on high-heat setting for 3 to 3½ hours. Transfer meat to a platter; cover and keep warm.

2. For sauce, skim fat from juices. Measure 2 cups of juices; transfer to a medium saucepan. In a small bowl combine cornstarch and the water; add to saucepan. Cook and stir on medium heat until thickened and bubbly; cook and stir for 2 minutes more. Serve roast with sauce and, if desired, rice pilaf.

MAKES 8 TO 10 SERVINGS

Per serving: 404 cal., 11 g total fat (3 g sat. fat), 100 mg chol., 124 mg sodium, 38 g carbo., 1 g fiber, 37 g pro.

BAKED RATATOUILLE-SAUSAGE
PENNE

4. Bake, covered, about 30 minutes or until heated through. Sprinkle with Parmesan cheese. Uncover and bake about 5 minutes more or until cheese melts. **MAKES 6 SERVINGS**

Per serving: 358 cal., 21 g total fat (7 g sat. fat), 46 mg chol., 525 mg sodium, 29 g carbo., 3 g fiber, 15 g pro.

Latin-Spiced Pork Tenderloins

Prep: 10 minutes **Roast:** 25 minutes
Stand: 15 minutes **Oven:** 425°F

    2 teaspoons chili powder
    1 teaspoon garlic powder
    1 teaspoon dried oregano, crushed
    ½ teaspoon salt
    ½ teaspoon black pepper
    ½ teaspoon ground cumin
    ¼ teaspoon cayenne pepper
    2 1-pound pork tenderloins

1. Preheat oven to 425°F. For rub, in a small bowl combine chili powder, garlic powder, oregano, salt, black pepper, cumin, and cayenne pepper. Sprinkle rub evenly over all sides of tenderloins; rub in with your fingers.
2. Place tenderloins on a rack in a shallow roasting pan. Roast, uncovered, for 25 to 35 minutes or until an instant-read thermometer inserted into thickest part of the tenderloins registers 155°F.
3. Remove tenderloins from oven. Cover meat tightly with foil; let stand for 15 minutes before slicing. The temperature of the meat after standing should be 160°F.

MAKES 8 SERVINGS

Per serving: 138 cal., 3 g total fat (1 g sat. fat), 73 mg chol., 198 mg sodium, 1 g carbo., 0 g fiber, 24 g pro.

Baked Ratatouille-Sausage Penne

Prep: 40 minutes **Bake:** 35 minutes
Oven: 350°F

    3 uncooked Italian sausage links (12 ounces)
    4 cloves garlic, minced
    1 teaspoon olive oil
    1 14.5-ounce can no-salt-added diced tomatoes
    3 tablespoons snipped fresh parsley
    ¼ teaspoon crushed red pepper (optional)
    1 pound eggplant, peeled and cut into ½-inch cubes
    6 ounces dried whole wheat penne pasta (about 2¼ cups)
    ⅓ cup finely shredded Parmesan cheese

1. Preheat oven to 350°F. Place sausage in an unheated skillet. Add ½ inch of water to the skillet. Bring to boiling; reduce heat. Simmer, covered, about 15 minutes or until juices run clear; drain off liquid. Cook for 2 to 4 minutes more or until browned, turning occasionally. Remove from heat. When cool enough to handle, cut sausages in half lengthwise; bias-cut into ½-inch slices. Set aside.
2. In a large skillet cook garlic in hot oil for 1 minute. Stir in undrained tomatoes, parsley, and, if desired, crushed red pepper. Bring to boiling. Stir in eggplant. Reduce heat. Simmer, covered, for 15 minutes.
3. Meanwhile, cook pasta according to package directions; drain. Return pasta to hot pan. Stir in eggplant mixture and sausage. Spoon into a 2-quart baking dish.

MEDITERRANEAN LAMB CHOPS

Spicy Apricot Lamb Chops

Prep: 20 minutes **Broil:** 10 minutes

    2   pounds broccoli rabe
    8   lamb rib chops, cut 1 inch thick (about
        2 pounds)
    1   tablespoon packed brown sugar
    1   teaspoon garlic salt
    1   teaspoon chili powder
    1   teaspoon paprika
    ½   teaspoon dried oregano, crushed
    ¼   teaspoon ground cinnamon
    ¼   teaspoon ground allspice
    ¼   teaspoon black pepper
    ¼   cup low-sugar apricot preserves
    1   tablespoon olive oil

1. Preheat broiler. Wash broccoli rabe; remove and discard woody stems. Coarsely chop the leafy greens; set aside.

2. Trim fat from chops. In a small bowl combine brown sugar, garlic salt, chili powder, paprika, oregano, cinnamon, allspice, and black pepper. Set aside 1 teaspoon of the spice mixture. Sprinkle the remaining spice mixture on all sides of the chops; rub in with your fingers.

3. Place chops on the unheated rack of a broiler pan. Broil 4 to 5 inches from the heat for 10 to 15 minutes or until done (160°F), turning meat and brushing with preserves halfway through broiling.

4. Meanwhile, in a very large skillet heat oil on medium-high heat. Add the 1 teaspoon reserved spice mixture. Cook and stir for 1 minute. Add broccoli rabe. Using tongs, toss and cook for 4 to 6 minutes or until broccoli rabe is crisp-tender.

5. Serve lamb chops with broccoli rabe mixture. **MAKES 4 SERVINGS**

Per serving: 335 cal., 12 g total fat (4 g sat. fat), 119 mg chol., 376 mg sodium, 14 g carbo., 4 g fiber, 42 g pro.

Mediterranean Lamb Chops

Prep: 10 minutes **Cook:** 15 minutes

    2   teaspoons vegetable oil
    6   lamb loin chops, cut 1½ inches thick
    1   medium red onion, cut into thin wedges
    1   26- to 28-ounce jar garlic and onion
        pasta sauce
    1   19-ounce can cannellini beans (white
        kidney beans), rinsed and drained
    ½   cup pitted kalamata olives, halved
    ½   cup bottled roasted red sweet peppers,
        cut into strips
    2   tablespoons balsamic vinegar
    2   teaspoons snipped fresh rosemary
        Hot cooked orzo or rice

1. Trim fat from chops. In a large skillet heat oil on medium heat. Cook chops in hot oil for 9 to 11 minutes for medium (160°F), turning once halfway through cooking. Transfer chops to a large bowl or platter; cover with foil to keep warm.

2. In the same skillet cook onion in lamb drippings on medium heat until tender. Add pasta sauce, beans, olives, roasted peppers, balsamic vinegar, and rosemary. Cook and stir on medium heat until heated through. Add chops to skillet; cover and heat through for 3 minutes.

3. Serve lamb chops and sauce over hot cooked orzo or rice. **MAKES 6 SERVINGS**

Per serving: 410 cal., 11 g total fat (3 g sat. fat), 40 mg chol., 798 mg sodium, 58 g carbo., 9 g fiber, 22 g pro.

GARLIC-CHILI-RUBBED LAMB

Garlic-Chili-Rubbed Lamb

Prep: 15 minutes **Marinate:** 4 to 24 hours
Grill: 16 minutes

    4 large cloves garlic, minced
  ½ teaspoon salt
    1 tablespoon chili powder
    1 teaspoon ground cumin
  ½ teaspoon sugar
  ½ teaspoon black pepper
  ½ teaspoon dried thyme, crushed
  ¼ teaspoon ground cinnamon
  ¼ teaspoon ground allspice
    2 to 3 teaspoons olive oil
    8 lamb rib or loin chops, cut 1 inch thick
        Grilled tomatoes (optional)

1. On a cutting board using the flat side of a chef's knife rub together garlic and salt to form a paste. Transfer garlic paste to a small bowl. Stir in chili powder, cumin, sugar, pepper, thyme, cinnamon, and allspice. Stir in enough olive oil to make a paste. Rub lamb chops all over with the paste. Cover and chill for 4 to 24 hours.
2. For a charcoal grill, arrange medium-hot coals around a drip pan. Test for medium heat above the pan. Place chops on grill rack over drip pan. Cover and grill to desired doneness, turning once halfway through grilling. Allow 16 to 18 minutes for medium rare (145°F) or 18 to 20 for medium (160°F). (For a gas grill, preheat grill. Reduce heat to medium. Adjust for indirect cooking. Grill as above.) If desired, serve with grilled tomatoes. **MAKES 4 SERVINGS**

Per serving: 199 cal., 12 g total fat (4 g sat. fat), 64 mg chol., 381 mg sodium, 3 g carbo., 1 g fiber, 20 g pro.

Greek Pita Pizzas ♡

Prep: 15 minutes **Bake:** 5 minutes
Oven: 400°F

    6 ounces lean ground lamb or beef
  ¼ cup finely chopped onion
    2 cloves garlic, minced
    1 8-ounce can no-salt-added tomato sauce
    1 teaspoon snipped fresh rosemary or
        ¼ teaspoon dried rosemary, crushed
    2 6-inch whole wheat or white pita bread
        rounds
  ½ cup shredded part-skim mozzarella cheese
        (2 ounces)
  ½ cup shredded fresh spinach
    1 small tomato, seeded and chopped
  ¼ cup crumbled reduced-fat feta cheese
        (1 ounce)
  12 pitted kalamata or ripe olives, quartered
        (optional)

1. Preheat oven to 400°F. In a medium nonstick skillet cook ground lamb, onion, and garlic until meat is browned; drain off fat. Stir tomato sauce and rosemary into meat mixture in skillet. Bring to boiling; reduce heat. Simmer, uncovered, for 2 minutes.
2. Carefully split pita bread rounds in half horizontally; place pita halves, rough sides up, in a single layer on a large baking sheet. Bake for 3 to 4 minutes or until lightly toasted.
3. Top toasted pita bread with meat mixture; sprinkle with mozzarella cheese. Bake for 2 to 3 minutes more or until cheese is melted. Remove from oven. Top with spinach, tomato, feta cheese, and, if desired, olives; serve immediately. **MAKES 4 PIZZAS**

Per pizza: 255 cal., 8 g total fat (4 g sat. fat), 38 mg chol., 432 mg sodium, 28 g carbo., 4 g fiber, 16 g pro.

Poultry

PROSCIUTTO-STUFFED CHICKEN
BREASTS WITH PEARS

Prosciutto-Stuffed Chicken Breasts with Pears

Prep: 30 minutes **Bake:** 45 minutes
Oven: 375°F

- 8 medium chicken breast halves with bone (about 4 pounds total)
- 1 5.2-ounce container semisoft cheese with herbs
- ½ cup shredded fontina or mozzarella cheese (2 ounces)
- ¼ cup grated Parmesan cheese
- ¼ cup chopped prosciutto (about 1½ ounces)
- 2 tablespoons butter or margarine, melted
- 1 tablespoon butter or margarine
- 4 medium pears, cored and thinly sliced
- 1 cup apple juice or apple cider
- 1 tablespoon cornstarch
- 2 teaspoons snipped fresh sage

1. Preheat oven to 375°F. Grease a 15×10×1-inch baking pan. Set aside.
2. Using your fingers, gently separate the chicken skin from the meat of the breasts, leaving the skin attached along one side; set aside.
3. For stuffing, in a medium bowl combine semisoft cheese, fontina cheese, Parmesan cheese, and prosciutto. Divide cheese mixture among chicken breast halves, spreading cheese mixture between the skin and meat of each breast half.
4. Place chicken pieces, bone sides down, in the prepared baking pan. Brush chicken with the 2 tablespoons melted butter. Bake for 45 to 55 minutes or until chicken is no longer pink (170°F).
5. Meanwhile, in a very large skillet melt the 1 tablespoon butter on medium heat. Add pear slices; cook and stir for 2 to 3 minutes or just until tender. In a small bowl whisk

together apple juice and cornstarch. Add to pears in skillet. Cook and stir until thickened and bubbly. Cook and stir for 2 minutes more. Remove from heat. Stir in sage. To serve, spoon pear mixture over baked chicken breasts. **MAKES 8 SERVINGS**

Per serving: 522 cal., 32 g total fat (14 g sat. fat), 152 mg chol., 356 mg sodium, 18 g carbo., 3 g fiber, 39 g pro.

Herbed Balsamic Chicken

Prep: 20 minutes **Cook:** 4½ hours (low) or 2 hours (high); plus 30 minutes (high)

- 1 medium onion, cut into thin wedges
- 1 tablespoon quick-cooking tapioca, crushed
- 6 bone-in chicken breast halves (3½ to 4 pounds), skinned
- 1 teaspoon dried rosemary, crushed
- 1 teaspoon dried thyme, crushed
- ½ teaspoon salt
- ¼ teaspoon black pepper
- ¼ cup balsamic vinegar
- 2 tablespoons chicken broth
- 1 9-ounce package frozen Italian green beans
- 1 medium red sweet pepper, seeded and cut into bite-size strips

1. Place onion in a 3½- or 4-quart slow cooker. Sprinkle with tapioca. Add chicken. Sprinkle with rosemary, thyme, salt, and black pepper. Pour balsamic vinegar and chicken broth over all.
2. Cover and cook on low-heat setting for 4½ hours or on high-heat setting for 2 hours.
3. If using low-heat setting, turn to high-heat setting. Add the green beans and sweet pepper. Cover and cook for 30 minutes more.
4. Using a slotted spoon, transfer chicken and vegetables to a serving platter. Spoon some of the sauce over chicken and vegetables. Pass remaining sauce. **MAKES 6 SERVINGS**

Per serving: 234 cal., 2 g total fat (1 g sat. fat), 100 mg chol., 308 mg sodium, 10 g carbo., 2 g fiber, 41 g pro.

Oven-Fried Parmesan Chicken

Prep: 30 minutes **Bake:** 45 minutes
Oven: 375°F

- 1   egg, lightly beaten
- 3   tablespoons milk
- ½   cup grated Parmesan cheese
- ¼   cup fine dry bread crumbs
- 1   teaspoon dried oregano, crushed
- ½   teaspoon paprika
- ⅛   teaspoon black pepper
- 2   to 2½ pounds meaty chicken pieces, skinned (breast halves, thighs, and drumsticks)
- 2   tablespoons butter or margarine, melted
     Snipped fresh oregano (optional)

1. Preheat oven to 375°F. In a small bowl combine egg and milk. In a shallow dish combine Parmesan cheese, bread crumbs, oregano, paprika, and pepper.

2. Dip chicken pieces into egg mixture; coat with crumb mixture. Arrange chicken pieces in a greased large shallow baking pan, making sure pieces don't touch. Drizzle chicken pieces with melted butter.

3. Bake for 45 to 55 minutes or until chicken is tender and no longer pink (170°F for breasts; 180°F for thighs and drumsticks). Do not turn chicken pieces during baking. If desired, garnish with fresh oregano.

MAKES 6 SERVINGS.

Per serving: 277 cal., 16 g total fat (5 g sat. fat), 112 mg chol., 306 mg sodium, 4 g carbo., 0 g fiber, 28 g pro.

Tender-Crisp Vegetable and Chicken Braise

Start to Finish: 50 minutes

- 3   tablespoons olive oil
- 8   ounces new potatoes, cut into ½-inch slices
- 4   small carrots with tops, trimmed and diagonally cut into 1-inch pieces
- 4   cups fresh mushrooms, halved (12 ounces)
- 1   large onion, cut into thin wedges
- 1   pound fresh asparagus, trimmed and cut into 1½-inch pieces

TENDER-CRISP VEGETABLE AND CHICKEN BRAISE

- 3   cloves garlic, peeled and sliced
- 2   skinless, boneless chicken thighs, cut into strips
- ½   teaspoon salt
- ¼   teaspoon black pepper
- ¾   cup reduced-sodium chicken broth
- 1   tablespoon snipped fresh tarragon

1. In a very large nonstick skillet heat 2 tablespoons of the oil on medium-high heat Evenly layer potatoes and carrots in skillet. Cook, uncovered, about 5 minutes or until potatoes are golden, turning once. Add mushrooms and onion. Cook for 5 to 6 minutes or until vegetables are crisp-tender, stirring often. Add asparagus and garlic; cook for 3 minutes. Transfer vegetables to a bowl; set aside.

2. In the same skillet heat the remaining olive oil. Sprinkle chicken with ¼ teaspoon of the salt and ⅛ teaspoon of the pepper. Cook chicken in hot oil about 3 minutes or until lightly browned, stirring occasionally. Add chicken broth; bring to boiling. Reduce heat. Simmer, covered, about 3 minutes or until no pink remains in chicken. Increase heat to medium-high. Stir in cooked vegetables; heat through. Stir in snipped tarragon and the remaining ¼ teaspoon salt and ⅛ teaspoon pepper. **MAKES 4 SERVINGS**

Per serving: 266 cal., 12 g total fat (2 g sat. fat), 29 mg chol., 483 mg sodium, 28 g carbo., 7 g fiber, 15 g pro.

CHICKEN À L'ORANGE

Apple-Glazed Chicken with Spinach ♡

Start to Finish: 30 minutes

⅓ cup apple jelly
2 tablespoons reduced-sodium soy sauce
1 tablespoon snipped fresh thyme or
1 teaspoon dried thyme, crushed
1 teaspoon finely shredded lemon peel
1 teaspoon grated fresh ginger or ¼ teaspoon ground ginger
4 skinless, boneless chicken breast halves (1 to 1¼ pounds)
¼ teaspoon salt
¼ teaspoon black pepper
Nonstick cooking spray
2 medium apples, cored and coarsely chopped
1 medium onion, sliced
2 cloves garlic, minced
12 cups packaged fresh baby spinach

1. Preheat broiler. For glaze, in a small microwave-safe bowl combine apple jelly, soy sauce, thyme, lemon peel, and ginger. Microwave, uncovered, on high for 1 to 1¼ minutes or just until jelly is melted, stirring once. Set aside ¼ cup of the glaze.
2. Sprinkle chicken with ⅛ teaspoon of the salt and ⅛ teaspoon of the pepper. Place chicken on the unheated rack of a broiler pan. Broil 4 to 5 inches from heat for 12 to 15 minutes or until chicken is tender and no longer pink (170°F), turning once and brushing with the remaining glaze during the last 5 minutes of broiling.
3. Meanwhile, lightly coat an unheated large saucepan with nonstick cooking spray. Preheat on medium heat. Add apples, onion, and garlic; cook and stir for 3 minutes. Stir in the reserved ¼ cup glaze; bring to boiling. Add spinach; toss just until wilted. Sprinkle with the remaining ⅛ teaspoon salt and ⅛ teaspoon pepper.
4. Serve chicken with spinach mixture.
MAKES 4 SERVINGS

Per serving: 268 cal., 2 g total fat (0 g sat. fat), 66 mg chol., 588 mg sodium, 35 g carbo., 4 g fiber, 30 g pro.

Chicken à l'Orange

Start to Finish: 20 minutes

4 skinless, boneless chicken breast halves
½ teaspoon salt
¼ teaspoon black pepper
1 tablespoon vegetable oil
¾ cup chopped green onions (6)
⅓ cup chicken broth
1 teaspoon cornstarch
2 navel oranges, peeled and sectioned, reserving any juice
1 tablespoon orange-flavor liqueur (such as Triple Sec) or orange juice
Dash cayenne pepper

1. Sprinkle chicken with salt and black pepper. In a large skillet heat oil on medium heat. Cook chicken in hot oil for 8 to 12 minutes or until chicken is no longer pink (170°F), turning once. Transfer chicken to a serving platter; keep warm.
2. For sauce, add ½ cup of the green onions to skillet; cook and stir about 3 minutes or until tender. In a small bowl stir together chicken broth and cornstarch; add to skillet. Stir in orange sections, reserved orange juice, and liqueur; cook and stir until thickened and bubbly. Cook and stir for 2 minutes more. Spoon sauce and oranges over chicken. Sprinkle with the remaining ¼ cup green onions and the cayenne pepper. **MAKES 4 SERVINGS**

Per serving: 275 cal., 6 g total fat (1 g sat. fat), 99 mg chol., 481 mg sodium, 12 g carbo., 1 g fiber, 40 g pro.

JERK CHICKEN BREASTS

Jerk Chicken Breasts

Prep: 20 minutes **Chill:** 30 minutes to 24 hours
Grill: 6 minutes

- 6 skinless, boneless chicken breast halves (about 2 pounds)
- 4 teaspoons Jamaican jerk seasoning
- 8 cloves garlic, minced
- 2 teaspoons snipped fresh thyme or ½ teaspoon dried thyme, crushed
- 2 teaspoons finely shredded lemon peel
- 2 tablespoons lemon juice
  Olive oil cooking spray or 2 teaspoons olive oil
  Lemon wedges

1. Place a chicken breast half between sheets of plastic wrap; pound gently with the flat side of a meat mallet until an even ½ inch thickness. Repeat with remaining chicken. In a small bowl combine jerk seasoning, garlic, thyme, and lemon peel. Brush chicken breasts with lemon juice. Sprinkle garlic mixture evenly over chicken breasts; rub in with your fingers. Place chicken in a resealable plastic bag set in a shallow dish; seal bag. Chill in the refrigerator for 30 minutes to 24 hours.
2. Lightly coat chicken with olive oil cooking spray or brush lightly with olive oil.
3. For a charcoal grill, place chicken on the grill rack of an uncovered grill directly over medium coals. Grill for 6 to 10 minutes or until chicken is tender and no longer pink, turning once halfway through grilling. (For a gas grill, preheat grill. Reduce heat to medium. Place chicken on grill rack over heat. Cover and grill as above.)
4. To serve, slice chicken; pass lemon wedges. **MAKES 6 SERVINGS**

Broiler method Preheat broiler. Place chicken on the unheated rack of a broiler pan. Broil 3 to 4 inches from heat for 6 to 10 minutes or until chicken is tender and no longer pink, turning once halfway through broiling.

Per serving: 180 cal., 2 g total fat (1 g sat. fat), 88 mg chol., 283 mg sodium, 2 g carbo., 0 g fiber, 35 g pro.

FETA-STUFFED CHICKEN BREASTS

Feta-Stuffed Chicken Breasts

Prep: 20 minutes **Stand:** 10 minutes
Cook: 12 minutes

- 1 tablespoon snipped dried tomatoes (not oil-packed)
- 4 skinless, boneless chicken breast halves (1 to 1½ pounds)
- ¼ cup crumbled feta cheese (1 ounce)
- 2 tablespoons softened fat-free cream cheese (1 ounce)
- 2 teaspoons snipped fresh basil or ½ teaspoon dried basil, crushed
- ⅛ teaspoon black pepper
- 1 teaspoon olive oil
  Fresh basil sprigs (optional)

1. Place tomatoes in a small bowl. Pour enough boiling water over the tomatoes to cover. Let stand for 10 minutes. Drain and pat dry; set aside.

2. Meanwhile, using a sharp knife, cut a pocket in each chicken breast by cutting horizontally through the thickest portion to, but not through, the opposite side. Set aside. In a small bowl combine feta, cream cheese, the 2 teaspoons basil, and the tomatoes. Spoon about 1 rounded tablespoon of the feta mixture into each pocket. If necessary, secure openings with wooden toothpicks. Sprinkle chicken with pepper.
3. In a large nonstick skillet heat oil on medium-high heat. Cook chicken in hot oil for 12 to 14 minutes or until tender and no longer pink, turning once (reduce heat to medium if chicken browns too quickly). Serve warm. If desired, garnish with basil sprigs.
MAKES 4 SERVINGS

Per serving: 168 cal., 5 g total fat (2 g sat. fat), 75 mg chol., 221 mg sodium, 1 g carbo., 0 g fiber, 29 g pro.

GREEK-STYLE CHICKEN SKILLET

*Tip For 2 cups cooked couscous, in a small saucepan bring 1 cup water and dash salt to boiling. Stir in ⅔ cup quick-cooking couscous. Remove from heat. Cover and let stand for 5 minutes. Fluff with a fork before serving.

Per serving: 401 cal., 10 g total fat (4 g sat. fat), 99 mg chol., 827 mg sodium, 36 g carbo., 4 g fiber, 41 g pro.

Keys-Style Citrus Chicken

Start to Finish: 25 minutes

    1 tablespoon canola oil
    4 skinless, boneless chicken breast halves
       (1 to 1¼ pounds)
    3 cloves garlic, peeled and thinly sliced
    1 teaspoon finely shredded lime peel
    2 tablespoons lime juice
    2 teaspoons snipped fresh cilantro
    ⅛ teaspoon crushed red pepper
    1 medium orange

1. In a large skillet heat oil on medium heat. Add chicken and garlic; cook for 8 to 10 minutes or until chicken is no longer pink (170°F), turning chicken once and stirring garlic occasionally.
2. Meanwhile, in a small bowl combine lime peel, lime juice, cilantro, and crushed red pepper; set aside. Peel and coarsely chop orange. Add lime juice mixture to skillet. Place chopped orange on chicken. Cover and cook for 1 to 2 minutes more or until heated through.
3. Serve any pan juices with chicken and chopped orange. **MAKES 4 SERVINGS**

Per serving: 175 cal., 5 g total fat (1 g sat. fat), 66 mg chol., 60 mg sodium, 5 g carbo., 1 g fiber, 26 g pro.

Greek-Style Chicken Skillet

Start to Finish: 40 minutes

    4   skinless, boneless chicken breast halves
        (about 1¼ pounds)
        Salt and black pepper
    1   tablespoon olive oil
    1½ cups sliced zucchini (1 medium)
    ¾   cup chopped green sweet pepper
    1   medium onion, sliced and separated
        into rings
    2   cloves garlic, minced
    ⅛   teaspoon black pepper
    ¼   cup water
    1   10.75-ounce can condensed tomato soup
    2   cups hot cooked couscous*
    ½   cup crumbled feta cheese (2 ounces)
        Lemon wedges

1. Sprinkle chicken with salt and black pepper. In a large skillet heat olive oil on medium heat. Add chicken; cook for 12 to 15 minutes or until no longer pink (170°F), turning once. Remove chicken from skillet; keep warm.
2. Add zucchini, sweet pepper, onion, garlic, and the ⅛ teaspoon black pepper to skillet. Add the water; reduce heat. Cover and cook for 5 minutes, stirring once or twice. Stir in tomato soup. Bring to boiling; reduce heat. Simmer, covered, for 5 minutes, stirring once.
3. To serve, divide couscous among 4 dinner plates. Place chicken on couscous. Spoon vegetable mixture over chicken and couscous. Sprinkle servings with feta cheese. Serve with lemon wedges. **MAKES 4 SERVINGS**

ROSEMARY CHICKEN WITH VEGETABLES

Tortilla-Crusted Chicken

Prep: 10 minutes **Bake:** 25 minutes
Oven: 375°F

　　Nonstick cooking spray
1　cup finely crushed multigrain tortilla chips
½　teaspoon dried oregano, crushed
¼　teaspoon ground cumin
¼　teaspoon freshly ground black pepper
1　egg
4　skinless, boneless chicken breast halves
　　(about 1¼ pounds)
　　Shredded romaine (optional)
　　Purchased salsa (optional)
　　Avocado slices (optional)

1. Preheat oven to 375°F. Coat a 15×10×1-inch baking pan with nonstick cooking spray; set aside. In a shallow dish combine tortilla chips, oregano, cumin, and pepper. Place egg in another shallow dish; beat lightly. Dip chicken in beaten egg, then coat with tortilla chip mixture.

2. Arrange chicken in the prepared baking pan. Bake about 25 minutes or until chicken is no longer pink (170°F). If desired, serve chicken on a bed of shredded romaine with salsa and avocado slices. **MAKES 4 SERVINGS**

Per serving: 230 cal., 6 g total fat (1 g sat. fat), 135 mg chol., 143 mg sodium, 7 g carbo., 1 g fiber, 35 g pro.

Rosemary Chicken with Vegetables

Start to Finish: 30 minutes

4　medium skinless, boneless chicken breast halves
½　teaspoon lemon-pepper seasoning
1　tablespoon olive oil
2　cloves garlic, minced
2　medium zucchini and/or yellow summer squash, halved lengthwise and cut crosswise into ¼-inch slices (2½ cups)
½　cup apple juice
2　teaspoons snipped fresh rosemary or ½ teaspoon dried rosemary, crushed
¼　teaspoon salt

2　tablespoons dry white wine or apple juice
2　teaspoons cornstarch
12　cherry tomatoes, halved (1 cup)
3　cups hot cooked couscous*
　　Fresh rosemary sprigs (optional)

1. Sprinkle chicken with lemon-pepper seasoning. In a large skillet heat olive oil on medium-high heat. Cook chicken in hot oil until brown, turning once. Cook on medium heat for 8 to 10 minutes more or until chicken is tender and no longer pink (170°F), turning once. Reduce heat to medium-low if chicken gets too brown. Transfer chicken to a platter; cover and keep warm.

2. Add garlic to skillet; cook and stir for 15 seconds. Add zucchini, apple juice, rosemary, and salt. Bring to boiling; reduce heat. Simmer, covered, for 2 minutes.

3. In a small bowl stir together wine and cornstarch until smooth; add to zucchini mixture in skillet. Cook and stir until thickened and bubbly; cook and stir for 2 minutes more. Stir in tomatoes. Serve vegetables and couscous with chicken. If desired, garnish with rosemary sprigs. **MAKES 4 SERVINGS**

*Tip For 3 cups cooked couscous, in a small saucepan bring 1½ cups water and ⅛ teaspoon salt to boiling. Stir in 1 cup quick-cooking couscous. Remove from heat. Cover and let stand for 5 minutes. Fluff with a fork before serving.

Per serving: 377 cal., 6 g total fat (1 g sat. fat), 82 mg chol., 378 mg sodium, 38 g carbo., 3 g fiber, 39 g pro.

GINGER CHICKEN STIR-FRY

Pasta and Sweet Peppers ♡

Start to Finish: 25 minutes

- 8 ounces dried whole wheat or multigrain rotini pasta (about 3¼ cups)
- 1 16-ounce package frozen yellow, green, and red peppers and onions stir-fry vegetables
  Nonstick cooking spray
- 12 ounces skinless, boneless chicken breasts, cut into bite-size pieces
- 4 cloves garlic, minced
- 1 cup chopped plum tomatoes
- ⅓ cup purchased dried tomato pesto
- ¼ cup snipped fresh basil
- ¼ cup finely shredded Parmesan cheese (1 ounce)
  Fresh basil leaves (optional)

1. In a large pot cook pasta according to package directions, adding stir-fry vegetables for the last 2 minutes of cooking.* Drain well; return to hot pot. Cover and keep warm.
2. Meanwhile, coat an unheated large nonstick skillet with nonstick cooking spray. Preheat on medium-high heat. Add chicken and garlic to hot skillet. Cook and stir for 3 to 4 minutes or until chicken is no longer pink.
3. Add chicken mixture to cooked pasta mixture along with tomatoes, pesto, and snipped basil. Toss to coat. Sprinkle with Parmesan cheese. If desired, garnish with fresh basil. **MAKES 6 SERVINGS**

*Tip Slowly add vegetables to pasta to prevent the water from cooling down too quickly. If water does stop boiling, return it to boiling, then begin timing for 2 minutes.

Per serving: 296 cal., 7 g total fat (2 g sat. fat), 36 mg chol., 199 mg sodium, 37 g carbo., 4 g fiber, 22 g pro.

Ginger Chicken Stir-Fry

Start to Finish: 25 minutes

- 1 tablespoon vegetable oil or peanut oil
- 2½ cups shredded green cabbage
- 1¼ cups sliced zucchini (1 medium)
- 1 small red sweet pepper, cut into strips
- ½ cup sliced carrot (1 medium)
- 1 medium onion, sliced
- 12 ounces skinless, boneless chicken breast halves or turkey tenderloins, cut into 1-inch pieces
- ½ cup bottled stir-fry sauce
- ½ teaspoon ground ginger
- 3 to 4 cups hot cooked white or brown rice
- ¾ cup chopped peanuts or cashews

1. In a wok or very large skillet heat oil on medium-high heat. Add half of the cabbage, zucchini, sweet pepper, carrot, and onion; stir-fry for 2 minutes or until crisp-tender. Remove vegetables from wok. Repeat with the remaining vegetables; remove from wok.
2. If necessary, add more oil to hot wok. Add chicken. Stir-fry for 3 to 5 minutes or until chicken is no longer pink. Push chicken from center of the wok. Add stir-fry sauce and ginger to center of the wok. Cook and stir until bubbly. Return vegetables to wok. Cook and stir about 1 minute more or until heated through. Serve over hot cooked rice. Sprinkle with nuts. **MAKES 6 SERVINGS**

Per serving: 355 cal., 14 g total fat (2 g sat. fat), 33 mg chol., 816 mg sodium, 37 g carbo., 5 g fiber, 22 g pro.

Mediterranean Pizza Skillet

Start to Finish: 30 minutes

- 2 tablespoons olive oil
- 3 skinless, boneless chicken breast halves, cut into ¾-inch pieces
- 2 cloves garlic, minced
- 4 plum tomatoes, chopped
- 1 14-ounce can artichoke hearts, drained and quartered
- 1 2.25-ounce can sliced pitted ripe olives, drained
- ½ teaspoon dried Italian seasoning, crushed
- ¼ teaspoon black pepper
- 2 cups romaine lettuce or hearty mesclun, chopped
- 1 cup crumbled feta cheese (4 ounces)
- ⅓ cup fresh basil leaves, shredded or torn
- 4 slices crusty Italian or French bread, toasted

1. In a large skillet heat oil on medium heat. Cook chicken and garlic in hot oil until chicken is brown. Stir in tomatoes, artichoke hearts, olives, Italian seasoning, and pepper. Bring to boiling; reduce heat. Simmer, covered, about 10 minutes or until chicken is no longer pink.

2. Top chicken mixture with romaine and cheese. Cover and cook for 1 to 2 minutes more or until romaine starts to wilt. Sprinkle with basil. Serve with bread. **MAKES 4 SERVINGS**

Per serving: 395 cal., 17 g total fat (6 g sat. fat), 82 mg chol., 1,003 mg sodium, 27 g carbo., 6 g fiber, 33 g pro.

Ginger Chicken with Rice Noodles

Prep: 20 minutes **Grill:** 12 minutes

- 2 tablespoons very finely chopped green onion
- 1½ teaspoons grated fresh ginger
- 3 cloves garlic, minced
- 3 teaspoons olive oil
- ⅛ teaspoon salt
- 2 skinless, boneless chicken breast halves (about 10 ounces)
- 2 ounces dried rice noodles
- ½ cup chopped carrot (1 medium)
- ½ teaspoon finely shredded lime peel
- 1 tablespoon lime juice
- 1 to 2 tablespoons snipped fresh cilantro
- 2 tablespoons coarsely chopped peanuts

1. For rub, in a small bowl combine green onion, ginger, garlic, 1 teaspoon of the olive oil, and the salt. Sprinkle evenly over chicken; rub in with your fingers.

2. For a charcoal grill, place chicken on the rack of an uncovered grill directly over medium coals. Grill for 12 to 15 minutes or until tender and no longer pink (170°F), turning once. (For a gas grill, preheat grill. Reduce heat to medium. Place chicken on grill rack over heat. Cover and grill as above.) Thinly slice chicken diagonally; set aside.

3. Meanwhile, in a large saucepan cook rice noodles and carrot in a large amount of boiling water for 3 to 4 minutes or just until noodles are tender; drain. Rinse with cold water; drain again. Use kitchen scissors to snip noodles into short lengths. In a medium bowl stir together lime peel, lime juice, and the remaining 2 teaspoons oil. Add noodle mixture and cilantro; toss gently to coat.

4. Divide noodle mixture between 2 individual bowls; arrange chicken slices on noodle mixture. Sprinkle with peanuts. Serve immediately. **MAKES 2 SERVINGS**

Per serving: 396 cal., 13 g total fat (2 g sat. fat), 82 mg chol., 369 mg sodium, 32 g carbo., 3 g fiber, 37 g pro.

VERDE CHICKEN ENCHILADAS

Verde Chicken Enchiladas

Prep: 35 minutes **Bake:** 30 minutes
Oven: 350°F

1 18-ounce tub refrigerated taco sauce with shredded chicken
2 cups shredded asadero, queso quesadilla, or Monterey Jack cheese (8 ounces)
⅓ cup thinly sliced green onions
1 16-ounce jar green salsa
12 6-inch corn tortillas
  Assorted toppers (such as purchased salsa, sour cream, guacamole, shredded lettuce, chopped tomato, and/or sliced ripe olives) (optional)

1. Preheat oven to 350°F. In a large bowl combine chicken, 1 cup of the cheese, and the green onions.
2. Spread ¼ cup of the green salsa in the bottom of a 3-quart rectangular baking dish. In a small saucepan heat the remaining green salsa until warm. Spread a little warm salsa over 1 of the tortillas; fill with about ¼ cup of the chicken mixture, spooning chicken mixture just below the center of tortilla. Roll up tortilla and place, seam side down, in baking dish. Repeat with remaining tortillas and remaining chicken mixture. Pour any remaining warm salsa over enchiladas. Sprinkle with the remaining 1 cup cheese.
3. Cover dish with tented foil and bake for 30 to 35 minutes or until heated through. If desired, serve with assorted toppers.
MAKES 6 SERVINGS

Per serving: 364 cal., 12 g total fat (6 g sat. fat), 71 mg chol., 1,317 mg sodium, 41 g carbo., 5 g fiber, 21 g pro.

Southwest Chicken Burgers

Prep: 15 minutes **Grill:** 14 minutes

1 egg, lightly beaten
¼ cup crushed nacho-flavor or plain tortilla chips
3 tablespoons finely chopped green sweet pepper
¾ teaspoon chili powder
¼ teaspoon salt
¼ teaspoon black pepper
1 pound uncooked ground chicken
4 Cheesy Corn Bread Slices
1 cup shredded Monterey Jack cheese with jalapeño peppers (4 ounces)
1 medium avocado, halved, seeded, peeled, and sliced (optional)
  Lettuce leaves (optional)
  Red onion slices (optional)
  Purchased or homemade salsa (optional)

1. In a large bowl combine egg, crushed tortilla chips, sweet pepper, chili powder, salt, and black pepper. Add chicken; mix well. Shape the chicken mixture into four ¾-inch-thick patties.

2. For a charcoal grill, grill patties on the rack of an uncovered grill directly over medium coals for 14 to 18 minutes or until no longer pink (165°F), turning once halfway through grilling. Add Cheesy Corn Bread Slices to grill during the last 2 minutes of grilling, turning once. Top burgers with cheese during the last 1 minute of grilling. (For a gas grill, preheat grill. Reduce heat to medium. Place patties on grill rack over heat. Cover; grill as above, adding Corn Bread Slices during the last 2 minutes.)
3. Serve patties on toasted Cheesy Corn Bread Slices. If desired, serve with avocado, lettuce, onion, and salsa. **MAKES 4 SERVINGS**

Cheesy Corn Bread Slices Preheat oven to 400°F. In a large bowl combine 1½ cups all-purpose flour, 1 cup yellow cornmeal, ¼ cup sugar, 4 teaspoons baking powder, and 1 teaspoon salt. In a small bowl whisk together 3 eggs, 1½ cups milk, and ⅓ cup vegetable oil; add all at once to flour mixture. Stir just until moistened. Fold in 1 cup shredded cheddar cheese (4 ounces). Pour batter into a well-greased 8×4×2-inch loaf pan. Bake about 30 minutes or until a wooden toothpick inserted in center comes out clean. Cool in pan on a wire rack for 10 minutes. Remove from pan; cool completely. Wrap and store corn bread overnight before slicing. Cut corn bread in half crosswise. Reserve half of the corn bread for another use. If desired, freeze in an airtight freezer container or bag for up to 3 months. Cut remaining half of corn bread into 4 lengthwise slices.

Per serving: 522 cal., 26 g total fat (5 g sat. fat), 66 mg chol., 698 mg sodium, 39 g carbo., 4 g fiber, 32 g pro.

CURRIED CHICKEN SKILLET

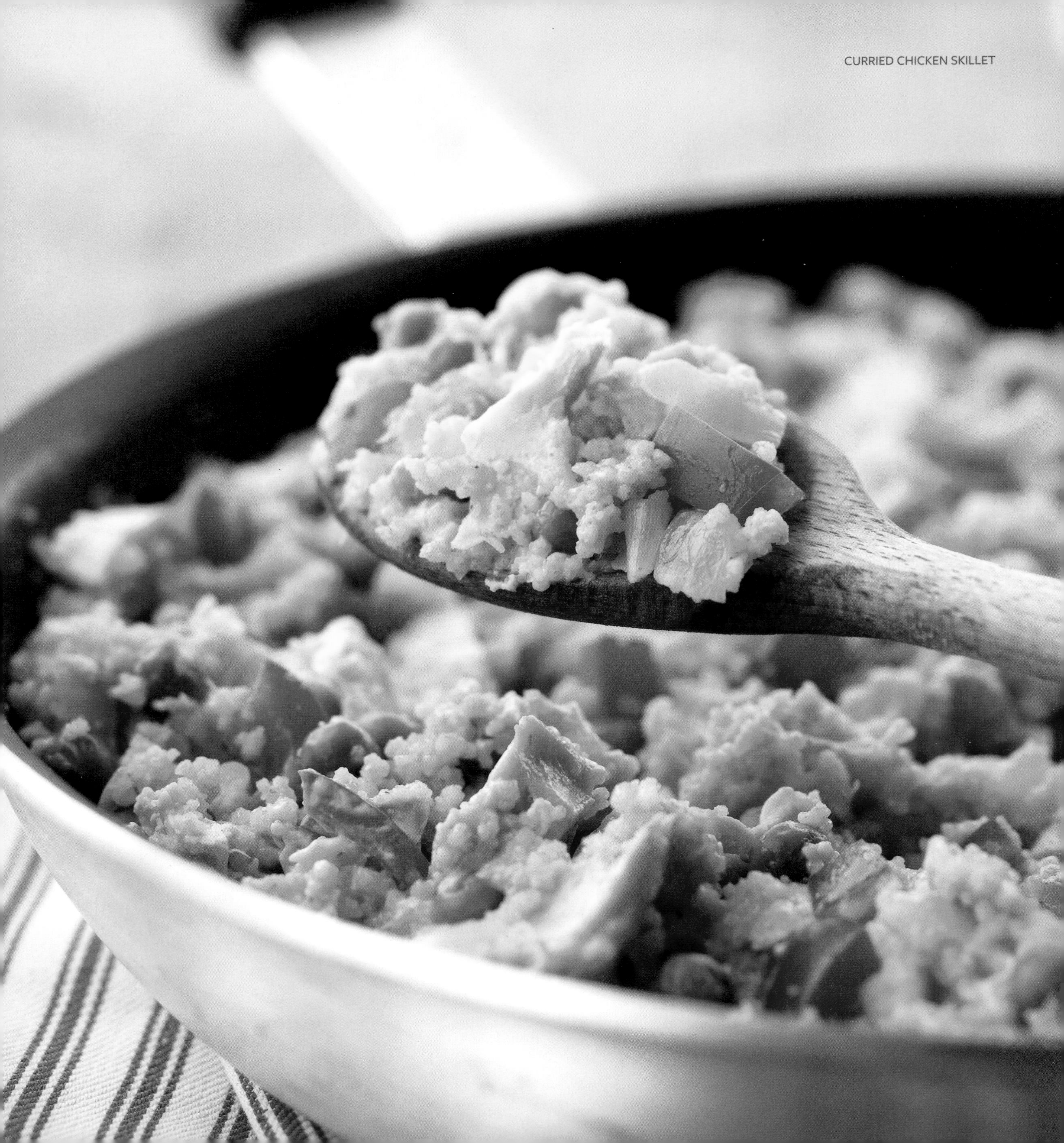

Curried Chicken Skillet ♥

Start to Finish: 25 minutes

    Nonstick cooking spray
1 cup chopped onion (1 large)
2 teaspoons curry powder
1⅓ cups water
⅔ cup whole wheat couscous
2 cups chopped cooked chicken breast (about 12 ounces)
1 cup frozen peas
1 cup chopped red sweet pepper (1 large)
½ cup light mayonnaise or salad dressing
3 tablespoons bottled mango chutney

1. Lightly coat an unheated large skillet with nonstick cooking spray. Preheat skillet on medium heat. Add onion; cook and stir until onion is crisp-tender. Stir in curry powder; cook for 1 minute more. Add the water and couscous to skillet; bring to boiling. Stir in chicken, peas, sweet pepper, mayonnaise, and chutney; return to boiling. Remove from heat. Cover and let stand for 5 minutes. **MAKES 6 SERVINGS**

Per serving: 287 cal., 9 g total fat (2 g sat. fat), 47 mg chol., 244 mg sodium, 33 g carbo., 5 g fiber, 20 g pro.

Roasted Pepper and Artichoke Pizza

Prep: 25 minutes **Bake:** 13 minutes
Oven: 425°F

1 12-inch whole wheat Italian bread shell (such as Boboli brand)
½ cup pizza sauce
1 cup coarsely chopped or shredded cooked chicken breast (about 5 ounces)
½ of a 14-ounce can artichoke hearts, drained and coarsely chopped
1 cup bottled roasted red sweet peppers, drained and cut into strips
¼ cup sliced green onions (2) or chopped red onion
¾ cup shredded reduced-fat mozzarella cheese (3 ounces)
2 ounces semisoft goat cheese (chèvre), crumbled

ROASTED PEPPER AND ARTICHOKE PIZZA

1. Preheat oven to 425°F. Place bread shell on a large baking sheet.
2. Spread pizza sauce evenly on crust. Top with chicken, artichokes, roasted red peppers, and green onions. Top with mozzarella cheese and goat cheese.
3. Bake for 13 to 15 minutes or until toppings are hot and cheese is melted. **MAKES 4 SERVINGS**

Per serving: 383 cal., 12 g total fat (6 g sat. fat), 52 mg chol., 935 mg sodium, 43 g carbo., 8 g fiber, 28 g pro.

Barbecue Quesadillas

Prep: 20 minutes **Cook:** 6 minutes per batch

    Nonstick cooking spray
4 7- or 8-inch flour tortillas
1 cup shredded extra-sharp cheddar cheese or Mexican-style four-cheese blend (4 ounces)
1 4-ounce can diced green chile peppers, drained
1 18-ounce tub refrigerated shredded chicken with barbecue sauce (2 cups)
1 cup bottled salsa
¼ cup sour cream
¼ cup sliced green onions (2)

1. Coat one side of each tortilla with nonstick cooking spray. Place, coated sides down, on cutting board or waxed paper. Sprinkle ¼ cup of the cheese over half of each tortilla. Top with chile peppers and barbecued chicken. Fold tortillas in half, pressing gently.
2. Heat a large nonstick skillet on medium heat. Cook quesadillas, 2 at a time, in hot skillet for 6 to 8 minutes or until golden brown, turning once. Remove quesadillas from skillet; place on a baking sheet. Keep warm in a 300°F oven for up to 30 minutes. Repeat with remaining quesadillas. To serve, cut each quesadilla into 3 wedges. Serve with salsa, sour cream, and green onions. **MAKES 4 SERVINGS**

Per serving: 469 cal., 21 g total fat (10 g sat. fat), 86 mg chol., 1,606 mg sodium, 44 g carbo., 2 g fiber, 25 g pro.

TURKEY TENDERLOINS WITH CILANTRO PESTO

Grilled Turkey Mole ♥

Prep: 30 minutes **Marinate:** 2 to 4 hours
Grill: 8 minutes

- 2 turkey breast tenderloins (about 1½ pounds)
- ¼ cup lime juice
- 1 tablespoon chili powder
- 2 teaspoons bottled hot pepper sauce
- 1 tablespoon canola oil
- ⅓ cup finely chopped onion (1 small)
- 1 clove garlic, minced
- 1 cup chopped tomato (1 large)
- 2 tablespoons canned diced green chile peppers
- 1 teaspoon unsweetened cocoa powder
- 1 teaspoon chili powder
- ⅛ teaspoon salt
  Fat-free sour cream (optional)

1. Split each turkey breast tenderloin in half horizontally. Place turkey in a resealable plastic bag set in a shallow dish. For marinade, in a small bowl stir together lime juice, the 1 tablespoon chili powder, and the hot pepper sauce. Pour over turkey. Seal bag; turn to coat turkey. Marinate in the refrigerator for 2 to 4 hours, turning bag occasionally.
2. For mole sauce, in a small saucepan heat oil on medium heat. Add onion and garlic; cook and stir for 4 to 5 minutes or until onion is tender. Stir in tomato, chile peppers, cocoa powder, the 1 teaspoon chili powder, and the salt. Bring to boiling; reduce heat. Simmer, covered, for 10 minutes. Remove from heat; set aside.
3. Drain turkey, discarding marinade. For a charcoal grill, place turkey on the lightly greased rack of an uncovered grill directly over medium coals. Grill for 8 to 10 minutes or until turkey is tender and no longer pink (170°F), turning once halfway through grilling. (For a gas grill, preheat grill. Reduce heat to medium. Place turkey on grill rack over heat. Cover and grill as above.) Serve turkey with mole sauce and, if desired, sour cream.
MAKES 4 SERVINGS

Per serving: 247 cal., 5 g total fat (1 g sat. fat), 105 mg chol., 223 mg sodium, 6 g carbo., 2 g fiber, 44 g pro.

Turkey Tenderloins with Cilantro Pesto

Prep: 20 minutes **Grill:** 12 minutes

- 1 pound turkey breast tenderloins
- ¾ cup lightly packed fresh cilantro sprigs
- 3 tablespoons walnuts
- 2 tablespoons olive oil
- 2 tablespoons lime juice
- 1 clove garlic, minced
- ⅛ teaspoon salt
- ¼ teaspoon salt
- ¼ teaspoon black pepper
  Lime wedges (optional)

1. Split each turkey breast tenderloin in half horizontally; set aside. For pesto, in a blender combine cilantro, walnuts, olive oil, lime juice, garlic, and the ⅛ teaspoon salt. Cover and blend until nearly smooth. Cover and store in the refrigerator until ready to use.
2. Sprinkle turkey with the ¼ teaspoon salt and the pepper. For a charcoal grill, place turkey on the rack of an uncovered grill directly over medium coals. Grill for 7 minutes; turn. Brush lightly with half of the pesto. Grill for 5 to 8 minutes more or until no longer pink (170°F). (For a gas grill, preheat grill. Reduce heat to medium. Place turkey on grill rack over heat. Cover and grill as above.)
3. Slice into serving-size pieces. Serve with the remaining pesto. If desired, serve with lime wedges to squeeze over turkey.
MAKES 4 SERVINGS

Per serving: 228 cal., 11 g total fat (2 g sat. fat), 70 mg chol., 268 mg sodium, 2 g carbo., 1 g fiber, 29 g pro.

CREOLE TURKEY MEATBALLS

Pineapple Turkey Kabobs ♡

Prep: 15 minutes **Marinate:** 4 to 24 hours
Grill: 12 minutes

 12 ounces turkey breast tenderloin, cut into
      1-inch cubes
 ⅓ cup unsweetened pineapple juice
 3 tablespoons rum or unsweetened
      pineapple juice
 1 tablespoon finely chopped fresh
      lemongrass or 2 teaspoons finely
      shredded lemon peel
 1 tablespoon olive oil
 1 medium red onion, cut into thin wedges
 2 plums or 1 nectarine, pitted and cut into
      thick slices
 1½ cups fresh or canned pineapple chunks
 2 cups hot cooked brown rice
 ¼ cup thinly sliced sugar snap peas

1. Place turkey in a resealable plastic bag set
in a shallow dish. For marinade, in a bowl
combine the ⅓ cup pineapple juice, the rum,
lemongrass, and olive oil. Pour over turkey;
close bag. Marinate in the refrigerator for 4 to
24 hours, turning bag occasionally.
2. Drain turkey, reserving marinade. In a small
saucepan bring marinade to boiling. Boil
gently, uncovered, for 1 minute. Remove from
heat. On eight 10- to 12-inch skewers,
alternately thread turkey and onion, leaving
about a ¼-inch space between each piece.
Thread plums and pineapple onto 4 skewers.
3. For a charcoal grill, grill turkey and fruit
kabobs on the rack of an uncovered grill
directly over medium coals until turkey and
onion are tender, turkey is no longer pink, and
fruit is heated through, turning once and
brushing occasionally with marinade during
the last half of grilling. (Allow 12 to 14 minutes
for turkey and onion and about 5 minutes for
fruit.) (For a gas grill, preheat grill. Reduce
heat to medium. Place turkey and fruit kabobs
on grill rack over heat. Cover and grill as above.)
4. To serve, toss hot cooked rice with snap
peas; serve turkey, onion, and fruit with rice.
MAKES 4 SERVINGS

Per serving: 326 cal., 5 g total fat (1 g sat. fat), 53 mg
chol., 41 mg sodium, 39 g carbo., 3 g fiber, 24 g pro.

Creole Turkey Meatballs

Prep: 15 minutes **Bake:** 25 minutes
Oven: 375°F

      Nonstick cooking spray
 ¾ cup chopped green sweet pepper
      (1 medium)
 ½ cup chopped onion (1 medium)
 ½ cup quick-cooking rolled oats
 ¼ cup refrigerated or frozen egg product,
      thawed, or 1 egg, lightly beaten
 2 tablespoons fat-free milk
 2 cloves garlic, minced
 1 teaspoon dried Italian seasoning, crushed
 1 teaspoon salt-free seasoning blend
 1 teaspoon Creole seasoning
 1 pound uncooked ground turkey

1. Preheat oven to 375°F. Lightly coat a
15×10×1-inch baking pan with nonstick
cooking spray; set aside. In a large bowl combine
sweet pepper, onion, rolled oats, egg, milk, garlic,
Italian seasoning, salt-free seasoning blend, and
Creole seasoning. Add turkey; mix well.
2. Using a small ice cream scoop or slightly
rounded measuring tablespoon, shape turkey
mixture into 1¼-inch balls. Arrange in
prepared pan.
3. Bake, uncovered, about 25 minutes or
until browned and no longer pink in center
(165°F).* **MAKES 10 SERVINGS**

*Tip The internal color of a meatball is not a
reliable doneness indicator. A turkey meatball
cooked to 165°F is safe, regardless of color.
To measure the doneness of a meatball,
insert an instant-read thermometer into the
center of the meatball.

Per serving: 94 cal., 4 g total fat (1 g sat. fat), 36 mg
chol., 104 mg sodium, 5 g carbo., 1 g fiber, 9 g pro.

PINEAPPLE TURKEY KABOBS

GREEK-STYLE TURKEY BURGERS

Turkey and Wild Rice Pilaf ♡

Prep: 25 minutes **Cook:** 45 minutes

- 1 tablespoon olive oil
- 1 cup sliced celery (2 stalks)
- ½ cup chopped onion (1 medium)
- ½ cup wild rice, rinsed and drained
- ½ cup uncooked regular brown rice
- 1 14-ounce can reduced-sodium chicken broth
- ¾ cup water
- 1 cup carrots cut into thin bite-size strips
- 2 medium red apples, cored and coarsely chopped
- 12 ounces cooked turkey breast or chicken breast,* cubed
- ¼ cup chopped walnuts, toasted

1. In a large skillet heat oil on medium heat. Add celery and onion; cook about 5 minutes or until tender, stirring occasionally. Add uncooked wild rice and brown rice; cook and stir for 2 minutes. Add chicken broth and the water.
2. Bring to boiling; reduce heat. Simmer, covered, for 40 minutes. Stir in carrots and apples. Cover and cook for 3 to 5 minutes more or until rice and vegetables are tender.
3. Stir in cubed turkey; heat through. Top servings with walnuts. **MAKES 6 SERVINGS**

*Tip For cooked turkey breast or chicken breast, place 1 pound turkey breast tenderloins, halved horizontally, or 1 pound skinless, boneless chicken breasts in a large skillet. Add 1½ cups water. Bring to boiling; reduce heat. Simmer, covered, for 12 to 14 minutes or until turkey or chicken is no longer pink (170°F). Drain well.

Per serving: 277 cal., 7 g total fat (1 g sat. fat), 47 mg chol., 218 mg sodium, 33 g carbo., 4 g fiber, 24 g pro.

Greek-Style Turkey Burgers ♡

Prep: 20 minutes **Grill:** 12 minutes

- ⅓ cup fine dry whole wheat bread crumbs*
- 1 egg white, lightly beaten
- 1 tablespoon plain low-fat yogurt
- 1 teaspoon snipped fresh rosemary or ½ teaspoon dried rosemary, crushed
- 1 teaspoon snipped fresh oregano or ½ teaspoon dried oregano, crushed
- 1 tablespoon crumbled feta cheese
- ⅛ teaspoon black pepper
- 1 pound uncooked ground turkey breast or chicken breast
  Mixed torn greens (optional)
- 1 recipe Olive-Tomato Salsa
- ¼ cup crumbled feta cheese (1 ounce)
- 2 whole wheat pita bread rounds, halved and lightly toasted

1. In a medium bowl combine bread crumbs, egg white, the 1 tablespoon yogurt, the rosemary, oregano, the 1 tablespoon feta cheese, and the pepper. Add turkey; mix well. Shape into four ¾-inch-thick patties.
2. Place patties on the greased rack of an uncovered grill directly over medium coals. Grill for 12 to 14 minutes or until no longer pink (165°F),** turning once halfway through grilling.
3. If desired, serve burgers on greens. Top burgers with Olive-Tomato Salsa and the ¼ cup feta cheese. Serve with pita bread.
MAKES 4 SERVINGS

Olive-Tomato Salsa In a small bowl stir together 1 cup chopped, seeded tomatoes; ¼ cup chopped, seeded cucumber; ¼ cup chopped, pitted kalamata or other ripe olives; ½ teaspoon snipped fresh rosemary or ¼ teaspoon dried rosemary, crushed; and ½ teaspoon snipped fresh oregano or ¼ teaspoon dried oregano, crushed. Makes about 1½ cups.

*Tip For bread crumbs. place 1 slice whole wheat bread, toasted, in a food processor. Cover; process until fine crumbs form.

**Tip The internal color of a burger is not a reliable doneness indicator. A turkey or chicken patty cooked to 165°F is safe, regardless of color. To measure the doneness of a patty, insert an instant-read thermometer through the side of the patty to a depth of 2 to 3 inches.

Per serving: 278 cal., 9 g total fat (3 g sat. fat), 26 mg chol., 379 mg sodium, 39 g carbo., 2 g fiber, 13 g pro.

TURKEY TETRAZZINI

Turkey Tetrazzini ♡

Prep: 30 minutes **Bake:** 10 minutes
Oven: 400°F

- 2 cups sliced fresh cremini, stemmed shiitake, or button mushrooms
- ¾ cup chopped red and/or green sweet pepper
- ½ cup cold water
- 3 tablespoons all-purpose flour
- 1 12-ounce can evaporated fat-free milk
- ½ teaspoon instant chicken bouillon granules
- ⅛ teaspoon salt
- ⅛ teaspoon black pepper
  Dash ground nutmeg
- 4 ounces dried whole wheat spaghetti, cooked and drained
- 1 cup chopped cooked turkey breast or chicken breast (5 ounces)
- ¼ cup finely shredded Parmesan cheese (1 ounce)
- 2 tablespoons snipped fresh parsley
  Nonstick cooking spray

1. Preheat oven to 400°F. In a covered large saucepan cook mushrooms and sweet pepper in a small amount of boiling water for 3 to 6 minutes or until the vegetables are tender. Drain well; return to saucepan.

3. In a screw-top jar combine the ½ cup cold water and the flour; cover and shake until well mixed. Stir flour mixture into the vegetable mixture in saucepan. Stir in evaporated milk, bouillon granules, salt, black pepper, and nutmeg. Cook and stir until thickened and bubbly. Stir in the cooked spaghetti, turkey, Parmesan cheese, and parsley.

4. Lightly coat a 2-quart square baking dish with nonstick cooking spray. Spoon spaghetti mixture into dish. Bake, covered, for 10 to 15 minutes or until heated through.
MAKES 6 SERVINGS

Per serving: 202 cal., 2 g total fat (1 g sat. fat), 24 mg chol., 253 mg sodium, 32 g carbo., 2 g fiber, 17 g pro.

Turkey Enchiladas

Prep: 20 minutes **Bake:** 35 minutes
Oven: 375°F

  Nonstick cooking spray
- 2 to 2½ cups shredded cooked turkey (10 to 12 ounces)
- 1 14.5-ounce can no-salt-added diced tomatoes
- 1 15-ounce can black beans, rinsed and drained
- 1½ cups bottled salsa
- ¾ cup shredded Colby and Monterey Jack cheese (3 ounces)
- ½ cup light sour cream
- ⅓ cup sliced green onions
- ¼ cup snipped fresh cilantro
- 1 teaspoon ground cumin
- ½ teaspoon salt
- ½ teaspoon black pepper
- 8 7- to 8-inch whole wheat or flour tortillas
- 1 teaspoon bottled hot pepper sauce
  Sliced green onions and snipped fresh cilantro (optional)

1. Preheat oven to 375°F. Lightly coat a 3-quart rectangular baking dish with nonstick cooking spray; set aside.

2. For filling, in a large bowl stir together turkey, half of the undrained tomatoes, the beans, ½ cup of the salsa, ½ cup of the cheese, the sour cream, the ⅓ cup green onions, ¼ cup cilantro, the cumin, salt, and pepper. Spoon about ⅔ cup filling on each tortilla. Roll up tortillas. Place enchiladas, seam sides down, in the prepared baking dish; set aside.

3. For sauce, stir together the remaining undrained tomatoes, the remaining 1 cup salsa, and the hot pepper sauce. Spoon over enchiladas. Cover with foil.

4. Bake, covered, for 30 minutes. Uncover; sprinkle with the remaining ¼ cup cheese. Bake for 5 to 10 minutes more or until heated through and cheese is melted. If desired, sprinkle with additional green onions and cilantro. **MAKES 8 SERVINGS**

Per serving: 305 cal., 26 g total fat (5 g sat. fat), 40 mg chol., 871 mg sodium, 29 g carbo., 14 g fiber, 26 g pro.

TURKEY ENCHILADAS

CHAPTER 8

Fish & Shellfish

ORANGE-GLAZED FISH

Orange-Glazed Fish

Prep: 15 minutes **Broil:** 8 minutes

- 1 pound fresh or frozen skinless fish steaks or fillets, 1 inch thick (halibut, salmon, sea bass, swordfish, tuna)
- 3 tablespoons orange marmalade
- 1 tablespoon lime juice
- 1 teaspoon prepared horseradish

1. Thaw fish, if frozen. Preheat broiler. For glaze, in a small bowl stir together orange marmalade, lime juice, and horseradish; set aside.
2. Rinse fish; pat dry with paper towels. If necessary, cut fish into 4 serving-size pieces. Place fish on the greased unheated rack of a broiler pan. Broil fish 4 inches from the heat for 8 to 12 minutes or until fish flakes easily when tested with a fork, carefully turning once halfway through broiling time and brushing with glaze during the last 2 to 3 minutes of broiling time.

MAKES 4 SERVINGS

Per serving: 274 cal., 15 g total fat (3 g sat. fat), 62 mg chol., 79 mg sodium, 10 g carbo., 0 g fiber, 23 g pro.

Asian-Glazed Fish Prepare as directed, except omit orange marmalade, lime juice, and horseradish For glaze, in a small bowl stir together 2 tablespoons hoisin sauce, 1 tablespoon soy sauce, 1 teaspoon toasted sesame oil, 1 teaspoon grated fresh ginger, and 1 clove garlic, minced. Broil fish as directed, brushing with glaze the last 2 to 3 minutes.

Sesame-Crusted Salmon

Start to Finish: 30 minutes

- 1 pound fresh or frozen skinless salmon or halibut fillets
- ½ cup mayonnaise
- ⅓ cup chopped bottled roasted red sweet pepper
- 2 teaspoons lemon juice
- 1 teaspoon snipped fresh chives
  Salt and black pepper
- ⅓ cup all-purpose flour
- 1 tablespoon white sesame seeds
- 1 tablespoon black sesame seeds*
- ¼ teaspoon salt
- ¼ cup milk
- 2 tablespoons vegetable oil
  Lemon or lime wedges (optional)
  Fresh watercress (optional)

1. Thaw fish, if frozen. Rinse fish; pat dry with paper towels. Cut into 4 serving-size pieces. Set aside.
2. For red pepper sauce, in a small bowl combine mayonnaise, roasted pepper, lemon juice, and chives. Season with salt and black pepper. Cover and chill until serving time.
3. In a shallow dish combine flour, white sesame seeds, black sesame seeds, and ¼ teaspoon salt. Place milk in another shallow dish. Dip salmon in milk. Firmly press both sides of fish in sesame seed mixture.
4. In a large skillet heat oil on medium-high heat; cook coated fish fillets in hot oil for 8 to 10 minutes or until fish flakes easily when tested with a fork, turning once. To serve, spoon red pepper sauce on dinner plates; top with fish. If desired, garnish with lemon wedges and fresh watercress.

MAKES 4 SERVINGS

*Tip If you can't find black sesame seeds, use all white sesame seeds.

Per serving: 539 cal., 44 g total fat (8 g sat. fat), 78 mg chol., 404 mg sodium, 10 g carbo., 1 g fiber, 25 g pro.

ASIAN SALMON WITH OVEN-ROASTED SWEET POTATOES

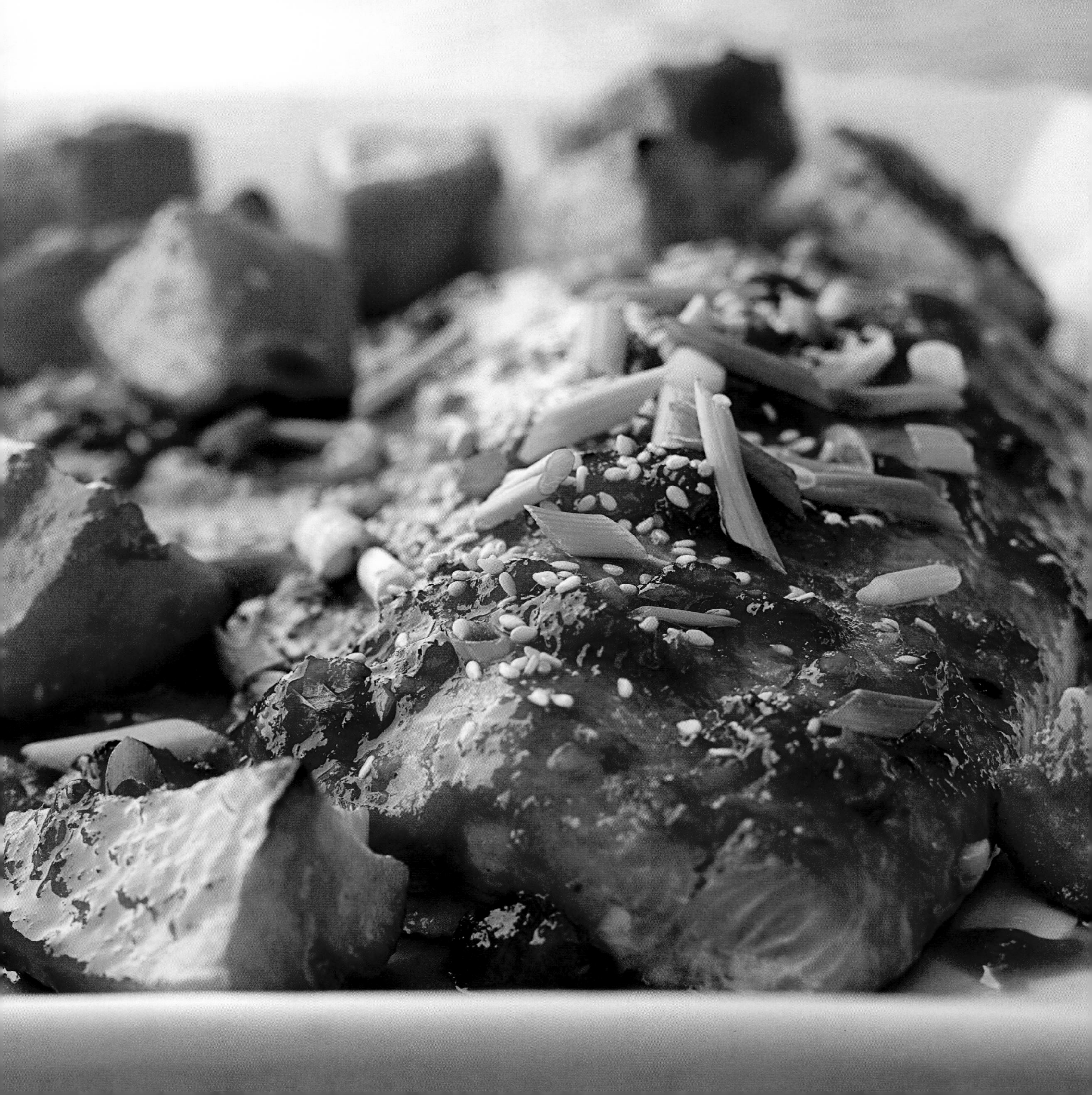

Asian Salmon with Oven-Roasted Sweet Potatoes

Prep: 30 minutes **Cook:** 5 minutes
Roast: 35 minutes **Oven:** 425°F

- 1 1¾-pound fresh or frozen salmon fillet, skinned
- 2 pounds sweet potatoes (4 medium)
- 1 tablespoon vegetable oil
- 2 tablespoons toasted sesame oil
  Salt and black pepper
- ⅓ cup reduced-sodium teriyaki sauce
- 2 tablespoons apricot or peach preserves
- 2 tablespoons dry sherry or orange juice
- 2 teaspoons grated fresh ginger
- 1 teaspoon Dijon mustard
- 2 cloves garlic, minced
- ¼ teaspoon freshly ground black pepper
- ¼ cup sliced green onions (2)
- 1 tablespoon sesame seeds, toasted

1. Thaw fish, if frozen. Rinse fish; pat dry with paper towels. Set aside.

2. Preheat oven to 425°F. Peel sweet potatoes. Cut into 1½-inch chunks. In a bowl toss together potatoes, vegetable oil, and 1 tablespoon of the sesame oil. Sprinkle with salt and pepper. Place sweet potatoes in a large roasting pan. Roast, uncovered, for 15 minutes.

3. Meanwhile, for sauce, in a small saucepan stir together teriyaki sauce, apricot preserves, dry sherry, ginger, mustard, garlic, pepper, and the remaining 1 tablespoon sesame oil. Bring to boiling; reduce heat. Simmer, uncovered, for 5 minutes or until slightly thickened, stirring occasionally. Set aside ¼ cup sauce.

4. Push potatoes to the outside of the pan; place salmon in center of pan. Spoon the remaining sauce over salmon and potatoes.

5. Roast, uncovered, for 20 to 25 minutes or until fish flakes easily when tested with a fork. Carefully transfer fish and potatoes to a serving platter. Drizzle with the reserved ¼ cup sauce. Sprinkle with green onions and sesame seeds. **MAKES 6 SERVINGS**

Per serving: 470 cal., 22 g total fat (4 g sat. fat), 77 mg chol., 500 mg sodium, 35 g carbo., 5 g fiber, 30 g pro.

BASIL-BUTTERED SALMON

Basil-Buttered Salmon

Prep: 15 minutes **Broil:** 8 minutes

- 4 fresh or frozen skinless salmon, halibut, or sea bass fillets (about 1¼ pounds)
- ½ teaspoon salt-free lemon-pepper seasoning
- 2 tablespoons butter, softened
- 1 teaspoon snipped fresh lemon basil, regular basil, or dill or ¼ teaspoon dried basil or dill, crushed
- 1 teaspoon snipped fresh parsley or cilantro
- ¼ teaspoon finely shredded lemon peel or lime peel
  Cooked asparagus spears (optional)
  Shredded Parmesan cheese (optional)

1. Thaw fish, if frozen. Preheat broiler. Rinse fish; pat dry with paper towels. Sprinkle with lemon-pepper seasoning.

2. Place fish on the greased unheated rack of a broiler pan. Turn any thin portions under to make uniform thickness. Broil fish 4 inches from the heat for 8 to 12 minutes or until fish flakes easily when tested with a fork, carefully turning once halfway through broiling time.

3. Meanwhile, for basil butter, in a small bowl stir together butter, basil, parsley, and lemon peel. To serve, spoon 1 teaspoon of the basil butter on top of each fish piece. (Cover and refrigerate remaining basil butter for another use.) If desired, top fillets with asparagus and Parmesan cheese. **MAKES 4 SERVINGS.**

Per serving: 294 cal., 19 g total fat (5 g sat. fat), 94 mg chol., 113 mg sodium, 0 g carbo., 0 g fiber, 28 g pro.

POTATO-SALMON BAKE

Potato-Salmon Bake

Prep: 25 minutes **Bake:** 57 minutes
Oven: 375°F /425°F

1¼ pounds fresh or frozen skinless salmon
    fillets
¾ cup panko (Japanese-style) bread crumbs
3 tablespoons coarsely chopped fresh dill
2 tablespoons butter, melted
2 teaspoons finely shredded lemon peel
3 tablespoons lemon juice (set aside)
2 pounds assorted potatoes (sweet
    potatoes, small Yukon Golds, and small
    red potatoes), cut into ⅜-inch slices
¾ teaspoon kosher salt
½ teaspoon black pepper
1¼ cups crumbled feta cheese (5 ounces)
¾ cup reduced-sodium chicken broth
    Fresh dill sprigs (optional)

1. Thaw fish, if frozen. Rinse fish; pat dry with
paper towels. Preheat oven to 375°F. In a small
bowl stir together panko, the 3 tablespoons
dill, 1 tablespoon of the melted butter, and
1 teaspoon of the lemon peel; set aside.
2. Layer half of the potatoes in a greased
2-quart casserole. Sprinkle with ¼ teaspoon
of the salt and ¼ teaspoon of the pepper;
sprinkle with half of the feta cheese. Repeat
layers with remaining potatoes, ¼ teaspoon
salt, ¼ teaspoon pepper, and the remaining
feta cheese. In a small bowl stir together the
chicken broth and the remaining 1 tablespoon
melted butter. Pour over potatoes. Bake,
covered, about 45 minutes or until potatoes
are tender.
3. Meanwhile, cut salmon into 2- to 3-inch
pieces. Toss salmon with lemon juice.
Sprinkle with the remaining ¼ teaspoon salt.

4. Remove potatoes from oven. Increase oven
temperature to 425°F. Place salmon on top of
potatoes. Sprinkle with panko mixture. Bake,
uncovered, for 12 to 15 minutes or until fish
flakes easily when tested with a fork. If desired,
garnish with fresh dill sprigs. **MAKES 6 SERVINGS**

Per serving: 430 cal., 21 g total fat (8 g sat. fat), 87 mg
chol., 724 mg sodium, 34 g carbo., 4 g fiber, 28 g pro.

Ancho-Glazed Salmon with Sweet Potato Fries

Start to Finish: 20 minutes

4 5- to 6-ounce fresh or frozen skinless
    salmon fillets
2 medium sweet potatoes, scrubbed
1 tablespoon sugar
1 teaspoon salt
1 teaspoon ground cumin
1 teaspoon ground ancho chili powder or
    chili powder
    Nonstick cooking spray
1 tablespoon olive oil
    Cilantro sprigs (optional)

1. Thaw salmon, if frozen.
2. Preheat broiler. Halve sweet potatoes
lengthwise. Cut potatoes lengthwise into
¼-inch slices. In a small bowl combine sugar,
salt, cumin, and chili powder. Place sweet
potatoes on the greased rack of an unheated
broiler pan. Coat both sides of potato slices
with nonstick cooking spray; sprinkle both
sides with about half the sugar mixture. Broil
4 inches from the heat about 10 minutes or
until tender, turning once halfway through
cooking.
3. Meanwhile, rinse salmon; pat dry with
paper towels. Sprinkle salmon with the
remaining sugar mixture. In a large skillet heat
olive oil on medium heat. Add salmon; cook
for 8 to 12 minutes or until fish flakes easily
when tested with a fork, turning once halfway
through cooking.
4. Serve salmon with sweet potatoes. If desired,
garnish with cilantro. **MAKES 4 SERVINGS**

Per serving: 363 cal., 19 g total fat (4 g sat. fat), 84 mg
chol., 710 mg sodium, 17 g carbo., 2 g fiber, 29 g pro.

ANCHO-GLAZED SALMON WITH
SWEET POTATO FRIES

Broiled Tuna Fajitas ♡

Prep: 20 minutes **Marinate:** 30 minutes
Broil: 8 minutes

2 5- to 6-ounce fresh or frozen tuna or
halibut steaks, cut 1 inch thick
¼ cup lime juice
2 tablespoons snipped fresh cilantro or
parsley
1 tablespoon olive oil
2 cloves garlic, minced
¼ teaspoon coarsely ground black pepper
⅛ teaspoon cayenne pepper
8 6-inch corn tortillas
Nonstick cooking spray
2 medium red and/or yellow sweet peppers,
quartered and stems and membranes
removed
1 cup purchased salsa

1. Thaw fish, if frozen. Rinse fish; pat dry with
paper towels. Place fish in a heavy, large
resealable plastic bag set in a shallow dish.
2. For marinade, in a small bowl stir together
lime juice, cilantro, olive oil, garlic, black
pepper, and cayenne pepper. Pour marinade
over fish in bag. Seal bag; turn to coat fish.
Marinate in the refrigerator for 30 minutes,
turning bag occasionally.
3. Wrap tortillas tightly in foil. Drain fish,
reserving marinade. Lightly coat the unheated
rack of a broiler pan with nonstick cooking
spray. Place fish on prepared broiler pan.
Place sweet pepper quarters on pan beside
fish. Place wrapped tortillas alongside the
broiler pan. Broil 4 to 5 inches from heat for
8 to 12 minutes or until fish flakes easily when
tested with a fork, brushing once with reserved
marinade after 3 minutes of broiling and
turning once halfway through broiling. Discard
any remaining marinade. Broil sweet peppers
about 8 minutes or until tender, turning
occasionally. Broil tortillas about 8 minutes or
until heated through, turning once.
4. Using a fork, break fish into chunks. Cut
sweet peppers into ½-inch strips. Fill warm
tortillas with fish and sweet pepper strips.
Serve with salsa. **MAKES 4 SERVINGS**

Per serving: 285 cal., 9 g total fat (2 g sat. fat), 27 mg
chol., 440 mg sodium, 33 g carbo., 6 g fiber, 21 g pro.

TUNA KABOBS WITH VEGETABLE RICE

Tuna Kabobs with Vegetable Rice

Prep: 15 minutes **Marinate:** 30 minutes
Broil: 5 minutes

1 pound fresh or frozen tuna or salmon
steaks, bones and skin removed
½ cup teriyaki sauce
2 tablespoons chopped green onion (1)
1½ to 2 teaspoons wasabi powder
1 cup uncooked brown rice
1 medium red sweet pepper, cut into strips
½ cup thinly sliced carrot (1 medium)
1 cup broccoli florets

1. Thaw fish, if frozen. Rinse fish; pat dry. Cut
fish into ¼-inch-thick pieces. Combine teriyaki
sauce, onion, and wasabi powder. In a shallow
dish combine fish and half of the teriyaki
mixture. Cover; chill for 30 minutes.
2. Meanwhile, in a medium saucepan combine
rice, sweet pepper, carrot, 2 cups *water*, and
¼ teaspoon salt. Bring to boiling; reduce heat.
Simmer, covered, for 25 minutes. Stir in
broccoli. Cook, covered, for 5 minutes. Remove
from heat. Let stand, covered, for 5 minutes.
Stir in remaining teriyaki mixture.
3. Preheat broiler. Thread tuna strips
accordion-style onto four 12-inch skewers;*
discard any remaining marinade. Place skewers
on the unheated rack of a broiler pan. Broil
4 to 5 inches from heat for 5 to 7 minutes or
until fish flakes easily when tested with a fork,
turning skewers once halfway through broiling.
Serve kabobs with rice. **MAKES 4 SERVINGS**

*Tip If using wooden skewers, soak in
enough water to cover for 30 minutes; drain
before using.

Per serving: 194 cal., 4 g total fat (1 g sat. fat), 22 mg
chol., 805 mg sodium, 23 g carbo., 2 g fiber, 17 g pro.

LEMON-HERB HALIBUT

Broiled Fillets with Tangerine Relish

Prep: 25 minutes
Broil: 4 to 6 minutes per ½-inch thickness

  6 4-ounce fresh or frozen skinless halibut,
      cod, sole, or other white fish fillets
  ¼ teaspoon salt
  ¼ teaspoon black pepper
  ⅓ cup orange juice
  ¼ cup finely chopped red onion or shallots
  2 teaspoons white balsamic vinegar or
      regular balsamic vinegar
  1 teaspoon snipped fresh tarragon or
      rosemary or ½ teaspoon dried tarragon or
      rosemary, crushed
  1 teaspoon olive oil
  1 clove garlic, minced
      Dash bottled hot pepper sauce
      Nonstick cooking spray
  4 medium tangerines, peeled
  2 tablespoons snipped fresh parsley
  6 cups torn mixed salad greens (optional)

1. Thaw fish fillets, if frozen. Rinse fish; pat dry with paper towels. Sprinkle with salt and pepper. Measure thickness of fish; set aside.
2. Preheat broiler. In a small saucepan combine orange juice, red onion, balsamic vinegar, tarragon, olive oil, garlic, and hot pepper sauce. Bring to boiling; reduce heat. Simmer, uncovered, for 5 to 6 minutes or until reduced to about ⅓ cup. Remove from heat. Remove 2 tablespoons of the orange juice mixture; set both mixtures aside.
3. Coat the unheated rack of a broiler pan with nonstick cooking spray. Place fish on rack. Brush both sides of fish with the reserved 2 tablespoons juice mixture. Turn under any thin portions of fish. Broil 4 inches from heat for 4 to 6 minutes per ½-inch thickness of fish or until fish flakes easily when tested with a fork.
4. For relish, separate tangerines into segments. Remove seeds; cut up segments. In a bowl combine chopped tangerines, the remaining juice mixture, and the parsley.
5. If desired, serve fish with greens. Spoon tangerine relish over fish. **MAKES 6 SERVINGS**

Per serving: 175 cal., 4 g total fat (1 g sat. fat), 36 mg chol., 161 mg sodium, 11 g carbo., 1 g fiber, 24 g pro.

Lemon-Herb Halibut

Prep: 15 minutes **Marinate:** 30 minutes
Broil: 8 minutes

  4 6-ounce fresh or frozen halibut steaks,
      cut 1 inch thick
  ¼ cup lemon juice
  2 tablespoons snipped fresh oregano or
      thyme or 1 teaspoon dried oregano or
      thyme, crushed
  4 teaspoons olive oil
  4 cloves garlic, minced
  2 teaspoons lemon-pepper seasoning
      Fresh oregano or thyme leaves (optional)
      Lemon wedges (optional)

1. Thaw fish, if frozen. Rinse fish; pat dry with paper towels. For marinade, in a shallow dish combine lemon juice, the 2 tablespoons oregano, the olive oil, garlic, and lemon-pepper seasoning. Add fish; turn to coat with marinade. Cover and marinate in refrigerator for at least 30 minutes or up to 1½ hours, turning fish occasionally.
2. Preheat broiler. Drain fish, reserving marinade. Place fish on the greased unheated rack of a broiler pan. Broil 4 inches from the heat for 8 to 12 minutes or until fish flakes easily when tested with a fork, turning once and brushing once with reserved marinade halfway through broiling. Discard any remaining marinade. If desired, garnish with fresh oregano leaves and serve with lemon wedges. **MAKES 4 SERVINGS**

Per serving: 238 cal., 8 g total fat (1 g sat. fat), 54 mg chol., 636 mg sodium, 3 g carbo., 0 g fiber, 36 g pro.

COD AMANDINE

Poached Halibut and Peppers

Start to Finish: 30 minutes

  4 fresh or frozen halibut, cod, or other white fish fillets (1 to 1½ pounds)
1½ cups dry white wine (Sauvignon Blanc or Pinot Grigio) or reduced-sodium chicken broth
  1 cup water
1½ cups chopped yellow and/or red sweet peppers (2 medium)
  3 tablespoons drained capers
  4 cloves garlic, minced
  ¼ to ½ teaspoon crushed red pepper
  ¼ teaspoon salt
  ⅛ teaspoon freshly ground black pepper
  1 tablespoon olive oil
      Coarsely chopped fresh basil

1. Thaw fish, if frozen. Rinse fish; pat dry with paper towels. Set aside.

2. In a large skillet combine wine, water, sweet peppers, capers, garlic, and crushed red pepper. Bring to boiling; reduce heat. Simmer, uncovered, for 7 minutes, stirring occasionally.

3. Place fish in a single layer in the wine mixture in the skillet. Sprinkle fish with salt and pepper. Spoon liquid over fish. Return to simmer. Cook, covered, for 4 to 6 minutes per ½-inch thickness of fish or until fish flakes easily when tested with a fork. Remove fish to serving platter and pour poaching liquid into a small serving pitcher. Drizzle cooked fish with olive oil and a little of the poaching liquid. Sprinkle with basil. Serve with remaining poaching liquid. **MAKES 4 SERVINGS**

Per serving: 260 cal., 6 g total fat (1 g sat. fat), 36 mg chol., 402 mg sodium, 9 g carbo., 1 g fiber, 25 g pro.

Cod Amandine

Prep: 20 minutes
Bake: 4 to 6 minutes per ½-inch thickness
Oven: 450°F

  4 4-ounce fresh or frozen skinless cod, tilapia, trout, or halibut fillets, ½ to 1 inch thick
  ¼ cup buttermilk
  ½ cup panko (Japanese-style) bread crumbs or fine dry bread crumbs
  2 tablespoons snipped fresh parsley or 2 teaspoons dried parsley flakes
  ½ teaspoon dry mustard
  ¼ teaspoon salt
  ⅛ teaspoon black pepper
  ¼ cup sliced almonds, coarsely chopped
  1 tablespoon olive oil
      Lemon wedges (optional)

1. Thaw fish, if frozen. Rinse fish; pat dry with paper towels. Measure thickness of fish. Preheat oven to 450°F.

2. Pour buttermilk into a shallow dish. In another shallow dish combine bread crumbs, parsley, dry mustard, salt, and pepper. Dip fish in buttermilk, then coat fish with crumb mixture. Place coated fish in a greased shallow baking pan.

3. Sprinkle fish with almonds. Drizzle olive oil over fish. Bake for 4 to 6 minutes per ½-inch thickness of fish or until fish flakes easily when tested with a fork. If desired, serve fish with lemon wedges. **MAKES 4 SERVINGS**

Per serving: 191 cal., 7 g total fat (1 g sat. fat), 49 mg chol., 245 mg sodium, 7 g carbo., 1 g fiber, 23 g pro.

PARMESAN-CRUSTED FISH

Parmesan-Crusted Fish

Prep: 15 minutes
Bake: 4 to 6 minutes per ½-inch thickness
Oven: 450°F

4 fresh or frozen skinless cod fillets
(1½ pounds)
Nonstick cooking spray
Salt and black pepper
⅓ cup panko (Japanese-style) bread crumbs
¼ cup finely shredded Parmesan cheese
(1 ounce)
½ cup water
1 10-ounce package julienned carrots
(3 cups)
1 tablespoon butter
¾ teaspoon ground ginger
Mixed fresh salad greens

1. Thaw fish, if frozen. Rinse fish; pat dry with paper towels. Preheat oven to 450°F. Lightly coat a baking sheet with nonstick cooking spray. Place fish on the prepared baking sheet. Sprinkle with salt and pepper. In small bowl stir together panko and cheese; sprinkle on fish.

2. Bake fish, uncovered, for 4 to 6 minutes for each ½-inch thickness of fish or until crumbs are golden and fish flakes easily when tested with a fork.

3. Meanwhile, in a large skillet bring the water to boiling; add carrots. Reduce heat. Cook, covered, for 5 minutes. Uncover; cook for 2 minutes more. Add butter and ginger to the carrots; toss to coat. Serve fish and carrots with greens. **MAKES 4 SERVINGS**

Per serving: 233 cal., 6 g total fat (3 g sat. fat), 84 mg chol., 407 mg sodium, 11 g carbo., 2 g fiber, 34 g pro.

Ancho and Lime Seared Scallops ♡

Start to Finish: 25 minutes

12 fresh or frozen sea scallops (1¼ to 1½ pounds)
½ teaspoon ancho chili powder or regular chili powder
⅛ teaspoon salt
Nonstick cooking spray
1 tablespoon lime juice
1 recipe Gingered Tropical Fruit Salsa

1. Thaw scallops, if frozen. Rinse scallops; pat dry with paper towels. In a small bowl combine chili powder and salt. Sprinkle chili powder mixture evenly over scallops; rub in with your fingers.

2. Lightly coat an unheated large nonstick skillet with nonstick cooking spray. Preheat on medium-high heat. Add scallops to hot skillet; cook for 4 to 6 minutes or until opaque, turning once. Transfer scallops to a serving plate. Drizzle with lime juice; cover to keep warm.

3. Add Gingered Tropical Fruit Salsa to skillet; cook and stir about 1 minute or until heated through, scraping up the browned bits from bottom of skillet. Serve warmed salsa with the scallops. **MAKES 4 SERVINGS**

Gingered Tropical Fruit Salsa In a medium bowl combine 1 tablespoon snipped fresh mint, 2 teaspoons seasoned rice vinegar, 2 teaspoons lime juice, ½ to 1 teaspoon grated fresh ginger or ¼ teaspoon ground ginger, and, if desired, ⅛ teaspoon crushed red peppers. Add ½ cup chopped fresh pineapple; ½ cup chopped mango or peach; ½ cup chopped, peeled kiwifruit; and one 5-ounce container mandarin orange sections, drained (½ cup). Toss gently to mix. Serve immediately or cover and chill for up to 24 hours. Makes 2 cups.

Per serving: 188 cal., 1 g total fat (0 g sat. fat), 47 mg chol., 333 mg sodium, 19 g carbo., 2 g fiber, 25 g pro.

ANCHO AND LIME SEARED SCALLOPS

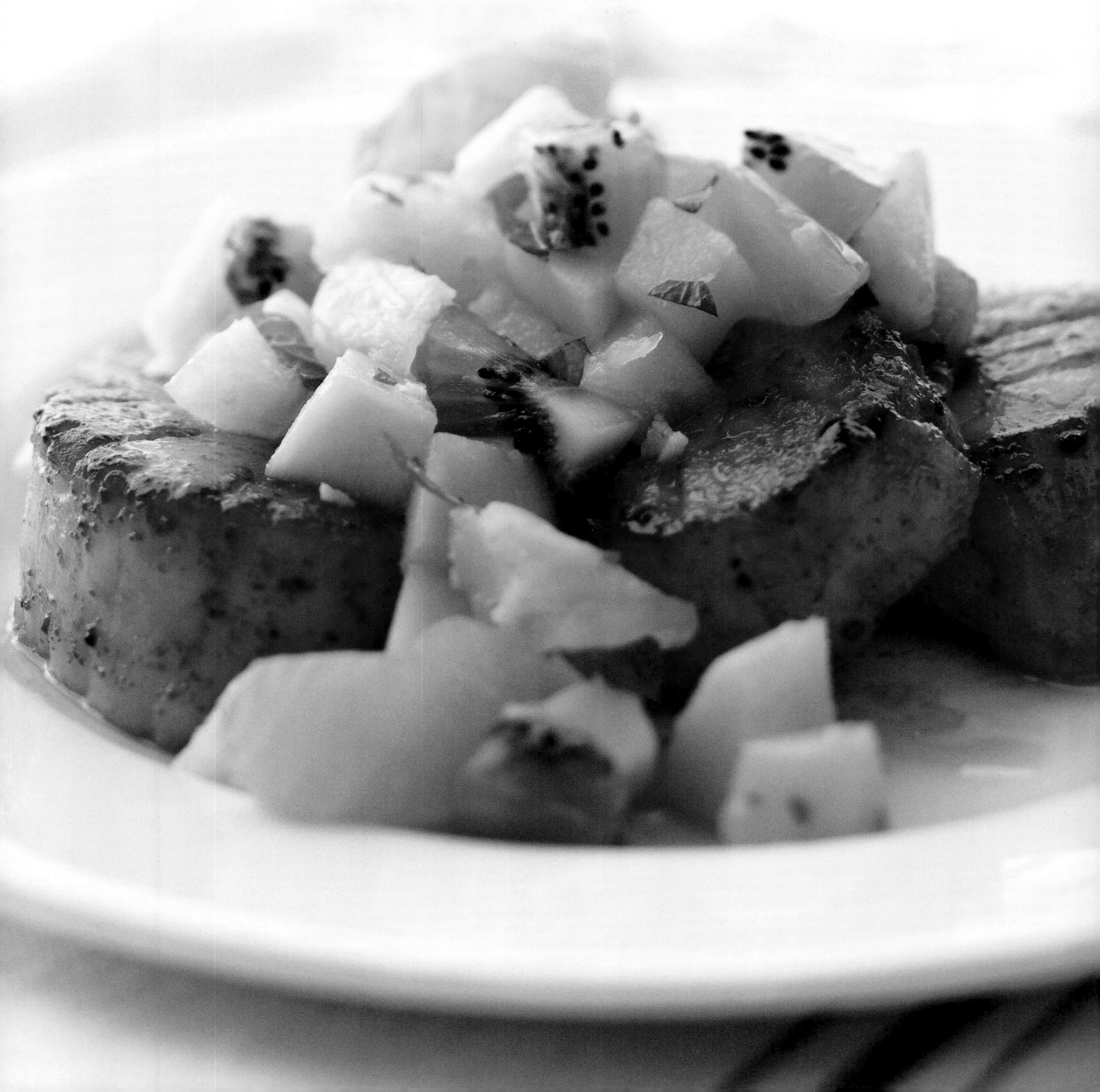

Cajun Shrimp with Mango-Edamame Salsa

Start to Finish: 30 minutes

1 pound fresh or frozen large shrimp with tails
2 teaspoons purchased salt-free Cajun seasoning or Homemade Cajun Seasoning
1 tablespoon soybean cooking oil
1 recipe Mango-Edamame Salsa
   Belgian endive leaves (optional)

1. Thaw shrimp, if frozen. Peel and devein shrimp, leaving tails intact if desired. Rinse shrimp; pat dry with paper towels. Set aside.
2. In a large bowl toss shrimp with Cajun seasoning. In a heavy large skillet heat oil on medium-high heat. Add shrimp; cook and stir about 5 minutes or until shrimp are opaque.
3. Serve shrimp with Mango-Edamame Salsa and, if desired, Belgian endive leaves.

MAKES 4 SERVINGS

Homemade Cajun Seasoning In a small bowl stir together ½ teaspoon onion powder, ½ teaspoon paprika, ¼ teaspoon ground white pepper, ¼ teaspoon garlic powder, ¼ teaspoon cayenne pepper, and ¼ teaspoon black pepper.

Mango-Edamame Salsa In a medium bowl combine 2 seeded, peeled, and chopped mangoes; 1 cup fresh or frozen shelled sweet soybeans (edamame), cooked and cooled; 1 red sweet pepper, chopped; ½ cup finely chopped green onion; ¼ cup snipped fresh cilantro; 2 teaspoons soybean cooking oil; and ¼ teaspoon salt. Toss gently to mix. Cover and chill until serving time or up to 2 hours. Makes 3 cups.

Per serving: 317 cal., 12 g total fat (2 g sat. fat), 129 mg chol., 287 mg sodium, 29 g carbo., 6 g fiber, 27 g pro.

SOY-LIME SCALLOPS WITH LEEKS

Soy-Lime Scallops with Leeks

Prep: 10 minutes **Marinate:** 30 minutes
Grill: 8 minutes

1 pound fresh or frozen sea scallops
¼ cup reduced-sodium soy sauce
¼ cup rice vinegar
4 baby leeks
8 medium green scallions, red scallions, or green onions
1 medium lime, halved

1. Thaw scallops, if frozen. Rinse scallops; pat dry with paper towels. For marinade, in a small bowl combine soy sauce and rice vinegar; set aside.
2. Trim root ends and green tops of leeks. Rinse leeks thoroughly to remove any grit.
3. Place leeks, scallops, and scallions in a resealable plastic bag set in a shallow dish.

Pour marinade over scallops and vegetables. Seal bag; turn to coat scallops and vegetables. Marinate in refrigerator for 30 minutes.
4. Remove scallops, leeks, and scallions from bag. Discard marinade. Place leeks, scallops, scallions, and lime halves (cut sides down) on the rack of an uncovered grill directly over medium coals. Grill for 8 to 10 minutes or until scallops are opaque, turning scallops and vegetables occasionally. Remove scallions from grill rack before they overbrown.
5. To serve, transfer leeks and scallions to 4 dinner plates. Top with scallops. Using grilling tongs, remove limes from grill and squeeze over scallops. **MAKES 4 SERVINGS**

Per serving: 130 cal., 1 g total fat (0 g sat. fat), 37 mg chol., 478 mg sodium, 9 g carbo., 1 g fiber, 20 g pro.

FETA SHRIMP KABOBS

Feta Shrimp Kabobs

Prep: 40 minutes **Grill:** 7 minutes

2 pounds fresh or frozen large shrimp (32 to 40 shrimp)
⅓ cup lemon juice
¼ cup olive oil
1 tablespoon snipped fresh rosemary
1 tablespoon snipped fresh oregano
3 cloves garlic, minced
1 teaspoon kosher salt
½ teaspoon crushed red pepper
1 lemon, cut into wedges
½ cup crumbled feta cheese

1. Thaw shrimp, if frozen. Peel and devein shrimp. Rinse shrimp; pat dry with paper towels. Place shrimp in a resealable plastic bag. Add lemon juice, olive oil, rosemary, oregano, garlic, salt, and crushed red pepper;

seal bag and turn to coat. Marinate in the refrigerator for 30 minutes to 1 hour.
2. Drain shrimp; discard marinade. Thread shrimp onto long skewers, leaving a ¼-inch space between pieces.
3. For a charcoal grill, place kabobs and lemon wedges on the greased rack of an uncovered grill directly over medium coals. Grill for 7 to 9 minutes or until shrimp are opaque and lemon wedges are lightly browned, turning once halfway through grilling. (For a gas grill, preheat grill. Reduce heat to medium. Place kabobs and lemon wedges on greased grill rack over heat. Cover and grill as above.) Before serving, sprinkle shrimp with feta cheese. **MAKES 6 SERVINGS**

Per serving: 225 cal., 9 g total fat (3 g sat. fat), 240 mg chol., 471 mg sodium, 5 g carbo., 1 g fiber, 33 g pro.

Shrimp with Vermicelli

Start to Finish: 35 minutes

12 ounces fresh or frozen peeled, deveined medium shrimp
4 ounces dried multigrain angel hair pasta
2 tablespoons butter
1 large onion, halved and thinly sliced
¼ to ½ teaspoon crushed red pepper
1 8-ounce can tomato sauce with basil, garlic, and oregano
1 medium yellow summer squash or zucchini, halved lengthwise and thinly sliced
⅛ teaspoon salt
4 cups prewashed baby spinach
1 cup cherry tomatoes, halved
2 tablespoons finely shredded Parmesan cheese

1. Thaw shrimp, if frozen. Rinse shrimp; pat dry with paper towels. Cook pasta according to package directions; drain.
2. Meanwhile, in a very large skillet melt butter on medium heat. Add onion; cook until tender. Add shrimp and crushed red pepper; cook and stir for 1 minute. Add tomato sauce, squash, and salt. Bring to boiling; reduce heat. Simmer, covered, for 5 minutes.
3. Stir drained pasta, spinach, and cherry tomatoes into shrimp mixture. Toss gently on medium heat until heated through. Sprinkle with Parmesan cheese. **MAKES 4 SERVINGS**

Per serving: 279 cal., 8 g total fat (4 g sat. fat), 114 mg chol., 588 mg sodium, 31 g carbo., 5 g fiber, 21 g pro.

SHRIMP WITH VERMICELLI

SHRIMP-ZUCCHINI KABOBS
WITH BASIL CREAM SAUCE

SZECHWAN SHRIMP

Shrimp-Zucchini Kabobs with Basil Cream Sauce

Prep: 40 minutes **Grill:** 10 minutes

1   8-ounce container light sour cream
½   cup snipped fresh basil
3   tablespoons snipped fresh chives
¾   teaspoon salt
⅛   teaspoon black pepper
1¼ pounds fresh or frozen large shrimp
2   medium zucchini (about 1 pound), halved lengthwise and cut into 1-inch slices
2   tablespoons olive oil
½   teaspoon finely shredded orange peel or lime peel
1   tablespoon orange juice or lime juice
¼   teaspoon cayenne pepper
5   cups fresh arugula, baby spinach, and/or romaine lettuce
    Fresh basil leaves (optional)

1. For sauce, in a food processor or blender combine sour cream, the snipped basil, the chives, ½ teaspoon of the salt, and the black pepper. Cover and process or blend until nearly smooth. Cover and chill until ready to serve.

2. Thaw shrimp, if frozen. Peel and devein shrimp, leaving tails intact. Rinse shrimp; pat dry with paper towels. On long skewers (see tip, page 211) alternately thread shrimp and zucchini, leaving a ¼-inch space between pieces. In a small bowl combine olive oil, orange peel, orange juice, cayenne pepper, and the remaining ¼ teaspoon salt; brush evenly on shrimp and zucchini.

3. Place skewers on the greased rack of an uncovered grill directly over medium coals. Grill about 10 minutes or until shrimp are opaque, turning once. (For a gas grill, preheat grill. Reduce heat to medium. Place skewers on greased grill rack over heat. Cover and grill as above.)

4. Arrange arugula on a serving platter. Top with kabobs. If desired, garnish sauce with basil leaves. Serve sauce with kabobs.

MAKES 6 SERVINGS

Per serving: 185 cal., 10 g total fat (3 g sat. fat), 121 mg chol., 434 mg sodium, 7 g carbo., 1 g fiber, 17 g pro.

Szechwan Shrimp

Start to Finish: 30 minutes

1   pound fresh or frozen medium shrimp in shells
3   tablespoons water
2   tablespoons ketchup
1   tablespoon reduced-sodium soy sauce
1   tablespoon rice wine, dry sherry, or water
2   teaspoons cornstarch
1   teaspoon honey
1   teaspoon grated fresh ginger or ¼ teaspoon ground ginger
½   teaspoon crushed red pepper
1   tablespoon peanut oil or vegetable oil
½   cup sliced green onions (4)
4   cloves garlic, minced
2   cups rice noodles or hot cooked rice
2   small fresh red chile peppers (such as Fresno or Thai), sliced (see tip, page 160) (optional)

1. Thaw shrimp, if frozen. Peel and devein shrimp; cut in half lengthwise. Rinse; shrimp pat dry with paper towels. Set aside.

2. For sauce, in a small bowl stir together the water, ketchup, soy sauce, rice wine, cornstarch, honey, ground ginger (if using), and crushed red pepper. Set aside.

3. Pour oil into a large skillet or wok. Heat on medium-high heat. Add green onions, garlic, and grated fresh ginger (if using); stir-fry for 30 seconds.

4. Add shrimp. Stir-fry for 2 to 3 minutes or until shrimp are opaque; push to side of skillet. Stir sauce; add to center of skillet. Cook and stir until thickened and bubbly. Cook and stir for 2 minutes more. Serve with rice noodles. If desired, garnish with sliced red chile peppers. **MAKES 4 SERVINGS**

Per serving: 249 cal., 5 g total fat (1 g sat. fat), 129 mg chol., 372 mg sodium, 30 g carbo., 0 g fiber, 19 g pro.

CURRIED SHRIMP WITH COUSCOUS

Curried Shrimp with Couscous ♡

Start to Finish: 40 minutes

1½ pounds fresh or frozen large shrimp
1½ cups water
1 cup whole wheat couscous
2 teaspoons olive oil
1 cup chopped onion
1 medium red sweet pepper, seeded and cut into bite-size strips
1 tablespoon grated fresh ginger
½ teaspoon curry powder
½ teaspoon ground cumin
¼ teaspoon cayenne pepper
6 ounces fresh pea pods, trimmed and halved lengthwise
¼ cup orange juice
3 tablespoons unsweetened light coconut milk
¼ teaspoon salt
½ cup snipped fresh cilantro

1. Thaw shrimp, if frozen. Peel and devein shrimp. Rinse shrimp; pat dry with paper towels. Set aside. In a medium saucepan bring the water to boiling; add couscous. Remove from heat; let stand for 5 minutes.
2. Meanwhile, in a very large nonstick skillet heat oil on medium heat. Add onion and sweet pepper; cook and stir about 5 minutes or just until tender. Add ginger, curry powder, cumin, and cayenne pepper; cook and stir for 1 minute. Add shrimp and pea pods, stirring to coat with the spices. Cook and stir about 3 minutes or until shrimp are opaque. Stir in orange juice, coconut milk, and salt; heat through.
3. Serve shrimp mixture with couscous. Sprinkle with cilantro.
MAKES 6 SERVINGS

Per serving: 315 cal., 5 g total fat (1 g sat. fat), 172 mg chol., 273 mg sodium, 39 g carbo., 7 g fiber, 30 g pro.

Mexican-Style Shrimp Pizza
Prep: 25 minutes **Bake:** 16 minutes
Oven: 400°F

4 8-inch whole wheat flour tortillas
2 teaspoons olive oil
  Nonstick cooking spray
2 large red and/or yellow sweet peppers, seeded and cut into bite-size strips
⅔ cup thinly sliced green onions
2 tablespoons water
¼ to ⅓ cup purchased green salsa
8 ounces peeled and deveined cooked medium shrimp
⅔ cup shredded reduced-fat or regular Monterey Jack cheese
2 tablespoons snipped fresh cilantro

1. Preheat oven to 400°F. Brush both sides of tortillas with oil; place tortillas in a single layer on 2 ungreased baking sheets. Bake about 10 minutes or until crisp, turning tortillas halfway through baking.
2. Coat an unheated skillet with cooking spray. Preheat skillet on medium heat. Add peppers and onions. Cook 5 minutes or until nearly crisp-tender. Add the water; cook, covered, for 2 minutes more.
3. Spread tortillas with salsa. Top with vegetable mixture, shrimp, and cheese. Bake about 3 minutes or until cheese is melted and shrimp is heated through. Sprinkle with cilantro. **MAKES 4 INDIVIDUAL PIZZAS**

Per pizza: 288 cal., 11 g total fat (4 g sat. fat), 125 mg chol., 673 mg sodium, 22 g carbo., 12 g fiber, 26 g pro.

CHAPTER 9 /

Vegetables & Sides

GREEK VEGETABLE SALAD

Marinated Vegetable Salad

Prep: 25 minutes **Stand:** 30 minutes to 1 hour

- 2 medium red and/or yellow tomatoes or 4 plum tomatoes, cut into wedges
- 1 cup thinly sliced zucchini or yellow summer squash (1 small)
- ¾ cup chopped green sweet pepper (1 medium)
- ½ of a small red onion, thinly sliced
- 2 tablespoons snipped fresh parsley
- 2 tablespoons extra virgin olive oil
- 2 tablespoons balsamic vinegar or wine vinegar
- 2 tablespoons water
- 1 tablespoon snipped fresh thyme or basil or 1 teaspoon dried thyme or basil, crushed
- 1 clove garlic, minced
  Pine nuts, toasted (optional)

1. In a medium bowl combine tomatoes, zucchini, sweet pepper, red onion, and parsley; set aside.
2. For dressing, in a screw-top jar combine olive oil, vinegar, the water, thyme, and garlic. Cover and shake well. Pour over vegetable mixture. Toss gently to coat.
3. Let salad stand at room temperature for 30 to 60 minutes, stirring occasionally. If desired, garnish with pine nuts. Serve with a slotted spoon. **MAKES 6 SERVINGS**

Make-ahead directions Prepare as above through Step 2. Cover and chill for 4 to 24 hours, stirring once or twice. Let stand at room temperature about 30 minutes before serving. If desired, garnish with pine nuts. Serve with a slotted spoon.

Per serving: 64 cal., 5 g total fat (1 g sat. fat), 0 mg chol., 7 mg sodium, 5 g carbo., 1 g fiber, 1 g pro.

Greek Vegetable Salad

Start to Finish: 30 minutes

- 1 cup chopped tomatoes (2 medium)
- ½ cup chopped cucumber
- ¼ cup chopped yellow, red, or green sweet pepper
- 2 tablespoons chopped red onion
- ¾ teaspoon snipped fresh thyme or ¼ teaspoon dried thyme, crushed
- ½ teaspoon snipped fresh oregano or ⅛ teaspoon dried oregano, crushed
- 1 tablespoon white balsamic vinegar or regular balsamic vinegar
- 1 tablespoon extra virgin olive oil
  Leaf lettuce (optional)
- ¼ cup crumbled reduced-fat feta cheese (1 ounce)

1. In a medium bowl combine tomatoes, cucumber, sweet pepper, red onion, thyme, and oregano. For dressing, in a small bowl whisk together balsamic vinegar and olive oil. Pour dressing over vegetable mixture. Toss gently to coat.
2. If desired, line a serving bowl with lettuce; spoon vegetable mixture into bowl. Sprinkle with feta cheese. **MAKES 4 SERVINGS**

Per serving: 65 cal., 5 g total fat (1 g sat. fat), 3 mg chol., 120 mg sodium, 4 g carbo., 1 g fiber, 2 g pro.

MARINATED VEGETABLE SALAD

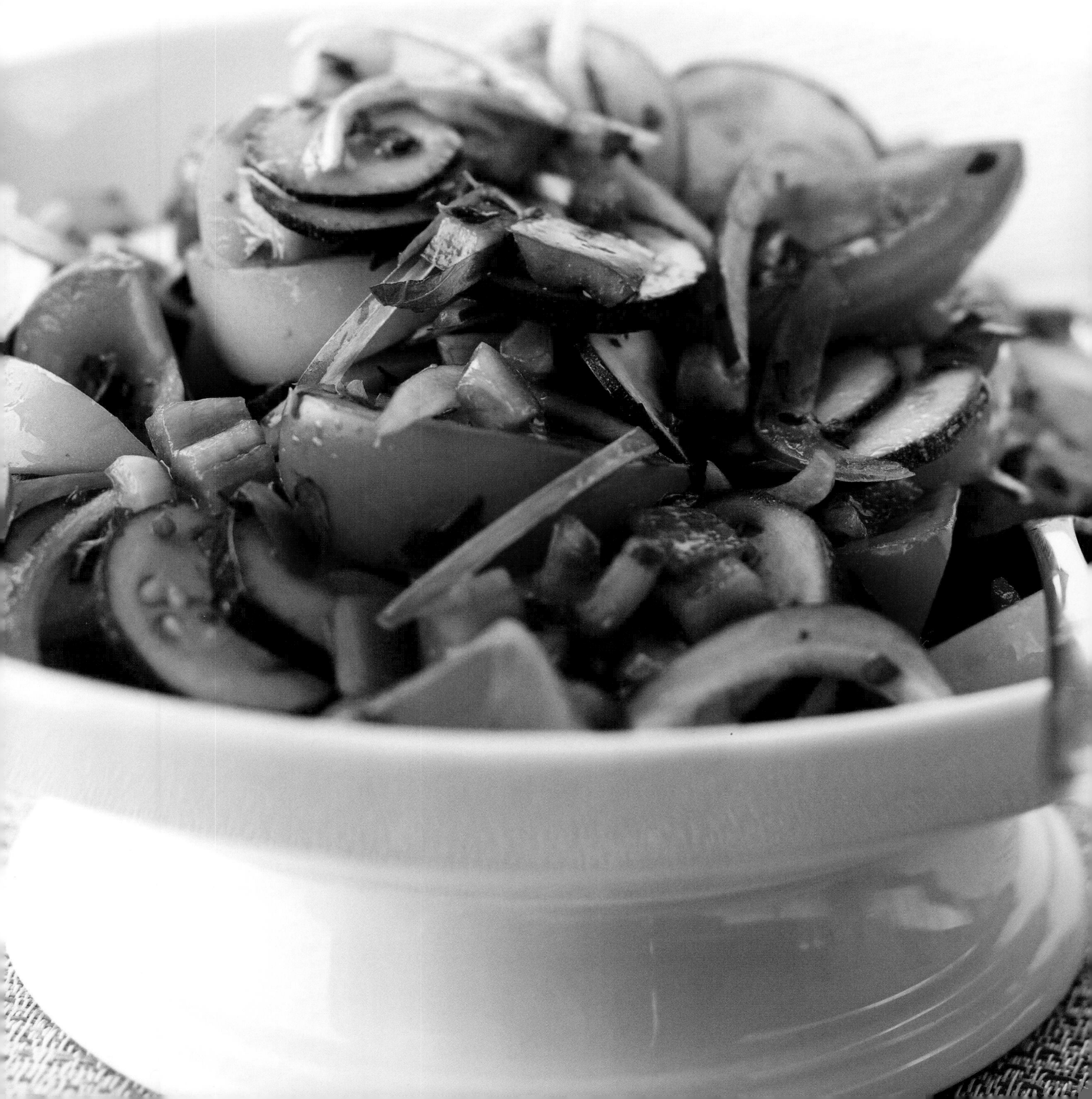

TOMATO AND RED ONION SALAD

Orange-Asparagus Salad ♡

Start to Finish: 20 minutes

 1 pound fresh asparagus
 ¼ cup orange juice
 4 teaspoons extra virgin olive oil
 1 teaspoon Dijon mustard
 ¼ teaspoon salt
 ⅛ teaspoon black pepper
 2 medium oranges, peeled and sectioned

1. Snap off and discard woody bases from asparagus. If desired, scrape off scales. Cut stems into 2-inch-long pieces. In a covered small saucepan cook asparagus in a small amount of boiling water for 1 minute; drain. Cool immediately in a bowl of ice water. Drain on paper towels.

2. For dressing, in a medium bowl whisk together orange juice, olive oil, mustard, salt, and pepper. Add asparagus and orange sections; stir gently to coat. Serve immediately or cover and chill for up to 6 hours.

MAKES 4 SERVINGS

Per serving: 74 cal., 5 g total fat (1 g sat. fat), 0 mg chol., 177 mg sodium, 8 g carbo., 2 g fiber, 2 g pro.

Tomato and Red Onion Salad ♡

Prep: 25 minutes **Stand:** 25 minutes

 4 cups ice-cold water
 2¾ teaspoons salt
 1 medium red onion, cut into ¼-inch slices
 ½ cup cider vinegar
 ¼ cup sugar
 ¾ teaspoon freshly ground black pepper
 8 cups chopped, seeded tomatoes* (about 3 pounds)

1. In medium bowl combine the 4 cups ice-cold water and 2 teaspoons of the salt; stir to dissolve salt. Add onion slices; stir to separate rings. Let stand for 20 minutes; drain.

2. Meanwhile, for dressing, in small bowl whisk together vinegar, sugar, pepper, and the remaining ¾ teaspoon salt.

3. For salad, in a very large bowl combine tomatoes and the onion. Add dressing; toss gently to coat. Let stand for 5 minutes before serving. **MAKES 6 TO 8 SERVINGS**

*Note Choose heirloom and cherry tomatoes in a variety of colors; if desired, halve the cherry tomatoes.

Per serving: 88 cal., 1 g total fat (0 g sat. fat), 0 mg chol., 401 mg sodium, 20 g carbo., 3 g fiber, 2 g pro.

Quick Bread Salad ♡

Prep: 20 minutes **Bake:** 8 minutes
Stand: 15 minutes **Oven:** 300°F

 3 cups Italian bread torn into bite-size pieces or cut into 1-inch cubes
 1½ cups coarsely chopped, seeded tomatoes (3 medium)
 ½ of a medium red onion, cut into thin wedges and separated
 ¼ cup snipped fresh basil or Italian (flat-leaf) parsley
 ¼ to ⅓ cup bottled Italian salad dressing
 4 cups torn or chopped romaine lettuce

1. Preheat oven to 300°F. Spread bread pieces in a shallow pan. Bake, uncovered, for 8 to 10 minutes, stirring once or twice until dry but not toasted. Cool on a wire rack. (Or let bread pieces stand overnight at room temperature, stirring once or twice.)

2. In a large bowl toss together bread pieces, tomatoes, onion, and basil. Pour the dressing over the bread mixture; toss to coat. Let stand for 15 minutes to allow the flavors to blend. Serve bread mixture over torn greens.

MAKES 4 SERVINGS

Per serving: 213 cal., 9 g total fat (1 g sat. fat), 0 mg chol., 417 mg sodium, 29 g carbo., 4 g fiber, 6 g pro.

ASIAN COLESLAW

2. Arrange watercress on a platter. Top with sweet pepper rings and tomato wedges. Shake dressing; drizzle over salad. Sprinkle with cheese. **MAKES 8 SERVINGS**

Herb-Dijon Vinaigrette In a screw-top jar combine 2 tablespoons extra virgin olive oil, 2 tablespoons white wine vinegar or balsamic vinegar, 1 tablespoon snipped fresh chives, 2 teaspoons snipped fresh basil, ½ teaspoon sugar, ½ teaspoon Dijon mustard, and ⅛ teaspoon black pepper. Cover and shake well to combine; use immediately or cover and chill for up to 3 days. Shake before serving. Makes ¼ cup.

Per serving: 85 cal., 5 g total fat (1 g sat. fat), 3 mg chol., 78 mg sodium, 9 g carbo., 2 g fiber, 3 g pro.

Peach and Blackberry Slaw

Start to Finish: 30 minutes

- ¼ cup white wine vinegar
- ¼ cup olive oil
- 1 tablespoon snipped fresh chives
- 1 teaspoon sugar
  Salt and black pepper
- 6 cups shredded cabbage
- 3 peaches, peeled and sliced
- ½ pint fresh blackberries
- 2 ounces coarsely crumbled blue cheese (optional)

1. For dressing, in a small bowl whisk together vinegar, olive oil, chives, and sugar. Season with salt and pepper; set aside.

2. In a large bowl toss together cabbage and peaches. Gently toss to combine. Drizzle with about half of the dressing; toss to coat. Top with blackberries and, if desired, crumbled cheese. Pass remaining dressing.

MAKES 6 SERVINGS

Per serving: 151 cal., 9 g total fat (1 g sat. fat), 0 mg chol., 116 mg sodium, 16 g carbo., 5 g fiber, 2 g pro.

Asian Coleslaw

Start to Finish: 25 minutes

- 4 cups packaged shredded cabbage with carrot (coleslaw mix)
- 1 medium yellow, orange, red, or green sweet pepper, seeded and thinly sliced (1 cup)
- ¼ cup thinly sliced green onions (2)
- ¼ cup snipped fresh cilantro
- ½ cup bottled low-fat sesame ginger salad dressing

1. In a large bowl combine coleslaw mix, sweet pepper, green onions, and cilantro. Pour dressing over cabbage mixture, tossing lightly to coat. Serve immediately or cover and chill up to 24 hours. **MAKES 6 SERVINGS**

Per serving: 68 cal., 3 g total fat (1 g sat. fat), 0 mg chol., 207 mg sodium, 9 g carbo., 1 g fiber, 1 g pro.

Tomato and Sweet Pepper Salad ♡

Start to Finish: 25 minutes

- 3 large yellow sweet peppers, seeded and thinly sliced in rings (about 3 cups)
- 4 cups fresh watercress or baby spinach
- 3 or 4 medium tomatoes (about 1 pound), cut into wedges
- 1 recipe Herb-Dijon Vinaigrette
- ¼ cup crumbled Gorgonzola or blue cheese (1 ounce)

1. In a covered 4-quart pot cook sweet pepper rings in a large amount of boiling water for 1 to 2 minutes or just until crisp-tender. Drain and rinse with cold water to cool. Drain well.

SWEET PEPPER AND FOUR-BEAN SALAD

Shredded Carrot Salad

Start to Finish: 20 minutes

  2 tablespoons lime juice
1½ teaspoons honey
  ½ teaspoon salt
  ⅓ cup extra virgin olive oil
 12 ounces carrots, peeled, trimmed, and shredded
  ⅓ cup coarsely chopped tart green apple
  2 tablespoons snipped fresh Italian (flat-leaf) parsley

1. For dressing, in a medium bowl whisk together lime juice, honey, and salt. Drizzle in olive oil, whisking until combined; set aside.
2. In a medium bowl combine carrots, apple, and parsley. Drizzle with dressing; toss to coat. Serve immediately or cover and chill for up to 12 hours. **MAKES 4 SERVINGS**

Per serving: 215 cal., 19 g total fat (3 g sat. fat), 0 mg chol., 351 mg sodium, 13 g carbo., 3 g fiber, 1 g pro.

Fig and Orange Salad

Start to Finish: 25 minutes

  6 cups mesclun or mixed salad greens
  3 green onions, thinly sliced
  2 tablespoons olive oil
  1 teaspoon finely shredded orange peel
  2 tablespoons orange juice
  1 tablespoon champagne vinegar or white wine vinegar
  1 8- or 9-ounce package dried Calimyrna figs, cut into thin wedges (about 1½ cups)
1⅓ cups orange sections (4 oranges)
   Salt and black pepper
  ¼ cup pecan pieces, toasted

1. In a large salad bowl; combine salad greens and green onions; set aside.
2. For dressing, in a small bowl whisk together olive oil, orange peel, orange juice, and vinegar. Pour dressing over greens mixture; toss gently to coat. Add figs and orange sections; toss gently to combine. Season with salt and pepper.
3. To serve, arrange greens mixture on salad plates. Sprinkle with pecans. **MAKES 6 SERVINGS**

Per serving: 198 cal., 8 g total fat (1 g sat. fat), 0 mg chol., 109 mg sodium, 32 g carbo., 6 g fiber, 3 g pro.

Sweet Pepper and Four-Bean Salad ♡

Prep: 20 minutes **Chill:** 4 to 24 hours

  4 cups fresh green and/or wax beans, trimmed and cut into 1½-inch pieces, or one 16-ounce package frozen cut green beans
  1 15- to 16-ounce can kidney beans, rinsed and drained
  1 15- to 16-ounce can garbanzo beans (chickpeas), rinsed and drained
  3 medium green, red, and/or yellow sweet peppers, seeded and cut into thin strips
  1 small red or white onion, thinly sliced and separated into rings
  ½ cup vinegar
  ¼ cup extra virgin olive oil
  1 tablespoon sugar
  2 teaspoons snipped fresh tarragon or thyme or ½ teaspoon dried tarragon or thyme, crushed
  ½ teaspoon black pepper

1. In a covered large saucepan cook fresh green and/or wax beans in a small amount of boiling water for 8 to 10 minutes or just until tender. (If using frozen green beans, cook according to package directions.) Drain beans; submerge in a bowl of ice water to cool quickly. Drain well.
2. In a large bowl combine green and/or wax beans, kidney beans, garbanzo beans, sweet peppers, and onion. For dressing, in a medium bowl whisk together vinegar, olive oil, sugar, tarragon, and black pepper until combined. Pour dressing over bean mixture. Toss gently to coat. Cover and chill for 4 to 24 hours, stirring occasionally. Serve with slotted spoon. **MAKES 14 SERVINGS**

Per serving: 117 cal., 4 g total fat (1 g sat. fat), 0 mg chol., 146 mg sodium, 17 g carbo., 5 g fiber, 5 g pro.

CONFETTI POTATO SALAD

Basil-Tomato Salad

Start to Finish: 30 minutes **Oven:** 425°F

> 1 recipe Lemon Vinaigrette
> ½ of a small baguette or French roll
> 2 tablespoons olive oil
> 2 cloves garlic, minced
> 1 small head green leaf lettuce, torn (6 cups)
> 3 cups fresh basil, torn
> 2 cups grape tomatoes, halved, or chopped plum tomatoes
> ½ cup pine nuts, toasted
> 2 ounces Parmesan cheese, shaved

1. Prepare Lemon Vinaigrette; set aside.
2. Preheat oven to 425°F. Split baguette in half horizontally. In small bowl combine olive oil and garlic. Brush onto cut sides of baguette. Cut each bread piece lengthwise into 3 or 4 breadsticks. Place on a baking sheet. Bake for 3 to 5 minutes or until toasted. Transfer to wire rack; cool.
3. In large bowl combine lettuce and basil. In 3- to 4-quart glass canister or desired container layer greens, tomatoes, pine nuts, and cheese. Serve with breadsticks and Lemon Vinaigrette. **MAKES 6 SERVINGS**

Lemon Vinaigrette In small screw-top jar combine ½ cup extra virgin olive oil, 1 teaspoon finely shredded lemon peel, ⅓ cup lemon juice (1 large lemon), 4 cloves minced garlic, 1 teaspoon sugar, ¼ teaspoon salt, and ¼ teaspoon black pepper. Cover; shake well.

Per serving: 449 cal., 33 g total fat (6 g sat. fat), 8 mg chol., 502 mg sodium, 30 g carbo., 3 g fiber, 13 g pro.

Confetti Potato Salad ♡

Prep: 30 minutes **Chill:** 4 to 24 hours

> 1½ pounds round red potatoes, cut into ½-inch cubes
> 1 cup fresh green beans cut into 2-inch-long pieces
> 2 cups broccoli and/or cauliflower florets
> ½ cup coarsely shredded carrot (1 medium)
> ½ cup bottled reduced-calorie ranch salad dressing
> ¼ teaspoon black pepper
> 1 to 2 tablespoons fat-free milk (optional)

1. Place cubed potatoes in a large saucepan; add enough lightly salted water to cover. Bring to boiling; reduce heat. Simmer, covered, for 5 to 7 minutes or just until tender. Drain well; cool.
2. In a small saucepan bring a small amount of lightly salted water to boiling. Add green beans; return to boiling. Cook, covered, about 3 minutes or until crisp-tender. Drain; rinse with cold water.
3. In a very large bowl combine cooked potatoes, green beans, broccoli and/or cauliflower, and carrot. Add salad dressing and pepper; toss to coat. Cover and chill for 4 to 24 hours. If necessary, stir in enough milk to reach desired consistency.
MAKES 8 (1-CUP) SERVINGS

Per serving: 108 cal., 3 g total fat (0 g sat. fat), 5 mg chol., 179 mg sodium, 18 g carbo., 3 g fiber, 3 g pro.

BASIL-TOMATO SALAD

NEW POTATO SALAD

Sweet and Fiery Polenta Fries

Start to Finish: 25 minutes

  1 teaspoon sugar
  ¼ teaspoon salt
  ¼ teaspoon ground cumin
  ¼ teaspoon chili powder
      Dash cayenne pepper
  ½ of a 16-ounce tube refrigerated cooked
      polenta, cut in half crosswise
  2 tablespoons all-purpose flour
  ¼ cup canola oil
  2 tablespoons finely chopped red sweet
      pepper
  1 tablespoon snipped fresh basil or Italian
      (flat-leaf) parsley

1. In a medium bowl combine sugar, salt, cumin, chili powder, and cayenne pepper; set aside. Cut each half of the polenta lengthwise into 6 thin slices; cut each slice lengthwise into 4 strips. Toss strips with flour to coat; shake off excess flour.

2. In a large nonstick skillet heat oil on medium-high heat. Cook polenta strips in hot oil for 7 to 8 minutes or until golden, turning occasionally. Remove polenta strips from skillet; drain on paper towels. Add polenta strips to sugar mixture in bowl; toss gently to coat. Sprinkle with sweet pepper and basil.

MAKES 4 SERVINGS

Per serving: 160 cal., 11 g total fat (5 g sat. fat), 0 mg chol., 367 mg sodium, 15 g carbo., 2 g fiber, 2 g pro.

New Potato Salad

Prep: 40 minutes **Chill:** 6 to 24 hours

  2 pounds tiny new potatoes
  1 cup low-fat mayonnaise or light salad
      dressing
  1 cup chopped celery (2 stalks)
  1 cup chopped onion (1 large)
  ⅓ cup chopped sweet or dill pickles
  ½ teaspoon salt
  ¼ teaspoon coarsely ground black pepper
  2 hard-cooked eggs, chopped
  1 to 2 tablespoons fat-free milk
      Coarsely ground black pepper

1. In a large saucepan combine potatoes and enough water to cover potatoes. Bring to boiling; reduce heat. Simmer, covered, for 15 to 20 minutes or just until tender. Drain well; cool potatoes. Cut potatoes into quarters.

2. In a large bowl combine mayonnaise, celery, onion, pickles, the ½ teaspoon salt, and the ¼ teaspoon pepper. Add the potatoes and eggs, gently tossing to coat. Cover and chill for 6 to 24 hours.

3. To serve, stir enough of the milk into salad to reach desired consistency. Season with additional pepper. **MAKES 16 SERVINGS**

Per serving: 86 cal., 3 g total fat (1 g sat. fat), 27 mg chol., 254 mg sodium, 14 g carbo., 1 g fiber, 2 g pro.

GREEN BEANS WITH TOASTED ALMONDS

NUTTY BROCCOLI

Green Beans with Toasted Almonds ♡

Start to Finish: 20 minutes

　3　cups fresh green beans (about 10 ounces), trimmed if desired
　¼　cup sliced almonds, toasted
　1　tablespoon olive oil
　½　teaspoon Homemade Spice Mix

1. In a covered large saucepan cook beans in a small amount of boiling water for 8 to 10 minutes or until crisp-tender. Drain well. Return to hot pan. Stir in almonds, olive oil, and Homemade Spice Mix. Heat through.
MAKES 6 SERVINGS

Homemade Spice Mix In a small bowl combine ½ teaspoon paprika, ½ teaspoon ground coriander, ½ teaspoon ground cumin, ¼ teaspoon garlic powder, ¼ teaspoon ground turmeric, ⅛ teaspoon salt, and ⅛ teaspoon cayenne pepper. Store leftover mix in an airtight container at room temperature for up to 6 months. Makes about 2¼ teaspoons.

Per serving: 59 cal., 4 g total fat (0 g sat. fat), 0 mg chol., 14 mg sodium, 5 g carbo., 2 g fiber, 2 g pro.

Nutty Broccoli

Start to Finish: 25 minutes

　1　pound broccoli, trimmed and cut into 2-inch pieces
　3　tablespoons butter
　2　tablespoons orange juice
　½　teaspoon finely shredded orange peel (set aside)
　¼　teaspoon salt
　3　tablespoons chopped walnuts, pine nuts, or pecans, toasted
　　　Orange wedges (optional)

1. If desired, cut broccoli stem pieces lengthwise in half. To steam, place a vegetable steamer basket in a 3-quart saucepan. Add water to reach just below the bottom of the basket. Bring water to boiling. Add broccoli to steamer basket. Cover and reduce heat. Steam for 8 to 10 minutes or just until broccoli stems are tender. Transfer broccoli to a serving dish.
2. Meanwhile, in a small skillet melt butter on medium-high heat; cook and stir butter for 3 to 4 minutes or until medium brown. Carefully add orange juice; cook for 10 seconds. Remove from heat; stir in orange peel and salt. Pour over broccoli. Sprinkle with walnuts. If desired, garnish with orange wedges.
MAKES 6 SERVINGS

Per serving: 94 cal., 8 g total fat (4 g sat. fat), 15 mg chol., 153 mg sodium, 4 g carbo., 1 g fiber, 2 g pro.

Roasted Asparagus

Prep: 10 minutes　**Roast:** 15 minutes
Oven: 450°F

　1　pound fresh asparagus
　⅛　teaspoon black pepper
　1　tablespoon olive oil
　3　tablespoons grated Parmesan cheese

1. Preheat oven to 450°F. Snap off and discard woody bases from asparagus. If desired, scrape off scales. Place asparagus in a 2-quart baking dish. Sprinkle with pepper. Drizzle with olive oil.
2. Roast, uncovered, about 15 minutes or until crisp-tender, using tongs to lightly toss twice during roasting. Transfer asparagus to a warm serving platter. Sprinkle with cheese.
MAKES 4 SERVINGS

Per serving: 58 cal., 5 g total fat (1 g sat. fat), 3 mg chol., 59 mg sodium, 3 g carbo., 1 g fiber, 3 g pro.

BROCCOLI AND CAULIFLOWER
SAUTÉ

Mustard-Glazed Brussels Sprouts and Oranges ♡

Start to Finish: 25 minutes

    3 medium blood oranges and/or oranges
    1 pound Brussels sprouts (about 4 cups)
    1 tablespoon butter or margarine
    2 teaspoons cornstarch
    ¼ teaspoon five-spice powder or dried dill
    2 tablespoons honey mustard

1. Finely shred enough peel from 1 of the oranges to make ½ teaspoon peel; set peel aside. Halve the orange; squeeze juice. Working over a bowl to catch the juices, peel and section the remaining 2 oranges; set orange sections aside. Combine the juices to make ⅓ cup, adding water if necessary. Set juice aside.

2. Trim stems and remove any wilted outer leaves from Brussels sprouts; wash. Halve any large sprouts. In a medium saucepan cook sprouts, uncovered, in a small amount of boiling water for 10 to 12 minutes or until tender. Drain; transfer to a serving bowl. Gently stir in the orange sections; cover and keep warm.

3. In the same saucepan melt butter. Stir in cornstarch and five-spice powder. Stir in reserved orange peel, the ⅓ cup orange juice, and the mustard. Cook and stir until thickened and bubbly. Cook and stir for 1 minute more. Spoon over Brussels sprouts and orange sections; toss gently to coat.

MAKES 5 OR 6 SERVINGS

Per serving: 103 cal., 3 g total fat (1 g sat. fat), 0 mg chol., 87 mg sodium, 19 g carbo., 5 g fiber, 3 g pro.

Broccoli and Cauliflower Sauté

Start to Finish: 20 minutes

    2 teaspoons olive oil
    1 cup broccoli florets
    1 cup cauliflower florets
    1 clove garlic, thinly sliced
    ¼ cup dry white wine or reduced-sodium
       chicken broth
    3 tablespoons water
    ⅛ teaspoon salt
    ⅛ teaspoon black pepper

1. In a large skillet heat oil on medium-high heat. Add broccoli, cauliflower, and garlic; cook for 2 minutes, stirring occasionally. Carefully add wine, the water, salt, and pepper; reduce heat to low. Cover and cook for 2 minutes. Uncover; increase heat to medium. Cook for 2 minutes or until vegetables are tender. **MAKES 4 SERVINGS**

Per serving: 47 cal., 2 g total fat (0 g sat. fat), 0 mg chol., 88 mg sodium, 4 g carbo., 1 g fiber, 1 g pro.

BUTTER-GLAZED CARROTS

Grilled Herb Corn on the Cob ♡

Prep: 20 minutes **Grill:** 25 minutes

6 fresh ears of corn
2 tablespoons snipped fresh oregano or
   2 teaspoons dried oregano, crushed
2 tablespoons snipped fresh thyme or
   2 teaspoons dried basil, crushed
1 tablespoon snipped fresh tarragon or
   1 teaspoon dried basil, crushed
2 tablespoons olive oil
½ teaspoon salt
¼ teaspoon black pepper

1. Peel back corn husks, but do not remove. Discard silks. Soak in cold water for 15 minutes; pat dry.
2. In a small bowl combine oregano, thyme, and tarragon; set aside. In another small bowl combine oil, salt, and pepper.
3. Brush corn with oil mixture. Sprinkle with herb mixture. Fold husks back around cobs. Tie with 100%-cotton kitchen string.
4. If desired, place corn in a grill basket. For a charcoal grill, grill corn on the rack of an uncovered grill directly over medium coals for 25 to 30 minutes or until kernels are tender, turning and rearranging ears occasionally. (For a gas grill, preheat grill. Reduce heat to medium. Place corn on grill rack over heat. Cover and grill as above.) **MAKES 6 SERVINGS**

Per serving: 174 cal., 6 g total fat (0 g sat. fat), 0 mg chol., 218 mg sodium, 30 g carbo., 4 g fiber, 6 g pro.

Butter-Glazed Carrots ♡

Start to Finish: 20 minutes

1 pound carrots, peeled and cut into ½-inch diagonal slices
2 tablespoons butter, softened
1 to 2 teaspoons dried tarragon or basil, crushed
   Salt and black pepper

1. In a medium saucepan cook carrots, covered, in ½ cup boiling water for 8 to 10 minutes or just until carrots are tender. Drain; return carrots to saucepan.
2. Add butter and tarragon to the saucepan; stir until combined. If necessary, heat on low heat to melt butter completely. Season with salt and pepper. Serve warm. **MAKES 4 SERVINGS**

Microwave directions In a microwave-safe baking dish or casserole combine carrots and ¼ cup water. Cover and microwave on high for 7 to 9 minutes or just until carrots are tender. Drain; return carrots to dish. Add butter and tarragon; stir until combined. If necessary, microwave for 10 to 20 seconds more to melt butter completely. Season with salt and pepper. Serve warm.

Per serving: 98 cal., 6 g total fat (4 g sat. fat), 15 mg chol., 261 mg sodium, 11 g carbo., 3 g fiber, 1 g pro.

Maple-Glazed Carrots Prepare as directed, except use 1 tablespoon butter, omit the herb, and add 2 tablespoons pure maple syrup and 1 tablespoon sesame seeds, toasted.

SKILLET SCALLOPED CORN

Herbed Leek Gratin
Prep: 20 minutes **Bake:** 35 minutes
Oven: 375°F

  3 pounds slender leeks
  ½ cup whipping cream
  ½ cup chicken broth
  2 tablespoons snipped fresh marjoram or
      1½ teaspoons dried marjoram, crushed
  ½ teaspoon salt
  ½ teaspoon freshly ground black pepper
1½ cups soft French or Italian bread crumbs
  3 tablespoons grated Parmesan cheese
  3 tablespoons butter, melted
      Fresh marjoram sprigs (optional)

1. Preheat oven to 375°F. Trim roots off leeks, leaving pieces 4 to 5 inches long with white and pale green parts. Cut leeks in half lengthwise. Rinse leeks thoroughly under cold running water; pat dry with paper towels. Arrange leeks, cut sides down, in a greased 2-quart au gratin dish or rectangular baking dish, overlapping leeks as necessary to fit. (Leeks should all be facing the same direction.)
2. In a small bowl combine whipping cream and chicken broth; pour over leeks. Sprinkle with half of the snipped or dried marjoram, the salt, and pepper. Cover tightly with foil. Bake for 20 minutes.
3. Meanwhile, in a small bowl combine bread crumbs, Parmesan cheese, and the remaining snipped or dried marjoram. Drizzle with melted butter; toss to coat.
4. Sprinkle leeks with bread crumb mixture. Bake, uncovered, for 15 to 20 minutes more or until leeks are tender and crumbs are golden brown. If desired, garnish with fresh marjoram sprigs. **MAKES 6 SERVINGS**

Per serving: 224 cal., 15 g total fat (9 g sat. fat), 45 mg chol., 457 mg sodium, 21 g carbo., 2 g fiber, 4 g pro.

Skillet Scalloped Corn ♡

Start to Finish: 15 minutes

  2 teaspoons butter
  ½ cup crushed rich round, wheat, or rye crackers
  1 11-ounce can whole kernel corn with sweet peppers, drained
  1 7- to 8.75-ounce can whole kernel corn with sweet peppers, whole kernel corn, or white (shoepeg) corn, drained
  2 1-ounce slices process Swiss cheese, torn
  ⅓ cup milk
  ⅛ teaspoon onion powder
      Dash black pepper

1. For topping, in a large skillet melt butter on medium heat. Add 2 tablespoons of the crushed crackers to the skillet. Cook and stir until lightly browned; remove and set aside.
2. In the same skillet combine remaining crushed crackers, corn, cheese, milk, onion powder, and pepper. Cook, stirring frequently, until cheese melts. Transfer to a serving dish; sprinkle with crumb topping. **MAKES 4 SERVINGS**

Per serving: 183 cal., 9 g total fat (4 g sat. fat), 18 mg chol., 704 mg sodium, 19 g carbo., 2 g fiber, 6 g pro.

HERBED LEEK GRATIN

Twice-Baked Jarlsberg Potatoes

Prep: 30 minutes **Bake:** 1 hour 5 minutes
Stand: 10 minutes **Oven:** 425°F/400°F

  8 baking potatoes (about 3 pounds total)
  ¼ cup butter
  ½ cup chopped leeks (white part and tender
     green part only)
  ¼ cup chopped shallots
  4 cloves garlic, minced
  1 tablespoon snipped fresh Italian (flat-leaf)
     parsley
  1 cup sour cream or plain yogurt
     Milk (optional)
     Salt and black pepper
  ¾ cup finely shredded Jarlsberg cheese
     (3 ounces)

1. Preheat oven to 425°F. Scrub potatoes;
pat dry. Prick potatoes with a fork. Bake
potatoes for 40 to 60 minutes or until tender.
Let baked potatoes stand about 10 minutes.
Cut a lengthwise slice from the top of each
potato; discard skin from slice and place pulp
in a medium bowl. Scoop pulp out of each
potato. Add the pulp to the bowl. Reduce
oven temperature to 400°F.
2. In a medium skillet melt butter on medium
heat. Add leeks, shallots, and garlic; cook and
stir for 5 to 7 minutes or until tender. Add
parsley; cook and stir for 30 seconds. Set aside.
3. Mash the potato pulp with a potato masher
or an electric mixer on low. Add sour cream
and butter-leek mixture; beat until almost
smooth. (If necessary, stir in 1 to 2 tablespoons
milk to reach desired consistency.) Season to
taste with salt and pepper. Stir in the Jarlsberg
cheese. Spoon the mashed potato mixture
into the potato shells.
4. Place stuffed potatoes in a 3-quart baking
dish. Bake for 25 minutes. **MAKES 8 SERVINGS**

Per serving: 273 cal., 14 g total fat (8 g sat. fat), 32 mg
chol., 153 mg sodium, 32 g carbo., 3 g fiber, 8 g pro.

Sweet Potatoes with Rosemary

Prep: 20 minutes **Cook:** 6 minutes
Broil: 5 minutes

  1½ pounds sweet potatoes, peeled and cut
      lengthwise into ½-inch-thick wedges
  1   cup water
  2   tablespoons Dijon mustard
  1   tablespoon olive oil
  1   tablespoon honey
  2   teaspoons snipped fresh rosemary or
      ½ teaspoon dried rosemary, crushed
  ⅛   teaspoon black pepper

1. Preheat broiler. Place sweet potatoes and
the water in a 2-quart microwave-safe baking
dish. Cover with vented plastic wrap.
Microwave on high for 6 to 8 minutes or until
potatoes are nearly tender, rearranging once
halfway through cooking. Drain well.
2. Meanwhile, in a small bowl combine
mustard, olive oil, honey, rosemary, and
pepper; set aside.
3. Place potatoes on the greased unheated
rack of a broiler pan. Broil 3 to 4 inches from
the heat for 4 minutes, carefully turning once
halfway through broiling. Brush with half of
the mustard mixture. Broil for 2 to
3 minutes more or until tender, turning and
brushing once with remaining mustard
mixture. **MAKES 4 SERVINGS**

Per serving: 159 cal., 3 g total fat (0 g sat. fat), 0 mg
chol., 249 mg sodium, 29 g carbo., 4 g fiber, 2 g pro.

CARAMEL ACORN SQUASH

Orange-Glazed Pearl Onions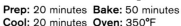

Start to Finish: 40 minutes

- 1 pound unpeeled pearl onions
- 1 tablespoon vegetable oil
- 1 clove garlic, thinly sliced
- ½ cup orange marmalade
- ½ teaspoon salt
- ⅛ teaspoon black pepper
- 1 tablespoon snipped fresh chives or parsley

1. In a medium saucepan cook onions in enough boiling water to cover for 1 minute; drain. Cool onions slightly; carefully remove skins. In the same saucepan cook onions, covered, in a small amount of boiling lightly salted water for 10 minutes or until tender; drain and set aside.

2. In a large skillet heat oil on medium-high heat. Add garlic; cook and stir about 30 seconds or until golden. Stir in marmalade until melted. Stir in cooked onions, salt, and pepper. Cook and stir for 3 to 5 minutes or until marmalade is slightly thickened and onions are coated. Stir in chives. **MAKES 4 TO 6 SERVINGS**

Per serving: 173 cal., 3 g total fat (1 g sat. fat), 0 mg chol., 316 mg sodium, 37 g carbo., 2 g fiber, 1 g pro.

Caramel Acorn Squash

Prep: 20 minutes **Bake:** 50 minutes
Cool: 20 minutes **Oven:** 350°F

- 2 1- to 1½-pound acorn squash
- ¼ cup butter
- ¼ cup packed brown sugar
- ¼ cup apple cider
- ½ teaspoon ground cinnamon
- ¼ teaspoon salt
- ¼ teaspoon freshly ground nutmeg

1. Preheat oven to 350°F. Line a shallow baking pan with parchment paper or aluminum foil. Cut each squash in half; discard seeds and remove fibrous material. Place halves, cut sides down, in the prepared baking pan. Bake, uncovered, for 40 to 45 minutes or until the squash is tender. Let stand until cool enough to handle; slice into 1-inch slices. (If desired, cover and refrigerate overnight. Let the squash come to room temperature before finishing the recipe.) Arrange squash slices in a 2-quart rectangular baking dish, overlapping as necessary.

2. In a large skillet heat butter, brown sugar, cider, cinnamon, salt, and nutmeg to boiling, stirring to dissolve sugar. Reduce heat and boil gently, uncovered, for 5 minutes or until syrupy. Drizzle glaze over squash. Bake, uncovered, about 10 minutes or until heated through. Spoon glaze over squash before serving. **MAKES 6 SERVINGS**

Per serving: 154 cal., 8 g total fat (5 g sat. fat), 20 mg chol., 160 mg sodium, 22 g carbo., 2 g fiber, 1 g pro.

ORANGE-GLAZED PEARL ONIONS

Desserts

DARK CHOCOLATE BROWNIES

Dark Chocolate Brownies

Prep: 25 minutes **Bake:** 25 minutes
Cool: 30 minutes **Oven:** 350°F

 14 ounces unsweetened chocolate, coarsely
   chopped
 1½ cups butter
 ½ cup water
 2 cups granulated sugar
 1½ cups packed brown sugar
 4 eggs
 2 teaspoons vanilla
 2⅔ cups all-purpose flour
 ¼ teaspoon salt
 ¼ teaspoon ground cinnamon
   Vanilla or coffee ice cream (optional)
   Chocolate-flavor syrup (optional)

1. Preheat oven to 350°F. Lightly grease a
13×9×2-inch baking pan; set aside.

2. In a large saucepan combine chocolate,
butter, and water; cook and stir on low heat
until chocolate is melted. Transfer to a large
mixing bowl.

3. Add granulated sugar and brown sugar to
the chocolate mixture; beat with an electric
mixer on low to medium until combined. Add
eggs and vanilla; beat on medium for 2 minutes.
Add flour, salt, and cinnamon; beat on low
until combined. Spread batter in prepared
baking pan.

4. Bake about 25 minutes or until a wooden
toothpick inserted near center comes out
clean. Cool in pan on a wire rack about
30 minutes or until brownies hold a cut edge.
Cut into bars.

5. If desired, top each brownie with a scoop
of ice cream and drizzle with chocolate syrup.
MAKES 40 BROWNIES

Per brownie: 214 cal., 13 g total fat (8 g sat. fat), 39 mg
chol., 76 mg sodium, 26 g carbo., 2 g fiber, 3 g pro.

Chocolate Cookie Treats

Prep: 45 minutes **Chill:** 1 hour
Bake: 10 minutes per batch
Cool: 1 hour **Oven:** 350°F

 1 ounce sweet baking, bittersweet, or
   semisweet chocolate, melted and cooled
   slightly
 5 tablespoons butter, softened
 ¾ cup granulated sugar
 1 large egg
 1 egg yolk
 1 teaspoon vanilla
 1⅓ cups all-purpose flour
 ⅓ cup walnuts, finely chopped
 32 walnut halves
 1 recipe Chocolate Glaze
   Powdered sugar (optional)

1. Preheat oven to 350°F. Line a baking sheet
with parchment paper; set aside. In a medium
bowl beat butter with an electric mixer on
medium-high about 2 minutes or until smooth.
Add granulated sugar, beating until creamy.
Add egg, egg yolk, and vanilla, beating well.
Stir in melted chocolate. Stir in flour and
chopped walnuts. Cover and chill for 1 hour.

2. Shape dough into 1-inch balls. Place on
prepared cookie sheets. Press a walnut half
into top of each cookie. Bake for 10 to
12 minutes or until centers are set. Remove
from pan and cool completely on a wire rack.

3. Spoon Chocolate Glaze evenly over cooled
cookies. Let stand until glaze is set. If desired,
sprinkle with powdered sugar. **MAKES ABOUT
32 COOKIES**

Chocolate Glaze In a small saucepan melt
1 ounce sweet baking, bittersweet, or
semisweet chocolate and 1 tablespoon butter.
Remove from heat. Add 1 cup powdered
sugar, 2 tablespoons fat-free milk, and
¼ teaspoon vanilla. Stir until well combined.

Per cookie: 99 cal., 5 g total fat (2 g sat. fat), 19 mg
chol., 19 mg sodium, 14 g carbo., 0 g fiber, 1 g pro.

Almond Flower Cake

Prep: 40 minutes **Bake:** 25 minutes
Cool: 1 hour **Oven:** 375°F

- 1 cup butter, softened
- 4 eggs
- 3 cups sifted cake flour
- 1½ teaspoons baking soda
- ½ teaspoon salt
- 1½ cups slivered almonds, toasted
- 2 cups sugar
- ½ teaspoon almond extract
- 1 cup buttermilk
  Sliced almonds, toasted
  Miniature candy-coated milk chocolate pieces
- 1 recipe Milk Chocolate Frosting

1. Let butter and eggs stand at room temperature for 30 minutes. Preheat oven to 375°F. Grease bottoms of three 8-inch round cake pans; line bottoms of pans with parchment paper. Grease and lightly flour pans. In a medium bowl stir together flour, baking soda, and salt; set aside.
2. In a food processor combine almonds and sugar; cover and process until almonds are finely ground. In a large mixing bowl beat butter and ground almond mixture until light and fluffy. Add eggs, 1 at a time, beating well after each addition. Beat in almond extract. Alternately add flour mixture and buttermilk, beating on low after each addition just until combined. Divide batter among prepared pans, spreading evenly.
3. Bake about 25 minutes or until a wooden toothpick inserted near the centers comes out clean. Cool layers in pans on wire racks for 10 minutes. Remove layers from pans; cool thoroughly on wire racks.
4. Prepare Milk Chocolate Frosting. Place 1 cake layer, bottom side up, on serving platter. Spread with ¾ cup frosting. Top with second layer, bottom side up; spread with ¾ cup frosting. Top with third layer, rounded side up. Spread top and sides with remaining frosting. Decorate with sliced almonds and candies, using almonds for petals and candies for the centers. **MAKES 14 SERVINGS**

Milk Chocolate Frosting In a medium saucepan combine ½ cup butter, ¾ cup unsweetened cocoa powder, and ½ cup milk. Cook on low heat until butter melts, stirring occasionally. Cool slightly. In a large mixing bowl beat 1 cup softened butter and 2 teaspoons vanilla with an electric mixer on medium for 30 seconds. Beat in cocoa mixture. Add sugar, ½ cup at a time, beating on medium after each addition. Beat until frosting is smooth and creamy.

Per serving: 918 cal., 44 g total fat (23 g sat. fat), 149 mg chol., 272 mg sodium, 128 g carbo., 4 g fiber, 10 g pro.

Blueberry-Mango Upside-Down Cake ♡

Prep: 35 minutes **Stand:** 30 minutes
Bake: 35 minutes **Cool:** 5 minutes **Oven:** 350°F

- 2 egg whites
- 1⅓ cups whole wheat pastry flour
- 2 teaspoons baking powder
- ½ teaspoon ground ginger
- 3 tablespoons packed brown sugar
- 2 tablespoons butter, melted
- 1½ cups peeled, pitted, and sliced fresh mangoes and/or unpeeled peach slices
- ½ cup fresh blueberries
- ½ cup granulated sugar
- ¼ cup butter, softened
- 1 teaspoon vanilla
- ⅔ cup fat-free milk
- ½ cup fresh blueberries and fresh peach and/or mango slices (optional)
- 3 cups vanilla frozen yogurt (optional)

1. Place egg whites in a medium bowl. Let stand at room temperature for 30 minutes. In a small bowl stir together flour, baking powder, and ginger; set aside.
2. Preheat oven to 350°F. Grease a 9×1½-inch round baking pan. In a small bowl stir together brown sugar and the 2 tablespoons melted butter. Spread in prepared pan. Arrange 1½ cups mango and/or peach slices over brown sugar mixture. Sprinkle with ½ cup blueberries.
3. Beat egg whites with an electric mixer on high until soft peaks form (tips curl). Gradually

add half of the granulated sugar, beating until stiff peaks form (tips stand straight). Set aside.
4. In a large bowl beat the ¼ cup butter with an electric mixer on medium for 30 seconds. Beat in the remaining half of the granulated sugar and the vanilla. Alternately add the flour mixture and milk, beating on low just until combined. Fold egg white mixture into batter; spoon over fruit in baking pan, spreading evenly.
5. Bake for 35 to 40 minutes or until a toothpick inserted near the center comes out clean. Cool cake in pan on a wire rack for 5 minutes.
6. Loosen side by running a knife around cake; invert onto serving plate. Cut into wedges. Serve warm. If desired, top with additional fruit and serve with frozen yogurt.
MAKES 12 SERVINGS

Per serving: 155 cal., 6 g total fat (4 g sat. fat), 16 mg chol., 97 mg sodium, 24 g carbo., 2 g fiber, 3 g pro.

BLUEBERRY-MANGO
UPSIDE-DOWN CAKE

PUMPKIN-PEAR CAKE

Pumpkin-Pear Cake

Prep: 25 minutes **Bake:** 35 minutes
Cool: 35 minutes **Oven:** 350°F

    1 cup packed brown sugar
   ⅓ cup butter, melted
 1½ teaspoons cornstarch
    2 15-ounce cans pear halves in light syrup
   ½ cup coarsely chopped pecans
    1 package 2-layer-size spice cake mix
    1 cup canned pumpkin

1. Preheat oven to 350°F. In a small bowl combine brown sugar, butter, and cornstarch. Drain pears, reserving 3 tablespoons of the syrup. Stir reserved syrup into brown sugar mixture. Pour mixture into a 13×9×2-inch baking pan. If desired, cut pear halves into fans by making 3 or 4 lengthwise cuts ¼ inch from the stem end of each pear half to the bottom of the pear half. Arrange whole or fanned pear halves on top of the syrup in pan, cored sides down. Sprinkle pecans evenly in pan.
2. Prepare cake mix according to package directions, except decrease oil to 2 tablespoons and add pumpkin. Slowly pour cake batter into pan, spreading evenly.
3. Bake for 35 to 40 minutes or until a wooden toothpick inserted near center comes out clean. Cool in pan on a wire rack for 5 minutes. Run a thin metal spatula around edges of cake. Carefully invert cake into a 15×10×1-inch baking pan or onto a very large serving platter with slightly raised sides. Cool about 30 minutes before serving. Serve warm. **MAKES 16 SERVINGS**

Per serving: 337 cal., 15 g total fat (4 g sat. fat), 51 mg chol., 254 mg sodium, 51 g carbo., 2 g fiber, 3 g pro.

Pineapple Cake with Macadamia-Apricot Topper

Prep: 25 minutes **Bake:** 35 minutes
Cool: 35 minutes **Oven:** 350°F

    6 egg whites
    3 egg yolks
 1⅔ cups cake flour
   ⅔ cup sugar
    2 teaspoons baking powder
   ¼ teaspoon salt
   ½ cup unsweetened pineapple juice
   ¼ cup canola oil
   ¼ teaspoon cream of tartar
    1 recipe Macadamia-Apricot Topper
    2 tablespoons shredded coconut, toasted

1. Allow egg whites and yolks to stand at room temperature for 30 minutes.
2. Preheat oven to 325°F. Meanwhile, in a large bowl combine flour, sugar, baking powder, and salt. Make a well in the center of the flour mixture.
3. Add egg yolks, juice, and oil to flour mixture. Beat with electric mixer on low until combined. Beat on high about 5 minutes or until batter is satin smooth. Wash and dry the beaters. In a very large bowl combine egg whites and cream of tartar; beat with an electric mixer on medium until stiff peaks form (tips stand straight). Pour batter in a thin stream over beaten egg whites, folding gently as you pour. Pour into an ungreased 10-inch tube pan.
4. Bake 45 to 50 minutes or until top springs back when lightly touched. Immediately invert cake (in the pan); cool completely. Loosen sides of the cake from the pan; remove cake from pan. Top with Macadamia-Apricot Topper and coconut. **MAKES 16 SERVINGS**

Macadamia-Apricot Topper Drain one 15-ounce can unpeeled apricot halves in light syrup; cut into strips. In a saucepan mix ⅔ cup unsweetened pineapple juice and 2 teaspoons cornstarch. Cook and stir until bubbly; cook and stir 2 minutes more. Stir in ½ cup chopped, toasted macadamia nuts. Stir in apricots. Makes 1¾ cups.

Per serving: 191 cal., 8 g total fat (1 g sat. fat), 39 mg chol., 91 mg sodium, 28 g carbo., 1 g fiber, 4 g pro.

Mocha Pound Cake

Prep: 25 minutes **Stand:** 30 minutes
Bake: 1 hour 15 minutes **Cool:** 1 hour
Oven: 325°F

- ⅔ cup butter
- 3 eggs
- 2 cups all-purpose flour
- 1¼ cups sugar
- ½ teaspoon cream of tartar
- ½ teaspoon salt
- ¼ teaspoon baking soda
- ½ cup cold water
- 1 tablespoon instant coffee crystals
- 1 teaspoon vanilla
- 2 ounces unsweetened chocolate, melted and cooled
- 1 recipe Coffee Cream (optional)
  Milk chocolate curls (optional)
  Instant coffee crystals (optional)

1. Allow butter and eggs to stand at room temperature for 30 minutes. Meanwhile, grease and lightly flour a 9×5×3-inch loaf pan; set aside. In a medium bowl stir together flour, sugar, cream of tartar, salt, and baking soda; set aside.

2. Preheat oven to 325°F. In a large mixing bowl beat butter with an electric mixer on medium to high for 30 seconds. Add flour mixture; beat for 2 to 3 minutes or until fine crumbs form.

3. In a small bowl combine the water and the 1 tablespoon coffee crystals, stirring until coffee crystals are dissolved. Add coffee mixture and vanilla to butter mixture; beat on low until combined. Beat on medium speed for 2 minutes. Beat in eggs and melted chocolate on low until combined. Beat on medium for 1 minute.

4. Pour batter into prepared pan, spreading evenly. Bake for 75 to 80 minutes or until a wooden toothpick inserted near center comes out clean.

5. Cool in pan on a wire rack for 10 minutes. Remove from pan; cool completely on rack. If desired, top each serving with Coffee Cream, chocolate curls, and additional coffee crystals. **MAKES 10 TO 12 SERVINGS**

Per serving: 350 cal., 17 g total fat (10 g sat. fat), 96 mg chol., 259 mg sodium, 46 g carbo., 2 g fiber, 5 g pro.

Coffee Cream In a medium bowl combine 1 cup whipping cream, 1 tablespoon powdered sugar, and 1 teaspoon instant coffee crystals. Cover and chill for 10 minutes. Beat with an electric mixer on medium to high until stiff peaks form (tips stand straight).

White Chocolate and Almond Pound Cake

Prep: 50 minutes **Stand:** 30 minutes
Bake: 55 minutes **Cool:** 15 minutes
Oven: 350°F

- 1 cup butter
- 6 eggs
- 4 ounces white baking chocolate with cocoa butter, chopped
- 3 cups all-purpose flour
- ¼ cup blanched almonds, finely ground
- 1 teaspoon baking powder
- ½ teaspoon baking soda
- ½ teaspoon salt
- 2 cups sugar
- 1 tablespoon vanilla
- 1½ teaspoons almond extract
- 1 8-ounce carton dairy sour cream
- 4 ounces white baking chocolate with cocoa butter, chopped
- 1 teaspoon shortening
- ¼ cup sliced almonds, toasted and chopped

1. Allow butter and eggs to stand at room temperature for 30 minutes. Meanwhile, grease and flour a 10-inch fluted tube pan; set aside.

2. Preheat oven to 350°F. In a small heavy saucepan cook and stir 4 ounces white chocolate on low heat until it melts. In a medium bowl combine flour, finely ground almonds, baking powder, baking soda, and salt. Set aside.

3. In a very large mixing bowl beat butter with an electric mixer on medium to high for 30 seconds. Gradually add sugar, beating about 10 minutes or until mixture is fluffy and lighter in color. Add eggs, 1 at a time, beating about 1 minute after each addition and scraping sides of bowl frequently. Add vanilla, almond extract, and the melted white chocolate; beat just until combined.

4. Alternately add flour mixture and sour cream to butter mixture, beating on low to medium after each addition just until combined. Do not overmix. Spread batter in the prepared pan.

5. Bake for 55 to 60 minutes or until a toothpick inserted near the center comes out clean. Cool cake in pan on a wire rack for 15 minutes. Remove cake from pan; cool completely on a wire rack.

6. For glaze, in a heavy small saucepan combine 4 ounces white chocolate and shortening. Cook and stir on low heat until melted. Spoon glaze over pound cake and sprinkle with the chopped almonds. Let stand until glaze is set. **MAKES 16 TO 20 SERVINGS**

Per serving: 447 cal., 23 g total fat (13 g sat. fat), 120 mg chol., 270 mg sodium, 53 g carbo., 1 g fiber, 7 g pro.

WHITE CHOCOLATE AND ALMOND POUND CAKE

RASPBERRY-LEMONADE SHORTCAKES

Raspberry-Lemonade Shortcakes ♡

Prep: 35 minutes **Stand:** 30 minutes
Bake: 20 minutes **Oven:** 350°F

- 2 eggs
- 1 cup all-purpose flour
- 1 teaspoon baking powder
- 1 teaspoon finely shredded lemon peel
- ¾ cup sugar
- ½ cup fat-free milk
- 2 tablespoons tub-style 60% to 70% vegetable oil spread
- 1 recipe Raspberry-Lemonade Sauce
  Small lemon wedges (optional)
  Fresh mint leaves (optional)

1. Allow eggs to stand at room temperature for 30 minutes. Meanwhile, grease a 9×9×2-inch baking pan. Line pan with waxed paper. Grease and flour waxed paper; set pan aside. In a small bowl stir together flour, baking powder, and lemon peel; set aside.
2. Preheat oven to 350°F. In a medium bowl beat eggs with an electric mixer on high about 4 minutes or until thick. Gradually add sugar, beating on medium for 4 to 5 minutes or until light and fluffy. Add flour mixture; beat on low to medium just until combined.

3. In a small saucepan heat and stir milk and vegetable oil spread until spread melts; add to batter, beating until combined. Pour batter into prepared pan.
4. Bake for 20 to 25 minutes or until a wooden toothpick inserted near center comes out clean. Cool cake in pan on wire rack for 10 minutes. Invert cake onto wire rack lined with waxed paper; carefully peel off top waxed paper and cool completely.
5. Cut cake into 12 pieces. Split each cake piece in half horizontally. Place cake piece bottoms on individual dessert plates. Spoon half of the Raspberry-Lemonade Sauce over cake bottoms. Top with cake piece tops. Spoon remaining sauce onto cakes. If desired, garnish with lemon wedges and mint leaves. **MAKES 12 SERVINGS**

Raspberry-Lemonade Sauce Place 3 cups fresh or frozen raspberries in a medium bowl. (Thaw frozen raspberries in the bowl, if using; do not drain.) Mash berries with a potato masher. In a small saucepan combine ⅓ cup sugar, ¾ teaspoon cornstarch, and ½ teaspoon finely shredded lemon peel. Add mashed raspberries. Cook and stir until thickened and bubbly; cook and stir for 2 minutes more. Remove from heat. Cool about 10 minutes. Stir in 4 cups fresh or frozen (thawed and drained) raspberries. Makes about 3½ cups.

Per serving: 175 cal., 3 g total fat (1 g sat. fat), 35 mg chol., 49 mg sodium, 35 g carbo., 5 g fiber, 3 g pro.

Chocolate-Almond Torte

Prep: 25 minutes **Stand:** 30 minutes
Bake: 25 minutes **Cool:** 15 minutes
Oven: 350°F

- ¾ cup fat-free milk
- ⅓ cup unsweetened cocoa powder
- 2 ounces unsweetened chocolate, chopped
- 1 tablespoon balsamic vinegar
- 3 egg whites
  Nonstick cooking spray
- ¾ cup all-purpose flour
- ⅔ cup granulated sugar
- ½ teaspoon baking powder
- ¼ teaspoon baking soda
- ⅛ teaspoon salt
- ¼ cup granulated sugar
- ¼ cup sliced almonds
- 1 to 2 teaspoons powdered sugar (optional)

1. In a small saucepan combine milk and cocoa powder. Heat on medium heat, whisking constantly, just until mixture comes to a boil. Remove from heat. Whisk in unsweetened chocolate and vinegar until smooth. Cool to room temperature. Meanwhile, in a medium mixing bowl allow egg whites to stand at room temperature for 30 minutes.
2. Preheat oven to 350°F. Lightly coat an 8×2-inch round tart pan with removable bottom or 8-inch springform pan with nonstick cooking spray; set aside. In a large bowl stir together flour, the ⅔ cup granulated sugar, the baking powder, baking soda, and salt. Stir cooled chocolate mixture into flour mixture until well combined (batter will be thick); set aside.
3. Beat egg whites with an electric mixer on medium until soft peaks form (tips curl). Gradually add the ¼ cup granulated sugar, about 1 tablespoon at a time, beating on high until stiff peaks form (tips stand straight). Gently fold one-third of the beaten egg whites into the chocolate mixture. Fold in the remaining beaten egg whites just until combined. Spread batter in prepared pan. Sprinkle almonds over batter.
4. Bake for 25 to 28 minutes or until a wooden toothpick inserted near the center comes out clean.
5. Cool in pan on wire rack for 15 minutes. Remove sides of pan. Cool completely. If desired, sprinkle lightly with powdered sugar before serving. **MAKES 12 SERVINGS**

Per serving: 144 cal., 4 g total fat (2 g sat. fat), 0 mg chol., 81 mg sodium, 25 g carbo., 1 g fiber, 4 g pro.

CHOCOLATE-ALMOND TORTE

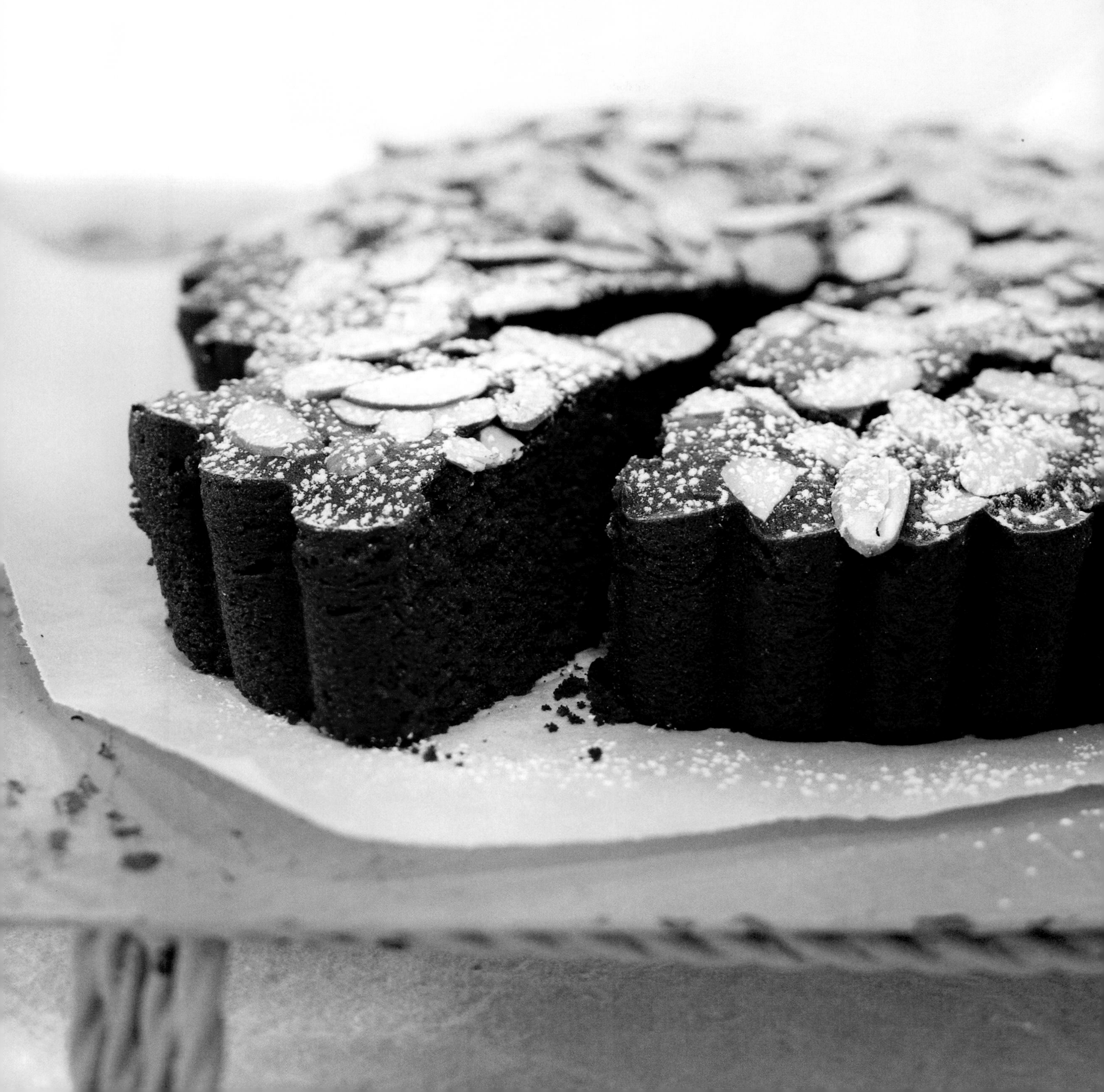

Berry-Cornmeal Shortcakes

Prep: 35 minutes **Stand:** 30 minutes
Bake: 15 minutes **Oven:** 425°F

- 1 pound small fresh strawberries (halve any large berries)
- ¼ cup orange marmalade
- 2 tablespoons finely snipped crystallized ginger
- 1¾ cups all-purpose flour
- ½ cup cornmeal
- 2 teaspoons baking powder
- ½ teaspoon salt
- 10 tablespoons butter
- ¾ to 1 cup whipping cream
- 2 tablespoons butter, melted
- 1 cup whipping cream
- 2 tablespoons sugar
- 1 teaspoon finely shredded orange peel

1. In a medium bowl combine strawberries, marmalade, and crystallized ginger. Cover and let stand at room temperature for 30 to 60 minutes.

2. Meanwhile, preheat oven to 425°F. Line a baking sheet with parchment paper or foil (or lightly grease a baking sheet); set aside.

3. In a large bowl stir together flour, cornmeal, baking powder, and salt. Using a pastry blender, cut in the 10 tablespoons butter until mixture resembles coarse crumbs. Add the ¾ cup cream, stirring with a fork just until moistened. (If necessary, stir in additional cream, 1 tablespoon at a time, to moisten.)

4. Turn out onto a lightly floured surface. Gently knead for 4 to 6 strokes or just until a ball forms. Pat or lightly roll dough until about ½ inch thick. Using a floured 3-inch round biscuit cutter, cut dough into 8 circles, dipping cutter into flour between cuts to prevent sticking. Place dough circles on prepared baking sheet. Brush tops with the 2 tablespoons melted butter. Bake for 15 to 18 minutes or until golden. Brush with any remaining melted butter. Cool shortcakes on a wire rack.

5. In a medium bowl combine the 1 cup cream, sugar, and orange peel. Beat with an electric mixer on medium to high just until stiff peaks form (tips stand straight).

6. To serve, split shortcakes in half. Spoon strawberry mixture over bottoms of shortcakes. Top with whipped cream; replace tops of shortcakes. **MAKES 8 SERVINGS**

Per serving: 530 cal., 37 g total fat (23 g sat. fat), 118 mg chol., 355 mg sodium, 48 g carbo., 2 g fiber, 5 g pro.

Apple-Almond Galette

Prep: 55 minutes **Bake:** 1 hour **Oven:** 375°F

- 1 7-ounce tube almond paste
- 1 egg
- 1 egg white
- 2 tablespoons all-purpose flour
- ¼ teaspoon salt
- 1¼ to 1½ pounds baking apples, peeled and cored
- 2 tablespoons lemon juice
- 2 tablespoons sugar
- ¾ to 1 teaspoon ground ginger
- ¼ teaspoon ground nutmeg
- ½ of a recipe Perfect Piecrust (page 266)
- 1 egg yolk
- 2 tablespoons water
  Sugar
- 2 tablespoons sliced almonds
  Whipped cream (optional)

1. In a large mixing bowl combine almond paste, egg, egg white, flour, and salt. Beat with an electric mixer on high about 1 minute or until fluffy; set aside.

2. Cut apples into ⅜-inch slices. In a large bowl toss apples with lemon juice, the 2 tablespoons sugar, the ginger, and nutmeg; set aside.

3. Preheat oven to 375°F. Line a baking sheet with parchment paper; set aside. On a lightly floured surface, roll out pastry to a 14-inch oval. Transfer to prepared baking sheet. Spread almond paste mixture over dough, leaving a 2-inch border around edge. Arrange apple slices on almond paste. Fold over border, pleating dough and covering outer edges of apples. Place in freezer for 10 minutes.

4. In a small bowl beat together the egg yolk and the water; brush over crust. Generously sprinkle crust and apples with sugar. Top with nuts.

5. Bake about 1 hour or until apples are tender and almond filling is golden. (If crust browns too quickly, cover the crust with foil.) Broil galette about 1 minute or until apples are slightly browned. Place a sheet of parchment paper on a wire cooling rack. Slide galette onto parchment on a wire rack. Cool slightly. If desired, serve with whipped cream.

MAKES 8 SERVINGS

Per serving: 375 cal., 21 g total fat (9 g sat. fat), 83 mg chol., 241 mg sodium, 43 g carbo., 4 g fiber, 7 g pro.

APPLE-ALMOND GALETTE

PEACH CRUMBLE TART

Peach Crumble Tart ♡

Prep: 35 minutes **Bake:** 63 minutes
Oven: 450°F/375°F

    1 recipe Oil Pastry
  ½ cup regular rolled oats
  ¼ cup all-purpose flour
    2 tablespoons packed brown sugar
1½ teaspoons ground cinnamon
    2 tablespoons butter or margarine, melted
  ¼ cup granulated sugar
    1 tablespoon all-purpose flour
    6 medium peaches (2 pounds), peeled and
       thinly sliced (about 6 cups), or two
       16-ounce packages frozen unsweetened
       peach slices, thawed and undrained
       (about 7 cups)

1. Preheat oven to 450°F. Prepare Oil Pastry.
On a floured surface, slightly flatten dough.
Roll dough from center to edges into a
12-inch circle. Ease pastry into a 10-inch tart
pan with removable bottom. Press pastry into
fluted sides of tart pan. Trim pastry to edge of
pan. Do not prick pastry. Line pastry with
double thickness of foil. Bake for 8 minutes.
Remove foil. Bake for 5 to 6 minutes more or
until golden brown. Cool on a wire rack.
Reduce oven temperature to 375°F.
2. Meanwhile, for topping, in a small bowl
combine oats, the ¼ cup flour, brown sugar,
and ½ teaspoon of the cinnamon. Stir in
melted butter. Set aside.

3. For filling, in a large bowl stir together
granulated sugar, 1 tablespoon flour, and the
remaining 1 teaspoon cinnamon. Add
peaches; toss gently to coat.
4. Spread filling evenly into tart shell. Sprinkle
with topping. Bake about 50 minutes or until
edge is bubbly and topping is browned.
Serve warm or cool. If desired, top with
additional peach slices and thawed *frozen
light whipped topping.* **MAKES 12 SERVINGS**

Oil Pastry In a medium bowl combine
1⅓ cups all-purpose flour and ¼ teaspoon
salt. Using a fork, stir ¼ cup vegetable oil and
3 tablespoons fat-free milk into flour mixture.
If necessary, stir in an additional 1 tablespoon
milk to moisten (dough will appear crumbly).
Form dough into a ball.

Per serving: 177 cal., 7 g total fat (2 g sat. fat), 5 mg
chol., 65 mg sodium, 27 g carbo., 2 g fiber, 3 g pro.

Pecan-Streusel Lattice Apple Pie

Prep: 1 minute **Bake:** 1 hour 40 minutes
Oven: 425°F/375°F

    1 recipe Perfect Piecrust
2½ to 3 pounds baking apples, peeled, cored,
       and sliced ½ to ¼ inch thick
  ½ cup granulated sugar
  ¼ cup cornstarch
  ¾ teaspoon ground cinnamon
  ½ teaspoon ground ginger
       Dash ground nutmeg
  ¾ cup coarsely chopped pecans
    3 tablespoons butter, melted
    2 tablespoons packed light brown sugar
    1 egg
    1 tablespoon water
       Sugar

1. Prepare Perfect Piecrust. On a lightly
floured surface, roll out half of the crust into a
circle 14 inches in diameter. Wrap pastry
around a rolling pin. Unroll pastry into a
9½-inch deep-dish pie plate. Trim pastry to
½ inch beyond edge of plate. Place in freezer
while preparing filling.

2. In a bowl toss together apples, the ½ cup
granulated sugar, the cornstarch, ½ teaspoon
of the cinnamon, the ginger, and nutmeg.
3. In a small bowl combine nuts, butter,
brown sugar, and the remaining ¼ teaspoon
cinnamon. Fill crust with half of the apples;
sprinkle with nut mixture. Top with remaining
apples. Return pie to freezer while making
lattice top.
4. Preheat oven to 425°F. On a lightly floured
surface, roll out remaining Perfect Piecrust
into a circle 14 inches in diameter. Using a
fluted pastry wheel, cut into eight 1-inch
strips. Place half of the pastry strips on filling
1 inch apart. Place remaining strips on pie,
weaving in a lattice pattern. Press strip ends
into bottom pastry; fold bottom crust over
strip ends; crimp edge. In a small bowl beat
together egg and the water; brush over lattice
top. Sprinkle with sugar.
5. Place pie on a baking sheet. Bake for
25 minutes. Reduce oven temperature to
375°F. Bake about 75 minutes more or until
apples are tender and filling is bubbly. If crust
browns too quickly, cover with foil. Cool on a
wire rack. **MAKES 8 SERVINGS**

Perfect Piecrust In a food processor
combine 2½ cups all-purpose flour,
1½ teaspoons sugar, and 1 teaspoon salt.
Add 1 cup cold butter, cut into ½-inch pieces;
process until mixture forms crumbs the size of
small peas. Combine 1 cup cold water and
1 tablespoon white vinegar. Add water mixture,
a little at a time, processing until a dough
starts to form (mixture will appear dry, but
form a dough when pressed with fingers). If
necessary, add additional water, 1 tablespoon
at a time. Turn dough out onto a lightly floured
surface; form mixture into a ball. Divide dough
in half. Shape each half into a flat disk. Wrap
disks individually in plastic wrap. Chill until ready
to use. To freeze, place in freezer bags and
freeze for up to 2 months. Thaw before using.

Per serving: 620 cal., 40 g total fat (18.5 g sat. fat), 99 mg
chol., 307 mg sodium, 72 g carbo., 5 g fiber, 7 g pro.

CHOCOLATE CHESS PIE

Chocolate Chess Pie

Prep: 25 minutes **Bake:** 1 hour **Oven:** 350°F

- ½ of a recipe Perfect Piecrust (page 266)
- 2 cups sugar
- ¼ cup unsweetened cocoa powder
- 1 tablespoon cornmeal
- 1 tablespoon all-purpose flour
- ½ teaspoon salt
- 4 eggs, lightly beaten
- ½ cup milk
- ½ cup butter, melted
- 1 teaspoon vanilla
- 1 cup chopped pecans

1. Preheat oven to 350°F. On a floured surface, roll pastry into a circle 12 inches in diameter. Line a 9-inch pie plate with pastry; crimp edge.

2. For filling, in a large bowl combine sugar, cocoa powder, cornmeal, flour, and salt. In a medium bowl whisk together eggs, milk, butter, and vanilla. Stir egg mixture into sugar mixture until smooth. Stir in pecans.

3. Pour filling into pastry-lined pie plate. Bake about 1 hour or until filling is set and crust is golden. If crust begins to brown too fast, reduce oven temperature to 325°F and cover edge of crust with foil. Cool on a wire rack. (Filling will fall slightly during cooling.) Cover and chill within 2 hours; chill for up to 24 hours. If desired, serve with *whipped cream.*

MAKES 8 TO 10 SERVINGS

Per serving: 599 cal., 33 g total fat (11 g sat. fat), 138 mg chol., 342 mg sodium, 71 g carbo., 2 g fiber, 8 g pro.

Black Bottom Pie

Prep: 1 hour **Bake:** 13 minutes **Oven:** 450°F

- ½ of a recipe Perfect Piecrust (page 266)
- 3½ cups half-and-half or light cream
- ¾ cup granulated sugar
- ½ cup cornstarch
- 3 tablespoons unsweetened cocoa powder
- 8 egg yolks
- 2 ounces bittersweet chocolate, chopped
- 2 teaspoons vanilla extract
- 1 tablespoon butter
- 1¼ cups whipping cream
- 3 tablespoons powdered sugar

1. Prepare Perfect Piecrust. Preheat oven to 450°F. On a floured surface, roll dough into a circle 12 inches in diameter. Wrap pastry around rolling pin; unroll pastry into a 9-inch pie plate. Ease into pie plate. Trim pastry to ½ inch beyond edges of pie plate. Fold under extra pastry; crimp edge. Prick bottom and sides of pastry with a fork. Line pastry with double thickness of foil. Bake for 8 minutes. Remove foil. Bake for 5 to 6 minutes more or until crust is golden. Cool on wire rack.

2. In a heavy medium saucepan whisk together 1¾ cups of the half-and-half, ½ cup of the sugar, ¼ cup of the cornstarch, and the cocoa powder. Cook and whisk on medium-high heat about 2 minutes or just until sugar is dissolved. Whisk in 4 egg yolks; reduce heat to medium. Cook, whisking constantly, until mixture thickens and just begins to boil. Remove from heat; stir in chocolate and 1 teaspoon of the vanilla. Place pan in a bowl of ice water until custard cools, stirring occasionally.

3. Remove pan from ice bath; dry pan bottom. Spread filling in prepared piecrust. Cover surface with plastic wrap; chill.

4. In clean heavy medium-size saucepan stir together the remaining 1¾ cups half-and-half, the remaining ¼ cup sugar, and the remaining ¼ cup cornstarch. Cook and whisk on medium-high heat for 2 minutes. Reduce heat to medium; whisk in 4 egg yolks. Cook, whisking constantly, until custard thickens and just begins to boil. Remove from heat; stir in the remaining 1 teaspoon vanilla and the butter. Place pan in a bowl of ice water until custard cools, stirring occasionally. Spread cooled custard on top of chocolate custard. Cover with plastic wrap; chill at least 3 hours.

5. In a chilled mixing bowl beat whipping cream and powdered sugar with an electric mixer on medium until soft peaks form. Top pie with whipped cream and, if desired, *chocolate curls.* **MAKES 8 SERVINGS**

Per serving: 668 cal., 47 g total fat (27 g sat. fat), 327 mg chol., 214 mg sodium, 56 g carbo., 2 g fiber, 9 g pro.

APPLE DUMPLINGS WITH CIDER SAUCE

Cherry Chip and Coconut Tartlets

Prep: 45 minutes **Bake:** 18 minutes
Chill: 30 minutes **Oven:** 325°F

```
 ¾  cup butter, softened
 1  8-ounce package cream cheese, softened
 2  tablespoons sugar
 1  teaspoon finely shredded lemon peel
 ⅛  teaspoon salt
1½  cups all-purpose flour
 ½  cup flaked coconut
 ½  cup white baking pieces, melted and
    cooled
 ⅓  cup lemon curd
 ¼  cup miniature cherry baking pieces
```

1. Preheat oven to 325°F. In a large mixing bowl beat butter and 4 ounces of the cream cheese with an electric mixer on medium to high for 30 seconds. Add sugar, lemon peel, and salt. Beat until combined, scraping sides of bowl occasionally. Beat in as much flour as possible. Stir in any remaining flour. Shape dough into a ball. If necessary, cover and chill dough about 30 minutes or until easy to handle.
2. Divide dough into 36 equal pieces. Press pieces evenly into bottoms and up the sides of 36 ungreased 1¾-inch muffin cups. Bake for 18 to 20 minutes or until lightly browned. Transfer pastry cups to a wire rack to cool.
3. Spread coconut in a single layer on a shallow baking pan. Toast in oven for 5 to 10 minutes or until golden brown, stirring occasionally. Cool.
4. For filling, in a medium mixing bowl beat the remaining 4 ounces cream cheese on medium to high for 30 seconds or until creamy. Beat in melted white baking pieces until smooth. Spoon about ½ teaspoon of the lemon curd into each pastry cup. Spoon cream cheese mixture over lemon curd or transfer cream cheese mixture to a decorating bag fitted with a large star tip and pipe over lemon curd. Sprinkle with toasted coconut and cherry baking pieces. **MAKES 36 TARTLETS**

Per tartlet: 115 cal., 8 g total fat (5 g sat. fat), 20 mg chol., 65 mg sodium, 10 g carbo., 1 g fiber, 1 g pro.

Apple Dumplings with Cider Sauce

Start to Finish: 1 hour

```
1¼  cups all-purpose flour
1½  teaspoons baking powder
 ¾  teaspoom ground cinnamon
 ½  teaspoon salt
    Dash ground nutmeg
 ¼  cup butter
 1  egg, lightly beaten
 ⅓  cup shredded, peeled apple
 1  tablespoon milk
 4  cups apple cider
 1  cup packed light brown sugar
    Crème fraîche (optional)
```

1. In a medium bowl stir together flour, baking powder, cinnamon, salt, and nutmeg. Using a pastry blender, cut butter into flour mixture until fine crumbs form. In a small bowl stir together egg, apple, and milk. Stir apple mixture into flour mixture (mixture will be dry). Turn dough out onto lightly floured surface. Knead a few strokes just until dough holds together. Divide dough into 8 portions; shape each portion into a ball.
2. In a large saucepan combine apple cider and brown sugar. Bring to boiling; reduce heat. Add 4 of the dumplings; return to simmer. Cook for 10 to 12 minutes or until dumplings are triple in size and golden brown, turning occasionally. Using a slotted spoon, remove dumplings to plate; cover loosely with foil. Repeat with the remaining 4 dumplings.
3. For cider sauce, return cider mixture in saucepan to boiling; cook about 5 minutes or until syrupy consistency. Serve warm dumplings with warm cider sauce and, if desired, crème fraîche. **MAKES 8 SERVINGS**

Per serving: 290 cal., 7 g total fat (4 g sat. fat), 42 mg chol., 232 mg sodium, 44 g carbo., 1 g fiber, 3 g pro.

Strawberry-Rhubarb Crisp ♡

Prep: 15 minutes **Bake:** 40 minutes
Cool: 20 minutes **Oven:** 375°F

⅓ cup low-sugar strawberry preserves
⅛ teaspoon ground cinnamon or nutmeg
2 cups sliced fresh strawberries
2 cups sliced fresh rhubarb
3 tablespoons all-purpose flour
½ cup quick-cooking rolled oats
2 tablespoons cornmeal
2 tablespoons honey
1 teaspoon vanilla

1. Preheat oven to 375°F. In a large bowl stir together preserves and cinnamon. Add strawberries and rhubarb; stir gently to coat. Add flour; stir gently until combined. Spoon into a 9-inch pie plate. Bake, uncovered, for 20 minutes.
2. Meanwhile, in a small bowl stir together rolled oats and cornmeal. Stir in honey and vanilla until combined. Sprinkle over strawberry mixture. Bake, uncovered, about 20 minutes or until topping is golden brown and fruit is tender and bubbly.
3. Cool about 20 minutes before serving. Serve warm. **MAKES 6 TO 8 SERVINGS**

Per serving: 117 cal., 1 g total fat (0 g sat. fat), 0 mg chol., 7 mg sodium, 26 g carbo., 3 g fiber, 2 g pro.

Peach Crisp Prepare as above, except substitute low-sugar apricot preserves for the strawberry preserves and 4 cups peeled and sliced fresh peaches or sliced nectarines for the strawberries and rhubarb. Stir 2 teaspoons lemon juice into the preserves mixture before adding fruit.

Per serving: 142 cal., 1 g total fat (0 g sat. fat), 0 mg chol., 2 mg sodium, 33 g carbo., 3 g fiber, 2 g protein

Peach-Blueberry Ginger-Oat Crisp ♡

Prep: 25 minutes **Bake:** 35 minutes
Cool: 30 minutes **Oven:** 375°F

4 cups sliced fresh peaches or frozen unsweetened peach slices, thawed and undrained
3 tablespoons packed brown sugar
2 tablespoons all-purpose flour
½ teaspoon ground ginger
1 cup fresh or frozen unsweetened blueberries, thawed
¼ cup water
8 gingersnaps
⅔ cup quick-cooking rolled oats
¼ cup chopped pecans (optional)
2 tablespoons butter, melted
1 cup frozen light whipped dessert topping, thawed (optional)

1. Preheat oven to 375°F. In a large bowl toss together peaches, brown sugar, flour, and ginger. Add blueberries and the water; toss to mix. Spoon fruit mixture into a 2-quart square baking dish. Bake, uncovered, for 20 minutes.
2. Meanwhile, place gingersnaps in a heavy plastic bag. Seal bag; using the flat side of a meat mallet or a rolling pin, crush cookies until in ¼- to ½-inch pieces. Transfer cookies to a medium bowl. Stir in rolled oats and, if desired, chopped pecans. Stir in butter until well mixed. Sprinkle over partially baked fruit mixture.
3. Bake for 15 to 20 minutes more or until fruit is bubbly and topping is lightly browned. Cool on a wire rack for 30 minutes. Serve warm. If desired, top with whipped topping.
MAKES 8 SERVINGS

Per serving: 153 cal., 4 g total fat (2 g sat. fat), 8 mg chol., 68 mg sodium, 29 g carbo., 3 g fiber, 2 g pro.

MAPLE BREAD PUDDING
WITH PECAN PRALINE

Maple Bread Pudding with Pecan Praline

Prep: 35 minutes **Chill:** 1 hour **Bake:** 40 minutes
Cool: 30 minutes **Oven:** 375°F

- 1 cup granulated sugar
- ¼ cup water
- ½ cup chopped pecans, toasted
- 8 eggs
- 4 cups half-and-half or light cream
- 1 cup packed brown sugar
- 1 cup maple syrup
- 1 tablespoon vanilla
- 1 1-pound loaf egg bread, torn into bite-size pieces (about 14 cups)
  Vanilla ice cream

1. Preheat oven to 375°F. For pecan praline, lightly grease a baking sheet; set aside. In a small saucepan combine granulated sugar and the water. Cook on medium heat, stirring to dissolve sugar. Bring to boiling; reduce heat. Without stirring, boil gently, uncovered, about 7 minutes or until mixture turns a deep amber color. Remove from heat. Stir in pecans. Quickly pour onto the prepared baking sheet. Cool. Break or chop into small pieces; set aside.

2. In a very large bowl whisk together eggs, half-and-half, brown sugar, maple syrup, and vanilla. Add bread pieces; stir to moisten evenly. Cover and chill for 1 hour.

3. Lightly grease a 3-quart rectangular baking dish. Transfer bread mixture to the prepared baking dish. Bake, uncovered, about 40 minutes or until golden brown and a knife inserted in the center comes out clean. Cool on a wire rack for 30 minutes. Serve warm bread pudding with scoops of ice cream. Sprinkle with pecan praline. **MAKES 12 TO 16 SERVINGS**

Per serving: 647 cal., 26 g total fat (13 g sat. fat), 222 mg chol., 331 mg sodium, 92 g carbo., 2 g fiber, 13 g pro.

Ricotta Cheesecake with Apple Topper

Prep: 30 minutes **Bake:** 1 hour **Cool:** 2 hours
Chill: 4 to 24 hours **Oven:** 325°F

Nonstick cooking spray
- 1 15-ounce carton light ricotta cheese
- 1½ 8-ounce packages reduced-fat cream cheese (Neufchâtel)
- ⅓ cup sugar
- ¼ cup honey
- ¼ cup unsweetened applesauce
- 2 tablespoons all-purpose flour
- 2 egg yolks
- 4 egg whites
- 1 recipe Apple Topper

1. Preheat oven to 325°F. Coat a 9-inch springform pan with cooking spray; set aside.
2. In large mixing bowl beat ricotta cheese, cream cheese, sugar, honey, applesauce, and flour with an electric mixer on medium until smooth. Add yolks all at once. Beat on low just until combined. In a clean large mixing bowl with clean beaters, beat whites on medium to high until stiff peaks form. Fold one-fourth of the egg whites into ricotta mixture. Fold in remaining egg whites. Spread filling evenly into prepared pan. Place in shallow baking pan.
3. Bake about 1 hour or until center appears nearly set when gently shaken.
4. Cool in pan on wire rack for 15 minutes. (Cheesecake will crack.) Using a thin metal spatula, loosen cheesecake from side of pan; cool for 30 minutes more. Remove side of pan; cool completely. Cover and chill for 4 to 24 hours. To serve, top sliced cheesecake with Apple Topper. **MAKES 12 SERVINGS**

Apple Topper In a large skillet toss 6 cups apple slices with 1 teaspoon apple pie spice or ground cinnamon. Add ¼ cup water; heat to boiling. Cook, covered, on medium-high heat about 5 minutes or just until tender, stirring occasionally. Drizzle with 2 tablespoons honey; toss gently to coat; cool.

Per serving: 212 cal., 9 g total fat (5 g sat. fat), 65 mg chol., 165 mg sodium, 26 g carbo., 1 g fiber, 8 g pro.

RICOTTA CHEESECAKE WITH APPLE TOPPER

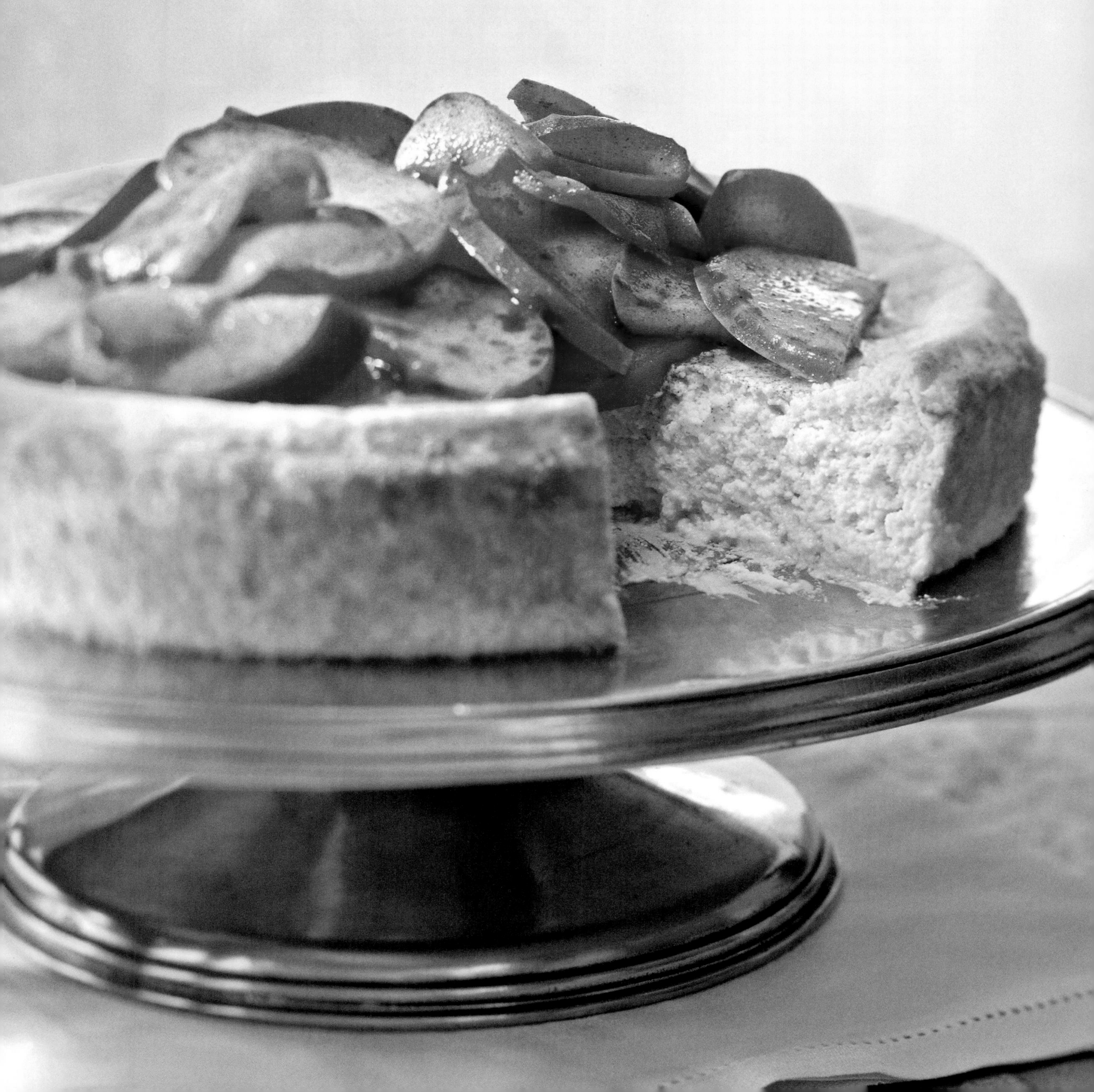

BERRY PUDDING CAKES

Raspberry Crème Brûlée

Prep: 25 minutes **Stand:** 15 minutes
Bake: 1 hour **Cool:** 30 minutes **Chill:** 1 hour
Oven: 325°F

- 2 cups whipping cream
- 1 4-inch vanilla bean,* split lengthwise
- 5 egg yolks, lightly beaten
- ½ cup sugar
- ¾ cup fresh raspberries or sliced small strawberries
  Raspberries or strawberries (optional)

1. Preheat oven to 325°F. In a heavy medium saucepan heat whipping cream and vanilla bean over medium-low heat about 15 minutes or just until simmering (do not boil), stirring often. Remove from heat and let steep for 15 minutes. Remove and discard the vanilla bean.
2. In a medium mixing bowl combine egg yolks and sugar. Beat with a wire whisk or with an electric mixer on low just until mixture is pale yellow and thick. Gradually add about half of the cream mixture to the egg mixture, stirring until well combined. Pour egg mixture into the remaining cream mixture, stirring until completely combined. Set aside.
3. Place eight 4-ounce ramekins or six 6-ounce custard cups in a 13×9×2-inch baking pan. Add 5 raspberries or strawberry slices to each ungreased ramekin. Pour egg mixture evenly into the ramekins. Set the pan on rack in oven. Pour boiling water into the baking pan around the ramekins until water is halfway up the sides of the ramekins.
4. Bake about 60 minutes or until custard is set. Carefully remove ramekins from water. Cool on a wire rack for 30 minutes. Cover and chill for 1 to 8 hours. If desired, garnish each crème brûlée with additional raspberries or strawberries. **MAKES 8 SERVINGS**

*Tip Or substitute 2 teaspoons vanilla extract. If using the vanilla extract, heat whipping cream just until warm; do not cook until bubbly and do not steep. Add the vanilla to the warm cream.

Per serving: 292 cal., 25 g total fat (15 g sat. fat), 210 mg chol., 28 mg sodium, 15 g carbo., 1 g fiber, 3 g pro.

Berry Pudding Cakes ♡

Prep: 20 minutes **Bake:** 20 minutes
Oven: 400°F

  Nonstick cooking spray
- 2 eggs, lightly beaten
- ¼ cup granulated sugar
- 1 teaspoon vanilla
  Dash salt
- 1 cup fat-free milk
- ½ cup all-purpose flour
- ½ teaspoon baking powder
- 3 cups fresh berries (such as raspberries, blueberries, and/or sliced strawberries)
- 2 teaspoons powdered sugar (optional)

1. Preheat oven to 400°F. Lightly coat six 6-ounce individual quiche dishes with nonstick cooking spray. Arrange in a 15×10×1-inch baking pan; set aside. In a medium bowl combine eggs, granulated sugar, vanilla, and salt; whisk until light and frothy. Whisk in milk until combined. Add flour and baking powder; whisk until smooth.
2. Divide berries among prepared quiche dishes. Pour batter over berries. (Batter will not cover berries completely.) Bake about 20 minutes or until puffed and golden brown. Serve warm. If desired, sift powdered sugar over each serving. **MAKES 6 SERVINGS**

Per serving: 141 cal., 2 g total fat (1 g sat. fat), 71 mg chol., 86 mg sodium, 26 g carbo., 3 g fiber, 5 g pro.

TRIPLE-CHOCOLATE TIRAMISU

Triple-Chocolate Tiramisu

Prep: 30 minutes **Chill:** 6 to 24 hours

- 2 3-ounce packages ladyfingers, split
- ¼ cup brewed espresso or strong coffee
- 1 8-ounce carton mascarpone cheese
- 1 cup whipping cream
- ¼ cup powdered sugar
- 1 teaspoon vanilla
- ⅓ cup chocolate liqueur
- 1 ounce white baking chocolate, grated
- 1 ounce bittersweet chocolate, grated
  Unsweetened cocoa powder
  Chocolate-covered coffee beans, chopped (optional)

1. Line bottom of an 8×8×2-inch baking pan with enough ladyfingers to cover, cutting to fit. Brush with half of the espresso; set aside.

2. In a medium bowl combine mascarpone cheese, whipping cream, powdered sugar, and vanilla. Beat with an electric mixer on medium just until stiff peaks form (tips stand straight). Add liqueur; beat just until combined.

3. Spread half of the mascarpone mixture over ladyfingers in pan. Sprinkle with white chocolate and bittersweet chocolate. Top with another layer of ladyfingers, cutting to fit (reserve any remaining ladyfingers for another use). Brush with remaining espresso. Spread remaining mascarpone mixture over ladyfingers in pan. Cover and chill for 6 to 24 hours.

4. Before serving, lightly sprinkle cocoa powder over top of dessert. If desired, garnish with coffee beans. **MAKES 12 SERVINGS**

Per serving: 256 cal., 19 g total fat (11 g sat. fat), 104 mg chol., 42 mg sodium, 17 g carbo., 0 g fiber, 6 g pro.

Crispy Ice Cream Bars

Prep: 40 minutes **Freeze:** 5 hours

- 4 cups crispy rice cereal
- ½ cup toffee pieces
- 1 cup unsalted peanuts
- ¾ cup sweetened shredded coconut
- ¾ cup packed brown sugar
- ½ cup butter
- ½ cup light-color corn syrup
- ½ teaspoon salt
- 4 pints ice cream (any flavor)

1. Line a 13×9×2-inch baking pan with parchment paper, extending parchment over edges of pan. In a large bowl combine cereal and toffee pieces; set aside. In a food processor combine peanuts and coconut. Cover and process until coarsely chopped. Add peanut mixture to cereal mixture; stir to mix.

2. In a medium saucepan combine brown sugar, butter, corn syrup, and salt. Bring to boiling; boil for 3 minutes. Pour brown sugar mixture over cereal mixture; toss to coat evenly. Press half of the mixture into prepared pan. Place in freezer for 10 minutes.

3. Spread softened ice cream evenly over cereal layer; freeze about 1 hour or until firm. Remove and quickly top with remaining cereal mixture. Freeze at least 4 hours or until firm.

4. To serve, lift bars from pan using parchment paper as handles. Cut into 3×1½-inch bars. Serve immediately. Wrap any leftovers tightly in freezer-proof wrap. Freeze for up to 1 week. **MAKES 24 BARS**

Per bar: 256 cal., 14 g total fat (8 g sat. fat), 35 mg chol., 158 mg sodium, 29 g carbo., 1 g fiber, 4 g pro.

Holiday Entertaining

ROASTED BUTTERNUT SQUASH SOUP

Fresh Oyster Stew

Start to Finish: 35 minutes

    4 cups shucked oysters (2 pints)
    2 tablespoons butter
    ⅔ cup sliced leeks (2 medium)
    2 tablespoons all-purpose flour
    ½ teaspoon salt
    ¼ teaspoon dried tarragon, crushed
   2½ cups half-and-half, light cream, or
        whole milk
        Sliced leeks (optional)

1. Drain oysters, reserving liquid. Strain liquid. Add enough water to strained liquid to measure 2 cups; set aside. Rinse the oysters thoroughly to remove any sand or shells.
2. In a large saucepan melt butter on medium heat. Cook the ⅔ cup leeks in hot butter about 4 minutes or until tender, stirring occasionally. Stir in flour, salt, and tarragon. Slowly stir in half-and-half. Cook and stir until slightly thickened and bubbly. Cook and stir for 1 minute. Keep warm.
3. In a medium saucepan combine reserved oyster liquid and oysters. Bring just to simmering on medium heat; reduce heat. Cook, covered, for 1 to 2 minutes or until oysters curl around the edges. Skim and discard fat from surface of cooking liquid. Stir oyster mixture into cream mixture. Heat through. If desired, garnish with additional sliced leeks. Serve immediately.
MAKES 6 SERVINGS

Per serving: 170 cal., 12 g total fat (7 g sat. fat), 77 mg chol., 358 mg sodium, 8 g carbo., 0 g fiber, 8 g pro.

Roasted Butternut Squash Soup

Prep: 30 minutes **Roast:** 1 hour **Oven:** 350°F

    3 pounds butternut squash, peeled, seeded,
        and cut into 1-inch cubes
    2 tablespoons olive oil
    1 teaspoon kosher salt
    ½ teaspoon freshly ground black pepper
    1 tablespoon butter
    1 cup chopped onion (1 large)
    7 to 8 cups vegetable broth
        Snipped fresh chives (optional)

1. Preheat oven to 350°F. In a large roasting pan toss together squash, olive oil, salt, and pepper. Roast about 1 hour or until tender, stirring once halfway through roasting.

2. Meanwhile, in an 8-quart pot melt butter on medium-low heat. Add onion and cook about 20 minutes on medium-low heat until tender and golden.
3. Add squash and 7 cups of the vegetable broth to pot. Bring to boiling; reduce heat. Simmer, uncovered, for 15 minutes. Transfer soup, in batches, to a blender and puree until smooth; return to pot. Add more broth, if needed, to reach consistency. Season with salt and pepper. If desired, garnish with fresh chives. **MAKES 10 SERVINGS**

Per serving: 130 cal., 5 g total fat (1.5 g sat. fat), 4 mg chol., 1,140 mg sodium, 22 g carbo., 3 g fiber, 2 g pro.

TRADITIONAL ROAST TURKEY

Traditional Roast Turkey

Prep: 20 minutes **Roast:** 3 hours
Stand: 15 minutes **Oven:** 425°F/325°F

  1 12- to 14-pound turkey
  1 tablespoon snipped fresh rosemary or
      1 teaspoon dried rosemary, crushed
  1 tablespoon snipped fresh thyme or
      1 teaspoon dried thyme, crushed
  1 tablespoon snipped fresh sage or
      1 teaspoon dried sage, crushed
  1 teaspoon kosher salt
  ½ teaspoon black pepper
  3 small onions, quartered (12 ounces)
  3 medium carrots, cut into 2-inch chunks
  3 stalks celery, cut into 2-inch chunks
  1 cup water
  1 tablespoon olive oil

1. Preheat oven to 425°F. Remove neck and giblets from turkey, reserving neck bone. Rinse the inside of the turkey; pat dry with paper towels. In a small bowl stir together rosemary, thyme, sage, salt, and pepper.

Season inside of body cavity with half of the herb mixture. Pull neck skin to the back; fasten with a skewer. Tuck the ends of the drumsticks under the band of skin across the tail. If there is no band of skin, tie the drumsticks securely to the tail with 100%-cotton kitchen string. Twist wing tips under the back.

2. Place turkey, breast side up, on a rack in a shallow roasting pan. Arrange onions, carrots, celery, and neck bone around turkey in roasting pan. Pour the water into the pan. Brush turkey with olive oil. Sprinkle turkey with remaining herb mixture. Insert an oven-going meat thermometer into the center of an inside thigh muscle; the thermometer should not touch bone. Cover turkey loosely with foil.

3. Roast for 30 minutes. Reduce oven temperature to 325°F. Roast for 2½ to 3 hours more or until the thermometer registers 180°F. About 45 minutes before end of roasting,

remove foil and cut band of skin or string between drumsticks so thighs cook evenly. When turkey is done, the juices should run clear and the drumsticks should move easily in their sockets.

4. Remove turkey from oven. Transfer to a serving platter (discard mixture in pan). Cover; let stand for 15 to 20 minutes before carving. If desired, garnish platter with *rosemary sprigs, sage leaves, pomegranate wedges, tiny apples or pears,* and/or *kumquats.* **MAKES 24 SERVINGS**

Per serving: 229 cal., 7 g total fat (2 g sat. fat), 137 mg chol., 155 mg sodium, 0 g carbo., 0 g fiber, 38 g pro.

Spice-Rubbed Rib Roast

Prep: 20 minutes **Roast:** 1 hour 45 minutes
Stand: 15 minutes **Oven:** 350°F

  2 tablespoons coriander seeds, crushed
  2 tablespoons finely shredded lemon peel
  1 tablespoon olive oil
  1 teaspoon cumin seeds, crushed
  ½ to 1 teaspoon crushed red pepper
  ¼ teaspoon salt
  1 4- to 5-pound beef rib roast
  8 cloves garlic, slivered

1. Preheat oven to 350°F. In a small bowl stir together coriander seeds, lemon peel, oil, cumin seeds, crushed red pepper, and salt; set aside.

2. Cut ½-inch slits randomly in top and sides of roast. Insert garlic slivers deep into slits. Rub lemon mixture onto surface of roast with your fingers.

3. Insert an oven-going meat thermometer in center of roast. (The thermometer should not touch bone.) Place roast, fat side up, in a shallow roasting pan. Roast, uncovered, to desired doneness. Allow 1¾ to 2¼ hours for medium rare (135°F) or 2¼ to 2¾ hours for medium (150°F).

4. Cover roast with foil and let stand 15 minutes. The temperature of the meat after standing should be 145°F for medium rare or 160°F for medium. **MAKES 12 SERVINGS**

Per serving: 163 cal., 9 g total fat (3 g sat. fat), 51 mg chol., 106 mg sodium, 1 g carbo., 1 g fiber, 17 g pro.

BEEF TENDERLOIN WITH
BLUE CHEESE-SHRIMP SAUCE

Beef Tenderloin with Blue Cheese-Shrimp Sauce

Prep: 25 minutes **Roast:** 45 minutes
Stand: 15 minutes **Oven:** 425°F

6 cloves garlic, minced
1 teaspoon salt
1 teaspoon coarsely ground black pepper
1 3- to 4-pound beef tenderloin roast
2 tablespoons butter
8 ounces medium shrimp, peeled and deveined
¼ cup dry white wine or chicken broth
½ cup whipping cream
½ cup crumbled blue cheese (2 ounces)
  Snipped fresh chives (optional)
  Fresh tarragon sprigs and/or thyme sprigs (optional)

1. Preheat oven to 425°F. In a small bowl combine 4 cloves of minced garlic, salt, and pepper. Sprinkle over roast; rub into meat with your fingers. Place roast on a rack in a shallow roasting pan.

2. Roast, uncovered, for 45 to 50 minutes or until thermometer registers 140°F for medium rare. Cover meat with foil. Let stand for 15 minutes. The temperature of the meat after standing should be 145°F.

3. While meat is standing, prepare sauce. In a large skillet melt butter on medium heat. Add the remaining 2 cloves minced garlic; cook and stir for 1 minute. Add shrimp; cook and stir about 2 minutes or until opaque. Remove skillet from heat. With a slotted spoon remove shrimp from skillet. Add wine. Return skillet to the heat. Cook for 2 to 3 minutes or until wine almost evaporates. Stir in whipping cream and blue cheese. Cook and stir about 3 minutes or until cheese melts and cream thickens to desired consistency. Stir in shrimp and heat through. Keep sauce warm.

4. Slice roast and serve with shrimp sauce. If desired, garnish with chives and tarragon.

MAKES 6 SERVINGS

Per serving: 539 cal., 29 g total fat (14 g sat. fat), 254 mg chol., 739 mg sodium, 3 g carbo., 0 g fiber, 61 g pro.

Pork with Cherry and Wild Rice Stuffing

Prep: 1 hour **Roast:** 1 hour 45 minutes
Stand: 15 minutes **Oven:** 325°F

⅓ cup wild rice
1¼ cups water
2 teaspoons snipped fresh rosemary or ½ teaspoon dried rosemary, crushed
½ teaspoon salt
¾ cup coarsely chopped dried cherries or cranberries
1 3-pound boneless pork top loin roast (single loin)
6 ounces bulk pork sausage
½ cup chopped onion (1 medium)
1 tablespoon snipped fresh parsley
1 teaspoon snipped fresh thyme or ¼ teaspoon dried thyme, crushed
¼ teaspoon freshly ground black pepper
  Salt and freshly ground black pepper
  Snipped fresh thyme
1 cup water
⅓ cup cold water
2 tablespoons all-purpose flour
  Fresh whole tart red cherries (optional)
  Fresh thyme sprigs (optional)

1. Rinse wild rice in a strainer, lifting the rice with your fingers to thoroughly clean; drain. In a small saucepan combine wild rice, 1¼ cups water, the rosemary, and the ½ teaspoon salt. Bring to boiling; reduce heat. Simmer, covered, for 40 to 45 minutes or until tender. Remove from heat. Stir in dried cherries. Set aside.

2. Trim fat from pork. Butterfly the meat by making a lengthwise cut down center of meat, cutting to within ½ inch of other side. Spread open. Place knife in the V of first cut. Cut horizontally to the cut surface and away from the first cut to within ½ inch of the other side of the meat. Repeat on opposite side of the V. Spread these sections open. Cover the roast with plastic wrap. Working from center (thicker part) to edges, pound with flat side of a meat mallet until meat is ½ to ¾ inch thick. Make sure the meat is a uniform thickness. Remove plastic wrap. Set meat aside.

3. For stuffing, in a large skillet cook sausage and onion until sausage is browned and onion is tender. Drain off fat. Stir in the

PORK WITH CHERRY AND WILD RICE STUFFING

parsley, 1 teaspoon thyme, and ¼ teaspoon pepper. If necessary, drain the cooked rice mixture to remove liquid. Stir cooked rice mixture into sausage mixture.

4. Preheat oven to 325°F. Spread the filling over the butterflied roast. Roll meat into a spiral from a short side. Tie with 100%-cotton kitchen string. Place on a rack in a shallow roasting pan. Sprinkle with salt, pepper, and snipped fresh thyme. Insert an oven-going meat thermometer in center of roast. Roast, uncovered, for 1¾ to 2¼ hours or until thermometer registers 155°F, covering ends of meat after 45 minutes to prevent stuffing from drying out. Transfer meat to serving platter. Cover loosely with foil; let stand for 15 minutes before carving. (Temperature of the meat after standing should be 160°F.)

5. For pan gravy, add the 1 cup water to pan, scraping up browned bits. In a small saucepan whisk together the ⅓ cup cold water and the flour. Whisk in pan juices. Cook and stir on medium heat until thickened and bubbly. Cook and stir for 1 minute. Season with salt and pepper.

6. Remove string from pork roast; discard. Slice roast; serve with pan gravy. If desired, garnish with tart red cherries and fresh thyme sprigs. **MAKES 8 TO 10 SERVINGS**

Per serving: 364 cal., 13 g total fat (4 g sat. fat), 122 mg chol., 406 mg sodium, 17 g carbo., 1 g fiber, 43 g pro.

FRUIT-STUFFED PORK TENDERLOINS
WITH MUSTARD-CRANBERRY SAUCE

Fruit-Stuffed Pork Tenderloins with Mustard-Cranberry Sauce

Prep: 45 minutes **Roast:** 50 minutes
Stand: 5 minutes **Oven:** 375°F

¼ cup butter
½ cup sliced celery (2 stalks)
½ cup finely chopped onion (1 medium)
1 clove garlic, minced
2 cups cooked brown rice
¼ cup dried cranberries
¼ cup snipped dried apricots
1 teaspoon finely shredded orange peel
½ teaspoon dried thyme, crushed
½ teaspoon salt
⅛ teaspoon black pepper
¼ cup apple juice (optional)
2 1-pound pork tenderloins
  Salt and black pepper
1 recipe Mustard-Cranberry Sauce

1. Preheat oven to 375°F. For stuffing, in a medium saucepan melt butter on medium heat. Cook celery, onion, and garlic in hot butter about 4 minutes or until tender. Remove from heat. Stir in rice, cranberries, apricots, orange peel, thyme, the ½ teaspoon salt, and the ⅛ teaspoon pepper. Stir in apple juice to moisten, if needed. Set stuffing aside.
2. Trim any fat from pork. Use a sharp knife to make a lengthwise cut down the center of each pork tenderloin, cutting to, but not through, the other side of the meat. Repeat by making 2 cuts on either side of the first

cut. Place each tenderloin between 2 pieces of plastic wrap. Pound lightly with the flat side of a meat mallet to make a 12×8-inch rectangle, working from the center out to the corners. Sprinkle pork with salt and pepper.
3. Spoon half of the stuffing over 1 of the tenderloins to within 1 inch of the edges. Roll tenderloin into a spiral, beginning with a short side. Tie meat with clean 100%-cotton string. Place, seam side down, on a rack in a shallow roasting pan. Repeat with remaining tenderloin and remaining stuffing, placing second tenderloin next to the first on the rack.
4. Roast, uncovered, for 50 to 60 minutes or until an instant-read thermometer inserted in the stuffing registers 165°F. Loosely cover with aluminum foil and let stand for 5 minutes.
5. Meanwhile, prepare Mustard-Cranberry Sauce. Slice tenderloins; serve with sauce.
MAKES 8 SERVINGS

Mustard-Cranberry Sauce In a small saucepan cook 1 clove garlic, minced, in 2 tablespoons hot butter on medium heat for 1 minute. Stir in 2 tablespoons all-purpose flour and 1 tablespoon Dijon mustard until combined. Stir in 1¼ cups chicken broth. Cook and stir until thickened and bubbly. Cook and stir for 1 minute. Stir in ¼ cup half-and-half or light cream and ¼ cup dried cranberries; heat through. Makes 1⅔ cups.

Make-ahead directions Prepare tenderloins through Step 3. Cover and chill up to 8 hours. Let stand at room temperature 15 minutes before roasting as directed in Step 4.

Per serving: 317 cal., 13 g total fat (7 g sat. fat), 98 mg chol., 550 mg sodium, 24 g carbo., 2 g fiber, 26 g pro.

Glazed Ham

Prep: 15 minutes **Bake:** 1 hour 30 minutes
Oven: 325°F

1 5- to 6-pound cooked ham (rump half or shank portion)
24 whole cloves (optional)
1 recipe Orange Glaze or Chutney Glaze
  Fresh bay leaves, cranberries, orange slices, and/or fresh rosemary sprigs

1. Preheat oven to 325°F. Score ham by making diagonal cuts in a diamond pattern. If desired, stud ham with cloves. Place ham on a rack in a shallow roasting pan. Insert an oven-going meat thermometer in center of ham so thermometer does not touch bone.
2. Bake, uncovered, for 1½ to 2¼ hours or until thermometer registers 140°F. Brush ham with some of the desired glaze during the last 20 minutes of baking. Serve with remaining glaze. Garnish with bay leaves, cranberries, orange slices, and/or fresh rosemary sprigs.
MAKES 16 TO 20 SERVINGS

Orange Glaze In a medium saucepan combine 2 teaspoons finely shredded orange peel, 1 cup orange juice, ½ cup packed brown sugar, 4 teaspoons cornstarch, and 1½ teaspoons dry mustard. Cook and stir on medium heat until thickened and bubbly. Cook and stir for 2 minutes. Makes 1¼ cups glaze.

Chutney Glaze In a food processor or blender combine one 9-ounce jar mango chutney, ¼ cup maple syrup, and 2 teaspoons stone-ground mustard. Cover and process or blend until smooth. Makes about 1¼ cups glaze.

Make-ahead directions Prepare desired glaze; cover and chill for up to 1 week. Reheat glaze before brushing on ham.

Per serving: 166 cal., 5 g total fat (2 g sat. fat), 47 mg chol., 1,078 mg sodium, 10 g carbo., 0 g fiber, 19 g pro.

ORANGE-GLAZED HAM

Apricot-Pecan Stuffing

Prep: 25 minutes
Cook: 3 hours 30 minutes to 4 hours (low)
Oven: 300°F

- 12 cups dry whole wheat or white bread cubes (18 to 20 bread slices)
- 6 tablespoons butter
- 1 cup sliced leeks (3 medium)
- 1 cup chopped onion (1 large)
- 2 large apples, peeled if desired, cored, and chopped (2 cups)
- 1 cup chopped pecans
- ¾ cup snipped dried apricots
- 1 teaspoon dried thyme, crushed
- ½ teaspoon salt
- ½ teaspoon ground nutmeg
- ⅛ teaspoon black pepper
- 1 14-ounce can chicken broth
  Nonstick cooking spray

1. Preheat oven to 300°F. Spread bread cubes in a 15½×10½×2-inch baking pan. Bake, uncovered, for 10 to 15 minutes or until cubes are dry, stirring twice; cool. (Cubes will continue to dry and crisp as they cool.)
2. In a large skillet melt butter on medium heat. Cook leeks and onion in hot butter about 5 minutes or until tender, stirring frequently. Stir in apples, pecans, apricots, thyme, salt, nutmeg, and pepper. Cook for 3 minutes, stirring occasionally.
3. In a very large bowl combine apple mixture and bread cubes. Drizzle broth over bread mixture to moisten, tossing gently. Lightly coat a 5- to 6-quart slow cooker with nonstick cooking spray. Transfer bread mixture to prepared cooker.
4. Cover and cook on low-heat setting (do not use high-heat setting) for 3½ to 4 hours. Transfer to a serving dish. **MAKES 12 SERVINGS**

Make-ahead directions Prepare toasted bread cubes as directed in Step 1. Store in an airtight container for up to 2 days.

Per serving: 348 cal., 17 g total fat (5 g sat. fat), 16 mg chol., 512 mg sodium, 47 g carbo., 6 g fiber, 7 g pro.

TANGERINE-CRANBERRY RELISH

Tangerine-Cranberry Relish ♡

Prep: 15 minutes **Chill:** 1 hour

- 1 12-ounce package fresh cranberries (3 cups)
- 2 medium tangerines or small oranges
- ¼ to ⅓ cup sugar

1. Rinse cranberries under running water and discard any soft or old berries; set aside. Slice each unpeeled tangerine into fifths; remove seeds. Place tangerine slices in a food processor; cover and process until coarsely chopped. Transfer to a medium bowl.

2. Add all but ½ cup of the cranberries to the food processor; cover and process until coarsely chopped. Add chopped cranberries to tangerines in bowl; stir in the remaining ½ cup cranberries. Stir in enough of the sugar to sweeten to taste; cover and chill for 1 hour. Stir before serving. **MAKES 12 SERVINGS**

Make-ahead directions Prepare as above. Cover and chill for up to 2 days. Stir before serving.

Per serving: 37 cal., 0 g total fat, 0 mg chol., 1 mg sodium, 10 g carbo., 2 g fiber, 0 g pro.

VEGETABLE TRIO WITH
ORANGE-THYME DRESSING

4. For dressing, whisk together orange juice, vinegar, and the remaining ¼ teaspoon salt. Whisk in the remaining 2 tablespoons olive oil. Add orange peel and the snipped thyme. Arrange vegetables on a serving dish. Serve with dressing. If desired, garnish with additional thyme sprigs. **MAKES 6 TO 8 SERVINGS**

Per serving: 118 cal., 7 g total fat (1 g sat. fat), 0 mg chol., 242 mg sodium, 13 g carbo., 3 g fiber, 1 g pro.

Brussels Sprouts with Apricot and Pistachio

Start to Finish: 30 minutes

1½ pounds Brussels sprouts
2   tablespoons olive oil
½   teaspoon kosher salt
⅓   cup shelled pistachio nuts, coarsely
    chopped
¼   cup snipped dried apricots

1. Trim stems and remove any wilted outer leaves from Brussels sprouts. Slice Brussels sprouts in half through the stem ends. In a large pot cook Brussels sprouts, uncovered, in a large amount of boiling water for 3 minutes; drain well. Pat dry with paper towels.
2. In a large skillet heat olive oil on medium-high heat. Add Brussels sprouts; sprinkle with salt. Cook for 5 to 7 minutes or until golden around the edges and heated through, stirring occasionally. Transfer to a serving dish. Sprinkle with pistachios and apricots.

MAKES 6 TO 8 SERVINGS

Make-ahead directions Prepare Brussels sprouts as directed in Step 1. Cover and chill for up to 24 hours. Continue as directed with Step 2.

Per serving: 102 cal., 6 g total fat (1 g sat. fat), 140 mg sodium, 11 g carbo., 4 g fiber, 4 g pro.

Vegetable Trio with Orange-Thyme Dressing

Prep: 30 minutes **Bake:** 1 hour 15 minutes
Oven: 375°F

3   medium beets, greens removed
1   pound carrots, peeled, cut into 2-inch
    lengths
1   2-pound acorn squash, cut into 1-inch
    slices
1   clove garlic, minced
    Fresh thyme sprigs
¾   teaspoon kosher salt
¼   teaspoon black pepper
4   tablespoons olive oil
1   tablespoon finely shredded orange peel
    (set aside)
⅓   cup orange juice
⅓   cup white wine vinegar
1   teaspoon snipped fresh thyme

1. Preheat oven to 375°F. Wrap beets in a double thickness of heavy foil. Bake for 40 minutes.
2. Meanwhile, in a large bowl toss together carrots, squash, garlic, and several thyme sprigs. Sprinkle with ½ teaspoon of the salt and the pepper. Drizzle with 2 tablespoons of the olive oil; toss to coat. Transfer mixture to a rimmed baking sheet. Place in oven alongside the beets. Roast for 35 to 40 minutes or just until vegetables are tender.
3. Unwrap cooked beets and rub with paper towels to remove skins. Cut beets into 1-inch pieces; set aside.

BRUSSELS SPROUTS WITH
APRICOT AND PISTACHIO

Maple-Glazed Sweet Potatoes and Apples

Prep: 25 minutes **Bake:** 1 hour 15 minutes
Oven: 350°F

- ⅓ cup butter
- ¼ cup maple or maple-flavor syrup
- ¼ cup apple cider or juice
- 3 pounds sweet potatoes, peeled and cut into 1½- to 2-inch chunks (8 cups)
- 1¾ pounds tart red and/or green apples (such as McIntosh, Granny Smith, or Rome Beauty), cored and cut into eighths (4½ cups)
- 1 cup pecan halves, toasted

1. Preheat oven to 350°F. In a medium saucepan combine butter, syrup, and apple cider; heat to boiling, stirring occasionally. Boil gently, uncovered, for 1 minute. Remove from heat; set aside. Place sweet potatoes in a 3-quart rectangular baking dish. Pour butter mixture over potatoes; stir to coat. Cover with foil and bake for 45 minutes.

2. Uncover dish; add apples and stir to coat evenly. Bake, uncovered, about 30 minutes or until sweet potatoes are tender, stirring once halfway through baking. Sprinkle with pecans before serving. **MAKES 10 SERVINGS**

Per serving: 278 cal., 14 g total fat (5 g sat. fat), 16 mg chol., 99 mg sodium, 38 g carbo., 6 g fiber, 3 g pro.

ROASTED ROOT VEGETABLES

Roasted Root Vegetables ♡

Prep: 20 minutes **Bake:** 1 hour 10 minutes
Oven: 325°F/425°F

- 12 ounces rutabaga, peeled and cut into ¾-inch pieces (about 3 cups)
- 8 ounces celery root, peeled and cut into 1-inch pieces (about 2 cups)
- 8 ounces whole baby carrots with tops, tops trimmed, or 8 ounces packaged peeled baby carrots (1½ cups)
- 8 ounces fingerling potatoes, halved if large
- 3 medium parsnips, peeled and cut into 1-inch slices (about 1½ cups)
- 1 medium fennel bulb, cored and cut into thin wedges (about 1 cup)
- 2 shallots, peeled and cut into thin wedges (1 cup)
- 2 tablespoons olive oil
- ½ teaspoon salt
- ½ teaspoon black pepper

1. Preheat oven to 325°F. In a shallow roasting pan combine rutabaga, celery root, baby carrots, fingerling potatoes, parsnips, fennel, and shallots. Add olive oil, salt, and pepper; toss to coat.

2. Bake, uncovered, for 1 hour, stirring occasionally. Increase oven temperature to 425°F. Bake, uncovered, about 10 minutes more or until vegetables are tender and lightly browned. **MAKES 12 SERVINGS**

Per serving: 82 cal., 2 g total fat (0 g sat. fat), 0 mg chol., 136 mg sodium, 14 g carbo., 3 g fiber, 2 g pro.

SAVORY HOLIDAY BREAD

Savory Holiday Bread

Prep: 25 minutes **Bake:** 40 minutes
Oven: 350°F

  3 cups all-purpose flour
  2 cups shredded Italian-blend cheeses
      (8 ounces)
  2 teaspoons baking powder
  1 teaspoon salt
 ½ teaspoon garlic powder
  3 eggs, lightly beaten
  1 5-ounce can (⅔ cup) evaporated milk
 ⅓ cup thinly sliced green onions
 ¼ cup butter, melted
 ¼ cup oil-packed dried tomatoes, drained
      and finely chopped
  1 egg yolk
  1 tablespoon water

1. Preheat oven to 350°F. Grease a large baking sheet; set aside. In a large bowl combine flour, cheese, baking powder, salt, and garlic powder. Add eggs, milk, green onions, melted butter, and dried tomatoes. Stir until combined.
2. Turn dough out onto a lightly floured surface. Knead dough by folding and gently pressing dough for 10 to 12 strokes or until dough holds together. Divide dough in 3 equal pieces. Roll each piece into a 14-inch rope. Place ropes 1 inch apart on prepared baking sheet; braid ropes, pinching ends to seal. Combine egg yolk and water; brush top of bread with egg yolk mixture.
3. Bake about 40 minutes or until golden brown. Transfer to a wire rack; cool completely. **MAKES 1 LOAF (18 SERVINGS)**

Per serving: 164 cal., 8 g total fat (4 g sat. fat), 65 mg chol., 280 mg sodium, 16 g carbo., 1 g fiber, 7 g pro.

Walnut-Sage Potatoes au Gratin

Prep: 30 minutes **Bake:** 1 hour 10 minutes
Stand: 10 minutes **Oven:** 350°F

  6 medium potatoes (2 pounds)
  3 tablespoons walnut oil or olive oil
 ½ cup chopped onion (1 medium)
  2 cloves garlic, minced
  3 tablespoons all-purpose flour
 ½ teaspoon salt
 ¼ teaspoon black pepper
2½ cups milk
  3 tablespoons snipped fresh sage
  1 cup shredded Gruyère cheese (4 ounces)
 ⅓ cup broken walnuts

1. If desired, peel potatoes; thinly slice potatoes to make about 6 cups. Place potato slices in colander. Rinse with cold water; drain.
2. Preheat oven to 350°F. For sauce, in a medium saucepan heat oil on medium heat. Cook onion and garlic in hot oil until tender. Stir in flour, salt, and pepper. Add milk all at once. Cook and stir until thickened and bubbly. Remove from heat; stir in sage.
3. Layer half of the potatoes in a greased 2-quart casserole. Top with half the sauce. Sprinkle with half of the cheese. Repeat layering with potatoes and sauce. (Cover and chill remaining cheese until needed.)
4. Bake, covered, for 40 minutes. Uncover and bake about 25 minutes or until potatoes are tender. Sprinkle with remaining cheese; top with walnuts. Bake, uncovered, for 5 minutes. Let stand for 10 minutes before serving. **MAKES 10 TO 12 SERVINGS**

Per serving: 217 cal., 12 g total fat (3 g sat. fat), 17 mg chol., 187 mg sodium, 20 g carbo., 2 g fiber, 9 g pro.

Pumpkin-Walnut Praline Pie

Prep: 40 minutes **Chill:** 30 minutes
Bake: 50 minutes **Oven:** 375°F

- 12 ounces cream cheese (four 3-ounce packages or one and one-half 8-ounce packages), softened
- ⅓ cup sugar
- 4 eggs
- 1 teaspoon finely shredded orange peel
- 1 recipe Pastry for Single-Crust Deep-Dish Pie
- 1 15-ounce can pumpkin puree
- ¾ cup sugar
- 2 teaspoons pumpkin pie spice
- ¾ cup half-and-half or light cream
- ¾ cup broken walnuts
- ½ cup milk chocolate-covered toffee pieces or chopped chocolate-covered English toffee bars
- ¼ cup packed brown sugar
  Hot fudge ice cream topping (optional)
  Whipped cream (optional)
  Pumpkin pie spice (optional)

1. In a medium mixing bowl combine cream cheese and the ⅓ cup sugar; beat with an electric mixer on low to medium until smooth. Beat in 1 of the eggs; stir in orange peel. Cover and chill for 30 minutes.

2. Preheat oven to 375°F. Prepare Pastry for Single-Crust Deep-Dish Pie. On a lightly floured surface, use your hands to slightly flatten pastry. Roll dough from center to edge into a circle about 13 inches in diameter. To transfer pastry, wrap it around the rolling pin. Unroll pastry into a 9½- to 10-inch deep-dish pie plate. Ease pastry into pie plate, taking care not to stretch pastry. Trim pastry to ½ inch beyond edge of pie plate. Fold under extra pastry. Crimp edge high. Do not prick pastry.

3. For pumpkin filling, in a large bowl combine pumpkin puree, the ¾ cup sugar, and the 2 teaspoons pumpkin pie spice. Add the remaining 3 eggs and beat lightly. Gradually beat in half-and-half. Spread cream cheese mixture in pastry-lined pie plate. Carefully spoon pumpkin filling over cream cheese

layer. To prevent overbrowning, cover edge of pie with foil. Bake for 25 minutes.

4. In a small bowl combine walnuts, toffee pieces, and brown sugar. Remove foil from pie. Sprinkle with walnut mixture.

5. Bake for 25 to 30 minutes or until a knife inserted near the center comes out clean. Cool on a wire rack. Cover and chill pie within 2 hours. If desired, top servings with hot fudge topping, whipped cream, and additional pumpkin pie spice. **MAKES 10 SERVINGS**

Pastry for Single-Crust Deep-Dish Pie

In a medium bowl stir together 1½ cups all-purpose flour and ¼ teaspoon salt. Use a pastry blender to cut in 6 tablespoons shortening until pieces are pea size. Sprinkle 1 tablespoon cold water over part of the mixture; gently toss with a fork. Push moistened dough to the side of the bowl. Repeat moistening dough, using 1 tablespoon cold water at a time, until all of the dough is moist (5 to 6 tablespoons cold water total). Form dough into a ball.

Per serving: 547 cal., 33 g total fat (13 g sat. fat), 133 mg chol., 255 mg sodium, 56 g carbo., 2 g fiber, 9 g pro.

Cranberry-Almond Bread ♡

Prep: 25 minutes **Bake:** 45 minutes
Cool: 10 minutes **Oven:** 350°F

- 1 cup whole bran cereal
- ¾ cup all-purpose flour
- ½ cup white whole wheat flour
- 1 teaspoon baking powder
- ¼ teaspoon baking soda
- ¼ teaspoon salt
- 1 egg, lightly beaten
- 1 cup fat-free milk
- ½ cup packed brown sugar
- 2 tablespoons canola oil
- ½ teaspoon almond extract
- ½ cup coarsely chopped dried cranberries
- ½ cup chopped almonds, toasted

CRANBERRY-ALMOND BREAD

1. Preheat oven to 350°F. Grease the bottom and ½ inch up sides of an 8×4×2-inch loaf pan; set aside. In a large bowl stir together whole bran cereal, all-purpose flour, white whole wheat flour, baking powder, baking soda, and salt. Make a well in center of the flour mixture; set aside.

2. In a medium bowl combine egg, milk, brown sugar, oil, and almond extract. Add milk mixture all at once to flour mixture. Stir just until moistened (batter should be lumpy). Fold in dried cranberries and almonds. Spoon batter into prepared pan.

3. Bake for 45 to 50 minutes or until a wooden toothpick inserted near center comes out clean. Cool in pan on a wire rack for 10 minutes. Remove from pan. Cool completely on wire rack. Wrap and store overnight before slicing. **MAKES 12 SERVINGS**

Per serving: 165 cal., 5 g total fat (0 g sat. fat), 18 mg chol., 137 mg sodium, 28 g carbo., 3 g fiber, 4 g pro.

NUTS ABOUT CRANBERRIES TART

Nuts About Cranberries Tart ♡

Prep: 45 minutes **Bake:** 31 minutes
Cool: 1 hour **Oven:** 450°F/375°F

- 1 recipe Rich Pastry
- ¼ cup packed brown sugar
- 2 tablespoons butter
- 1 cup fresh cranberries
- 1 medium pear, cored and chopped
- ⅓ cup lightly salted pistachio nuts
- ⅓ cup sliced almonds
- ½ teaspoon vanilla

1. Preheat oven to 450°F. On a lightly floured surface, roll Rich Pastry dough to a 15×6-inch rectangle.* Transfer dough to an ungreased 13¾×4-inch tart pan with a removable bottom.* Ease pastry into tart pan. Press pastry into the fluted sides of pan. Trim pastry even with edges of pan. Line pastry with a double thickness of foil. Bake for 8 minutes. Remove foil. Bake for 3 to 4 minutes more or until set and dry. Cool in pan on wire rack. Reduce oven temperature to 375°F.

2. In a medium saucepan cook and stir brown sugar and butter until combined. Add the cranberries and pear; cook and stir until bubbly. Remove from heat. Stir in pistachios, almonds, and vanilla. Spoon into crust. Place tart on baking sheet.

3. Bake for 20 to 25 minutes or until filling is bubbly around edges and pastry is golden. Cool in pan on a wire rack. Remove sides of pan. **MAKES 12 SERVINGS**

Rich Pastry In a medium bowl combine 1 cup all-purpose flour, ¼ cup whole wheat pastry flour, and 1 tablespoon granulated sugar. Cut in ¼ cup butter until pieces are pea size. Combine 2 tablespoons refrigerated or frozen egg product, thawed, and 2 tablespoons ice water. Gradually stir water mixture into flour mixture until moistened. (If necessary, stir additional cold water, 1 teaspoon at a time, into mixture to moisten.) Shape into a ball.

***Tip** Or roll dough to a 10-inch circle and ease pastry into an ungreased 9-inch tart pan with removable bottom.

Per serving: 165 cal., 9 g total fat (4 g sat. fat), 15 mg chol., 62 mg sodium, 20 g carbo., 2 g fiber, 3 g pro.

Black Forest Tartlets

Prep: 30 minutes **Bake:** 15 minutes
Cool: 5 minutes **Chill:** 5 minutes **Oven:** 350°F

- ⅓ cup tub-style 60% to 70% vegetable oil spread
- ½ of an 8-ounce package reduced-fat cream cheese (Neufchâtel), softened
- 2 tablespoons packed brown sugar
- 2 tablespoons unsweetened cocoa powder
- 1 cup all-purpose flour
- 1 4-serving-size package sugar-free, fat-free instant chocolate pudding mix
- 1¾ cups fat-free milk
- ½ teaspoon almond extract
- 2 tablespoons snipped dried tart cherries
- 24 frozen unsweetened tart red cherries, thawed and drained

1. Preheat oven to 350°F. In a large bowl beat vegetable oil spread, cream cheese, sugar, and cocoa powder with an electric mixer on medium until mixed. Stir in flour. Press a teaspoon of dough into bottom and up sides of 24 ungreased 1¾-inch muffin cups.

2. Bake 15 minutes or until set. Cool in muffin cups on a wire rack for 5 minutes. Remove pastry cups from pans; cool on wire rack.

3. Meanwhile, in a medium bowl whisk pudding mix, milk, and extract for 1 minute. Chill 5 minutes or until mixture sets up slightly. Transfer half of the mixture to an airtight container and refrigerate for another use. Fold dried cherries into remaining mixture. Spoon pudding mixture into pastry cups. Top with tart cherries. **MAKES 24 TARTS**

Per tart: 65 cal., 3 g total fat (1 g sat. fat), 4 mg chol., 197 mg sodium, 6 g carbo., 0 g fiber, 2 g pro.

Mocha Fudge Cookies

Prep: 35 minutes **Stand:** 30 minutes
Bake: 12 minutes per batch **Oven:** 350°F

  2 6-ounce packages bittersweet chocolate, chopped
 ½ cup butter
1½ cups sugar
  4 eggs
  1 tablespoon instant espresso coffee powder or instant coffee crystals
 ⅓ cup all-purpose flour
 ¼ teaspoon baking powder
 ⅛ teaspoon salt
  1 cup semisweet chocolate pieces
 ¾ cup chopped toasted hazelnuts (filberts) or almonds
1¼ cups white baking pieces
 ¾ teaspoon shortening

1. In a medium saucepan combine chopped chocolate and butter. Heat and stir on low heat until melted. Cool for 10 minutes.
2. In a large bowl combine sugar, eggs, and espresso powder. Beat with an electric mixer on medium to high for 2 to 3 minutes or until well mixed and color lightens slightly. Add cooled chocolate mixture; beat until combined. In a small bowl stir together flour, baking powder, and salt. Add to chocolate mixture; beat until combined. Stir in chocolate pieces, nuts, and ½ cup of the white baking pieces.
3. Cover; let stand about 20 minutes or until mixture thickens slightly. Preheat oven to 350°F. Line 2 cookie sheets with foil or parchment paper. Using a rounded tablespoon, drop dough about 2 inches apart onto prepared cookie sheets. Bake for 12 to 13 minutes or until tops are cracked and appear set. Cool on cookie sheets for 1 minute. Transfer to wire rack; cool.
5. For drizzle, in a saucepan melt remaining ¾ cup white baking pieces and shortening on low heat, stirring often. Cool slightly. Drizzle over cookies. **MAKES ABOUT 42 COOKIES**

To store Place cookies in layers separated by waxed paper in an airtight container. Store at room temperature for up to 3 days.

Per cookie: 171 cal., 10 g total fat (6 g sat. fat), 26 mg chol., 44 mg sodium, 20 g carbo., 1 g fiber, 2 g pro.

PECAN SHORTBREAD RASPBERRY COOKIES

Pecan Shortbread Raspberry Cookies

Prep: 40 minutes **Bake:** 7 minutes per batch
Chill: 1 to 2 hours **Oven:** 350°F

  1 cup butter, softened
 ⅔ cup granulated sugar
  1 teaspoon vanilla
 ½ teaspoon almond extract
  2 cups all-purpose flour
  1 cup ground pecans
     Powdered sugar
 ⅓ cup seedless raspberry preserves

1. In a large mixing bowl beat butter with an electric mixer on medium to high for 30 seconds. Add granulated sugar, vanilla, and almond extract; beat until light and fluffy, scraping bowl often. Beat in flour and pecans until combined. Wrap dough in plastic wrap; chill for 1 to 2 hours or until the dough is easy to handle.
2. Preheat oven to 350°F. On a lightly floured surface, roll half of the dough at a time until ⅛ inch thick. Using a 2-inch round scalloped cookie cutter, cut rounds from dough. Place 1 inch apart on ungreased cookie sheets. Using a 1-inch round cutter, cut centers from half of the unbaked cookies. Remove centers; reroll dough to make more cookies. Bake for 7 to 9 minutes or until edges are firm and bottoms are lightly browned. Transfer to wire racks; let cool.
3. To assemble, sift powdered sugar over tops of cookies with holes; set aside. Spread about ½ teaspoon preserves onto bottom of each cookie without a hole. Top with a cookie with a hole, sugar side up.
MAKES ABOUT 40 COOKIES

To store Place cooled cookies, without preserves, in an airtight container; cover. Store at room temperature for up to 3 days or freeze for up to 3 months. Assemble as above before serving.

Per cookie: 101 cal., 7 g total fat (3 g sat. fat), 12 mg chol., 34 mg sodium, 10 g carbo., 0 g fiber, 1 g pro.

GINGERBREAD COOKIES

Walnut-Raspberry Thumbprints

Prep: 40 minutes **Chill:** 2 hours
Bake: 7 minutes **Oven:** 375°F

¼ cup butter, softened
¼ cup granulated sugar
¼ cup packed brown sugar
½ teaspoon baking powder
¼ teaspoon ground cinnamon or ground cardamom
⅛ teaspoon baking soda
2 egg whites
½ teaspoon vanilla
½ cup all-purpose flour
¼ cup whole wheat pastry flour or whole wheat flour
1 cup quick-cooking rolled oats
1 egg white, lightly beaten
¾ cup finely chopped walnuts and/or pecans
¼ cup low-sugar strawberry, apricot, and/or red raspberry preserves

1. In a large bowl beat butter with an electric mixer on medium to high for 30 seconds. Add granulated sugar, brown sugar, baking powder, cinnamon, and baking soda. Beat until combined, scraping sides of bowl occasionally. Beat in the 2 egg whites and the vanilla until combined. Beat in as much of the all-purpose flour and whole wheat flour as you can with the mixer. Using a wooden spoon, stir in any remaining flour and the oats. Cover and chill dough about 2 hours or until easy to handle.
2. Preheat oven to 375°F. Lightly grease cookie sheets. Shape dough into ¾-inch balls. Roll balls in the 1 egg white; roll in nuts to coat. Place on prepared cookie sheets. Using your thumb, make an indentation in the center of each cookie.
3. Bake for 7 to 8 minutes or until edges are golden brown. If indentations puff during baking, gently press the back of a measuring teaspoon into indentations when cookies are removed from oven. Cool cookies on cookie sheet for 1 minute. Transfer to a wire rack; cool. Just before serving, spoon preserves into indentations. **MAKES ABOUT 36 COOKIES**

Per cookie: 60 cal., 3 g total fat (1 g sat. fat), 3 mg chol., 22 mg sodium, 7 g carbo., 1 g fiber, 1 g pro.

Gingerbread Cookies

Prep: 35 minutes **Chill:** 2 hours
Bake: 4 minutes per batch **Oven:** 375°F

¼ cup butter, softened
¼ cup 50% to 70% vegetable oil spread
½ cup packed brown sugar
2 teaspoons ground ginger
1 teaspoon baking soda
1 teaspoon ground cinnamon
¼ teaspoon salt
¼ teaspoon ground cloves
¼ cup full-flavor molasses
¼ cup refrigerated or frozen egg product, thawed, or 1 egg
2 cups all-purpose flour
¾ cup white whole wheat flour

1. In a large bowl beat butter and vegetable oil spread with an electric mixer on medium to high for 30 seconds. Add brown sugar, ginger, soda, cinnamon, salt, and cloves. Beat until well mixed, scraping bowl occasionally. Beat in molasses and egg. (Mixture will look curdled.) Add all-purpose flour and whole wheat flour, beating just until combined. Divide dough in half. Cover and chill the dough for 2 to 3 hours or until easy to handle.
2. Preheat oven to 375°F. On a lightly floured surface, roll dough, half at a time, to ⅛-inch thickness. Using a 2- to 3-inch gingerbread person cookie cutter, cut out shapes. Place cutouts 1 inch apart on greased cookie sheets.
3. Bake for 4 to 6 minutes or until edges are firm and centers are set. Cool on cookie sheets on wire racks for 1 minute. Transfer to wire racks; cool. **MAKES 36 (3-INCH) COOKIES**

Per 3-inch cookie: 73 cal., 2 g total fat (1 g sat. fat), 3 mg chol., 73 mg sodium, 12 g carbo., 0 g fiber, 1 g pro.

Index